J
"Cl

# John Tortes "Chief" Meyers

## A Baseball Biography

WILLIAM A. YOUNG

McFarland & Company, Inc., Publishers
*Jefferson, North Carolina, and London*

LIBRARY OF CONGRESS CATALOGUING-IN-PUBLICATION DATA

Young, William A.
    John Tortes "Chief" Meyers : a baseball biography /
William A. Young.
        p.      cm.
    Includes bibliographical references and index.

    ISBN 978-0-7864-6801-0
    softcover : acid free paper ∞

    1. Meyers, Chief, 1880–1971.    2. Indian baseball players—
Biography.    3. Cahuilla Indians—Sports.    4. Baseball
players—United States—Biography.    I. Title.
GV865.M493Y68  2012
796.357092 — dc23
[B]                                                        2012023786

BRITISH LIBRARY CATALOGUING DATA ARE AVAILABLE

On the cover: New York Giants catcher "Chief" Meyers (National
Baseball Hall of Fame Library, Cooperstown, New York)

Front cover design by Cindy LaBreacht

Manufactured in the United States of America

*McFarland & Company, Inc., Publishers
    Box 611, Jefferson, North Carolina 28640
    www.mcfarlandpub.com*

# Table of Contents

# *Preface*

It has been for me a privilege and a pleasure to research and write the story of John Tortes "Chief" Meyers, one of the first Native Americans to rise to stardom in baseball's major leagues. The inspiration came from my son Matt, who shares my love for baseball. Several summers ago Matt and I were standing together in front of the plaque honoring Charles Albert "Chief" Bender at the National Baseball Hall of Fame in Cooperstown, New York. Bender was another Native American who excelled during the early years of major league baseball. "You should write a biography of Bender," Matt said, knowing such a project would combine my interest in Native American history and cultures with my passion for the national pastime. However, I soon learned that several fine biographies of Chief Bender had recently been published.

As I did more reading about the first American Indians in the major leagues, I soon encountered a friend of Bender, a man who had his own distinguished career, winning the highest honors given to baseball players at the time. The more I learned about John Tortes Meyers, the more convinced I became that his remarkable story should be told.

Meyers was one of the best catchers of the Deadball Era, playing for the New York Giants under famed manager John McGraw from 1908 through 1915. He was a fine hitter whose offensive statistics compare favorably with a majority of the catchers in the Hall of Fame. He was also heralded for his work behind the plate. A strong-armed, agile catcher who developed a rapport with his pitching staff, Meyers spent seven years as trusted battery mate of one of the best hurlers of all time, Christy Mathewson. Meyers played in three World Series with the Giants (1911–1913) and one with the Brooklyn Dodgers (1916).

While his outstanding career in major league baseball during the formative years of the game is reason enough for a full biography of John Tortes Meyers, there are other compelling reasons. As a member of the Santa Rosa Band of the Cahuilla tribe of southern California, Meyers grew up at a time when the Cahuilla and other Native Americans were under intense pressure

1

to leave behind their traditional ways and assimilate to the dominant culture. Stereotypes, ranging from the vicious to the inane, dominated the public discourse about Native Americans. While most American Indian major leaguers tried to leave behind tribal identities and immersed themselves in the white man's world in order to try to escape these prejudices, Meyers did not. He spent time on the Santa Rosa Reservation as a boy, absorbing Cahuilla values that guided and sustained him for the rest of his life. When his baseball career ended, Meyers returned to his Cahuilla homeland and became a leader in his tribe.

Though he remained true to his Cahuilla heritage, Meyers also understood the importance of learning how to succeed in the dominant culture. He spent a year at Dartmouth College, where he developed a passion for history, art, literature, and philosophy that never left him. He was widely known as one of the most learned and cultured major leaguers of his era. For the Native Americans who followed him into careers not only in baseball but other professions, Meyers left a valuable legacy: work hard to excel at the highest levels in the wider world, but always remain rooted in the heritage and values of your own people.

This biography draws on the myriad of colorful stories in the contemporary press about Meyers and the teams on and against which he played. In the halcyon days of baseball writing, gifted journalists like Damon Runyon, Grantland Rice, Fred Lieb, Bozeman Bulger, Sid Mercer, and Ring Lardner brought games and players vividly to life. Reflecting the racial biases of the time that cast Native American ball players as "savage warriors," sports writers typically portrayed Chief Meyers through prejudicial filters. However, they also recognized and recorded his stature and achievements on and off the baseball diamond.

Other primary sources come from the National Baseball Hall of Fame Library; the Alumni Archives in the Rauner Special Collections Library at Dartmouth College; the lending library of the Society for American Baseball Research; the Riverside, California, Metropolitan Museum; the San Diego History Center; and the Agua Caliente Cultural Museum in Palm Springs, California. I am indebted to the librarians and archivists at these institutions for their gracious assistance.

As the list of references will attest, there is no shortage of excellent books and articles on the early history of baseball. Among those most helpful in this project was the late Lawrence Ritter's acclaimed *The Glory of Their Times: The Story of the Early Days of Baseball Told by the Men Who Played It.* I also drew on the groundbreaking work by Jeffrey P. Beck on the American Indian integration of baseball. Dr. Beck and Robert Peyton Wiggins, author of an excellent biography of Charles Bender and an expert on the Deadball Era, graciously agreed to read a draft of the manuscript and made valuable suggestions. I am also indebted to Professor Henry Koerper for his research on Meyers.

Particularly helpful to me in accessing even the most obscure works relevant to my research were Cindy Schoolcraft, Resource Sharing Assistant at Reeves Library (Westminster College; Fulton, Missouri), and Nina Stawski, Access Librarian at Hugh Stephens Library (Stephens College; Columbia, Missouri).

I also extend my appreciation to the following members of the Meyers family who generously shared their memories with me: Colonel John V. Meyers, Shanna Meyers, Michele Meyers Cornejo, and Anne-Margaret Meyers. Their obvious pride in their Uncle Jack inspired me, and their active leadership in the Santa Rosa Band of the Cahuilla is a lasting tribute to his legacy.

Finally, I am deeply grateful for the love and support of my family throughout the long and sometimes tedious journey from that day in Cooperstown to the completion of this project. My son Matt planted the seed and nurtured its growth along the way. My daughter Rachel gave me helpful writing and editing tips. My son-in-law Gabe and daughter-in-law Carrie urged me on when my enthusiasm waned. Spending many hours with my grandchildren Noah and Sadie helped rescue me when it felt like I was sinking into the quicksand that a lengthy writing project can become. My wife Sue was the insightful reader every writer needs, helping me to let go of words that were not needed and to find those that made the difference at crucial points in the story. Beyond her invaluable help as an editor extraordinaire, she is and always will be my best friend and soul mate.

# Prologue: An Evening at Shea Stadium, 1965

Shortly before the end of the 1965 season 85-year-old former major leaguer John Tortes Meyers stood proudly at home plate in Shea Stadium, home of the New York Mets. Like most other Native American major leaguers, Meyers, a member of the Santa Rosa Band of the Cahuilla tribe of southern California, had been known by the nickname "Chief" throughout his baseball career. Still called Chief in retirement, Meyers had flown east for a Mets–Dodgers series. Although six decades earlier most of his major league career was spent with the New York Giants, as their star catcher, he also played for the Dodgers. In Meyers's later years Dodgers owner Walter O'Malley gave the former Dodgers catcher *carte blanche* to travel with the team any time he liked.

Standing beside Meyers at home plate that night was future Hall of Fame New York Yankees catcher Yogi Berra, who was then a coach for the Mets. Reading from a script prepared by Meyers, the stadium announcer explained that the Chief had been Mets manager Casey Stengel's teammate a half-century earlier when both played for the Dodgers during the 1916 World Series. As one of the best catchers of the old days, the announcer intoned, Chief Meyers would now present the uniform he wore on that occasion to one of the greatest catchers of modern times.

The exchange was quickly made and after polite applause the two star catchers from different eras walked together to the Mets dugout. As Berra put the uniform down on the bench, Meyers said to him, "You don't really want that, do you, Yogi?" Berra shrugged. Meyers nodded and stuffed his old Dodgers uniform back into a brown paper bag. Then, after shaking Berra's hand and patting him on the back, the old catcher turned to sportswriter Donald Honig, who was observing the scene, and said with a gleam in his eye, "One ceremony to go."

Waiting for Meyers in the stands was Lawrence Ritter, who had met the Chief a year earlier during an interview for Ritter's acclaimed book, *The Glory*

4

*Of Their Times: The Story of the Early Days of Baseball Told by the Men Who Played It.* When later recalling the evening at Shea Stadium, Ritter said that as they left the Dodgers' hotel to go to the game he couldn't help but notice the paper bag Chief was carrying. Aware of Ritter's curiosity Meyers had simply winked and said, "All shall be revealed, young man, to those who bide their time."

Now, as he returned to the stands, Meyers said to Ritter, "Come on, let's have some fun." The Cahuilla catcher led the way, followed by Ritter and Honig, to the offices of George Weiss, President of the Mets. "I don't know if you fellows realize it," Meyers said as they approached the Mets administrative offices, "but Mr. Weiss was once my employer. The year was 1917 and he hired me as playing manager for his minor league New Haven team. Well, you know that there was a war on then, World War I, and on Opening Day when the band played and they raised a flag out in center field, I was stricken with an acute attack of patriotism that refused to go away. After the game, without a word to anyone, I went downtown and joined the Marines. Never did return to the ballpark. At the very least, I certainly owe Mr. Weiss an apology."

The Mets president, who was expecting the visit, was clearly pleased to see Chief Meyers again and invited the trio into his office. Meyers pulled out a small drawstring bag and placed it on Weiss's desk. The old catcher explained that while barnstorming in Vancouver in 1910 he had been given some stones as a special gift by the Kwakiutl Indians, who told him the stones would bring good fortune and long life. "I have enjoyed both. And now, with the same sentiments, I would like to present them to you. I hope you will accept them as a belated but heartfelt apology for my sudden and inexcusable departure from your New Haven team," he said to Weiss. With that, Meyers pulled open the drawstrings of the little bag and poured out some small, nondescript rocks. Weiss then looked up at the somber-faced Meyers. Each seemed to be daring the other to smile, but neither did.

After a few moments of silence Weiss said, "Thank you, Chief, no apology has ever been necessary, considering the cause for which you departed." He stood up, shook the old catcher's hand, and the second of the two rituals Meyers had orchestrated for the evening was over.

As they walked away, Honig turned to the Meyers and said, "Chief, was that true about those stones, that those 'what's-their-name-Indians' gave them to you?"

The Cahuilla catcher calmly replied, "Kwakiutl. They live in the Vancouver area. A noble people."

"But what about the stones?" Honig asked.

Meyers's eyes twinkled yet again, and he said, "God knows where they came from. They've been at the bottom of an empty flowerpot in my basement ever since I can remember. But it was a fine little ceremony, wasn't it? Now, let's go sit somewhere and I'll tell you some stories about the olden days, about Christy Mathewson and John McGraw and Honus Wagner and anything else you want to hear."[1]

Jack Meyers, as those who knew him best called him, *was* an outstanding major league baseball player, as prominent during the period known as the Deadball Era (1901–1919) as Yogi Berra was in the 1950s and 60s. Although Meyers did not reach the major leagues until he was nearly thirty, an age when many players were beginning to losing their edge, he was the star catcher for the New York Giants between 1909 and 1915 and finished his career in 1916 and 1917 with the Dodgers and Boston Braves. Decades before the establishment of the National Baseball Hall of Fame at Cooperstown, New York, Meyers was accorded one of the greatest honors of his day, selection to the Grand National All-American team.

Meyers's powerful hitting and his success "behind the bat" make him, in the estimation of STATS, Inc., one of the two top catchers of the Deadball Era. The other was another New York Giant — Hall of Famer Roger Bresnahan.[2] Meyers caught Hall of Fame hurlers Christy Mathewson and Rube Marquard and other pitching greats while playing for legendary Giants manager John J. McGraw. On the Giants he was also a teammate of the best overall athlete of the 20th century, Jim Thorpe. In the California Winter Leagues and on a barnstorming tour he caught the legendary Walter Johnson. He also played against and had stories to tell about Honus Wagner, Grover Cleveland Alexander and other baseball immortals. The baseball story of John Tortes Meyers, star catcher of the New York Giants and Brooklyn Dodgers, is fascinating in its own right.

However, there is another dimension that makes the tale of this outstanding athlete even more important. Because John Tortes Meyers was a Native American, his story epitomizes the challenges and struggles faced by American Indians at a critical time of transition. The plan to assimilate Native Americans to Euroamerican culture was in place and gaining momentum during Meyers's formative years and throughout his baseball career.

According to the popular narrative, as the quintessential American game, baseball was a microcosm of the ideal "melting pot" in which men of different ethnic groups came together as Americans. Although African Americans were excluded from major league baseball until 1947, this version of events claims Native Americans were fully accepted in America's game. Meyers and other baseball players of Indian heritage were lifted up as examples of what all Native Americans and others in minority groups could achieve if they were willing to commit themselves to assimilate fully to the dominant culture. In language typical of the era the claim was made by *The Sporting News*: "The Mick, the Sheeney, the Wop, the Dutch, and the Chink, the Cuban, the Indian, the Jap, or the so-called Anglo-Saxon — his 'nationality' is never a matter of moment if he can pitch, or hit, or field."[3]

A casual observer might conclude the life and baseball career of John Tortes Meyers is an assimilation success story. Although he grew up at a time when many Cahuilla people were still following their traditional way of life, by his own admission Meyers was of the younger generation who turned from the old Cahuilla customs and embraced the modern, Euroamerican lifestyle. He reached the pinnacle of success in that world. But to portray Meyers as finding his home comfortably in the white man's world would be misleading. His is a more nuanced and complicated story. Though he was, to the casual observer, fully immersed in the dominant culture, he never felt fully at home there. He knew that no matter how successful he became as a major league ballplayer he would always remain a foreigner. As he told a reporter in 1909, and reaffirmed over a half-century later, near the end of his life, he always felt like a "stranger in a strange land."[4]

With fellow American Indian major leaguers of the Deadball Era, Meyers bore the burden of always being portrayed through a prism of stereotypes and clichés that ridiculed the native nations from which they came and distorted the multifaceted individual human beings they were.

The story of John Tortes Meyers therefore must be seen within the context of the struggles of Native Americans in general, and athletes in particular, to maintain their dignity and self-respect. How Meyers coped with the raw prejudice he encountered on and off the field of play in comparison to other Native American ball players is a critically important dimension of his story.

For too many Native Americans, at the height of the pressures of assimilation, the inescapable tension of feeling trapped between two worlds without being fully at home in either was overwhelming. Leaving behind their Native American heritage only to feel the stinging rejection of racism despite their achievements in the dominant culture caused some to seethe with rage that sometimes turned outward but more often was directed inward in spirals of self-destructive behavior.

Such was not the case for John Tortes Meyers. Though it was not an easy passage, he did successfully negotiate the treacherous boundaries between the Native American and Euroamerican worlds. Though he entered the white man's world willingly and was able to compete on its playing fields, according to its rules, he was also intensely proud of his Native American identity and heritage. Throughout his life he drew on the Cahuilla values he learned as a child.

Meyers was rooted in his Cahuilla tradition, but he also benefitted from the best of what the white world had to offer him. During a year at Dartmouth College he began a life-long love of learning, especially in the areas of philosophy, literature and art. For the rest of his life he read widely and enjoyed visiting museums and art galleries. John Tortes Meyers "did as much as any Native American of his generation to shatter the stereotypical image of the dumb Indian. [He] was more sophisticated than nearly all of his fellow players."[5] Meyers, those who knew him best said, was "an intelligent man" who had "an imposing personal dignity."[6]

John Tortes Meyers excelled in America's national sport when most American Indians could not vote in America's elections. He deserves to be recognized and remembered as the baseball star he was. His is also the story of a Native American athlete who found a balance between assimilation to the dominant culture and remaining rooted in his Cahuilla heritage. As he said to Lawrence Ritter a year before the ceremonies at Shea Stadium, "I guess I'm like the venerable old warrior Chief of the Great Six Nations, who announced his retirement by saying, 'I am like an old hemlock. My head is still high, but the winds of close to a hundred winters have whistled through my branches, and I have been witness to many wondrous things and many tragic things. My eyes perceive the present, but my roots are imbedded deeply in the grandeur of the past.'"[7]

# ONE

## *Early Life and Beginning a Career in Baseball (1880–1905)*

A sportswriter once reported that John Tortes Meyers had revealed to him something about his heritage few people knew — that his "first name is Tortes, but calling him Chief is no misnomer. His father and granddad were *bona fide* feathered chiefs of the Cohuilla [sic] tribe."[1]

Throughout his life Meyers employed the ironic humor of his Cahuilla heritage to expose the naïveté of journalists and others about Native American cultures by drawing on and manipulating popular stereotypes. Sportswriters often called this quality Chief Meyers's "sly wit." However, for Meyers such humor was not just a way to have fun. It was a strategy he used over the years to cope, by exposing and subtly mocking the contradictions and absurdities he observed and experienced in the world in which he was viewed as a foreigner because he was an Indian.

The "feathered chiefs" reference evokes an image more appropriate to Plains Indians in war bonnets than to the Cahuilla of California. Meyers would sometimes put on a long "war bonnet" himself to pose for photographs, saying "he always wore this traditional Indian garb in the off-season."[2] When asked by reporters about his tribal heritage, he sometimes told them he was the "son of a royal house," and they dutifully described him that way in their stories.[3]

Rather than being a "feathered chief," John Tortes Meyers's father, John Mayer (not Meyers) was a German-American from Terre Haute, Indiana, who served as a captain in the Union Army during the Civil War. Like many other veterans of that war he traveled to California after the conflict ended. Captain Mayer settled in Riverside sometime during the 1870s and took ownership of a saloon. One of his son Jack's grade school teachers, or perhaps a school administrator, transformed "Mayer" to "Meyer," and somewhere along the way the "s" was added.

Like other Cahuilla women of the era, Meyers's mother Felicité Tortes (1840–1916) was a skilled basket maker who sold her wares to earn cash to support her family. She may have met Captain Mayer while living in Spring Rancheria and selling baskets in Riverside. Or perhaps she met him while working as a maid for one or more prominent Riverside families. She was, according to an early twentieth century history of Riverside, "much esteemed by those she had faithfully served."[4]

After their marriage John and Felicité lived in a home behind the saloon in Riverside, but they also spent time with Felicité's family on the Santa Rosa Reservation. They had three children. Their oldest son, Marion, was a year older than Jack. Their daughter Mary Christine, called Christine in the family, was two years younger than Jack. As an adult Marion was a plasterer in Riverside. Christine was the valedictorian of her high school class and worked as a registered nurse throughout her life.[5] She was very active in tribal affairs, always speaking out for the rights of her people. "I think she got that," Christine's granddaughter and Jack's grandniece, Shanna Meyers, remembers, "from her mother, my great-grandmother, Felicité."[6]

After her husband's death in 1887 Felicité took a job working as a cook at the Glenwood Hotel in Riverside, which would later become the famed Mission Inn.[7]

When Meyers began his major league baseball career in 1908, he gave his birthdate as July 29, 1882. That date appeared on official baseball publications and trading cards throughout his career. He also listed 1882 as the year of his birth on U.S. Indian Census surveys while he was playing professional baseball and during the early years of his retirement.[8] However, Meyers was actually born two years earlier, to the day, on July 29, 1880. There was a practical reason for his misrepresentation. Already 28 when he broke into major league ball, he was concerned about age discrimination and later admitted he moved his birth date forward two years, telling one reporter, "I was 28 years old before I got to the major leagues, but I didn't want them to know it."[9] The date 1883 is also found in some publications, suggesting he may have shaved as many as three years off his birth date in some contexts.[10]

At times Meyers would say he had been born "in a small Cahuilla village, and I went to school there."[11] In fact, he was born in the family's downtown Riverside home behind his father's saloon, located on the current Seventh Street, between Main and Market.[12] Meyers remembered as a boy selling spring water, perhaps from the transient Cahuilla village at Spring Rancheria, on the streets of Riverside "for two bits a bucket."[13]

Meyers recalled his mother Felicité "spoke German, French and English in addition to several dialects of Cahuilla, and frequently enjoined her children to speak their language properly, without admixture of Spanish, English

Meyers's mother Felicité Tortes and younger sister Christine in Riverside, California (about 1900). Their active leadership in the Santa Rosa Band of the Cahuilla inspired Meyers to become a tribal leader himself when his baseball career ended (courtesy Riverside Metropolitan Museum, Riverside, California).

or slang."[14] His careful use of language throughout his life may trace to his mother's influence. The knowledge of Cahuilla he acquired from his mother and her family while living on the Santa Rosa Reservation as a young boy is also an indication that John Tortes Meyers was well aware of the cultural perspective and values embedded in the language.

According to Meyers's grandniece, Shanna, her great-grandmother, Felicité, was the first Cahuilla woman to take individual title to communal land on the Santa Rosa Reservation.[15] Felicité's foresight enabled her children, grandchildren, and great-grandchildren to remain connected to the Reservation to this day.

After a few years on the Santa Rosa Reservation, at about age ten or eleven, Meyers returned to Riverside and attended Sixth Street School, later known as Lincoln School, and, for a time, Riverside High School, located at 14th Street and Brockton Avenue.[16]

# The Impact of the Policy of Assimilation (1880–1920)

Throughout the first half of John Tortes Meyers's life, the policy of the United States government toward American Indians was dominated by the view that Indians must "assimilate" to Euroamerican civilization. The underlying rationale was that by embracing values such as individualism and private property ownership, Indians would become productive citizens able to make lives for themselves rather than remain as wards of the government. In addition, most of their collectively held lands would become available for settlement by whites. Assimilation policy was based on the belief that "once 'freed' from their 'savage' heritage, [Indians] would participate fully in the nation's institutions."[17]

Supporters of the policy considered Native Americans the test case in a wider project of assimilating all minorities, including freed African American slaves and their descendants as well as the Asian workers flooding the west coast. Baseball would become one of the arenas in which the social experiment of assimilating American Indians would take place, and Meyers, along with other Native American major league baseball players, would be a major participant in the test.

A major element in assimilation policy was an educational program designed in the words of one of its first architects, Captain Richard Pratt, to "kill the Indian, and save the man."[18] In 1878, two years before John Tortes Meyers was born, the first off-reservation boarding school was created at Hampton Institute in Virginia when the school founded to educate blacks expanded its enrollment to include Indians.

The next year Captain Pratt founded the first all–Indian boarding school — Carlisle Indian School in Pennsylvania, which Meyers's friend and opponent in two World Series, Albert Bender, and his New York Giants teammate Jim Thorpe attended. The programs at the boarding schools like Carlisle varied, but had in common the goal of stripping Indian students of their tribal identities, replacing them with new American identities. Upon arrival, students' traditional clothes were removed, replaced by Euroamerican dress. If boys had long hair, it was cut. The students were punished for speaking their native languages and forbidden to practice their traditional rituals. Boys were prepared for lives as manual laborers and girls trained to be domestic workers.

By the year Meyers was born, 7,000 Indian children were attending Hampton, Carlisle and other boarding schools. Sports, especially football, track, and baseball, were soon used at Carlisle and other schools to assimilate Indian boys through teaching them the dominant society's games.[19]

Soon after it opened in 1902, Sherman Institute in Meyers's hometown of Riverside, California, became "one of the largest off-reservation Indian boarding schools in North America and served as a flagship Indian school for the U.S. government." Like other boarding schools Sherman was created "to assimilate ... Indian pupils into mainstream white society."[20]

Another linchpin in the assimilation policy was evangelization by Christian churches. Not only were Indian students forbidden to practice their traditional religions at boarding schools, they were forced to attend Christian worship services. Christian missionaries had long worked to convert Native Americans. During the administration of President Ulysses S. Grant (1869–1877) and continuing into the twentieth century, various Christian denominations were given supervisory responsibility on many reservations and assigned the role of "civilizing" native peoples by convincing them to give up their "heathen" lifestyles for the path of the "Christian way of life."

Because of its small size and relative isolation, the Santa Rosa Reservation was probably not as directly impacted by the policy of assimilation as the larger reservations. However, the curriculum of the government school Meyers attended on the reservation was decidedly assimilationist. For example, Meyers would not have been allowed to speak Cahuilla, even though he had learned the language from his mother. He was also exposed to the off-reservation boarding school milieu through his proximity to Sherman Institute in Riverside. Finally, even before the policy of the Grant administration, the Catholic Church into which Meyers had been baptized was a "civilizing influence" at Santa Rosa.

Throughout his life Meyers experienced the various economic, social, political, educational, and religious pressures to assimilate fully to Euroamerican culture. However, he was able to rise above these pressures and refused to give up his Cahuilla identity. Meyers charted his own course by drawing on opportunities to participate in the dominant culture, but never at the expense of denying or downplaying his Cahuilla heritage.

## A Start in Baseball (1893–1902)

Before Meyers was born the Cahuilla and tribes throughout California had adopted baseball as a popular form of recreation.[21] Meyers was likely introduced to the game as a little boy on the Santa Rosa Reservation. By the time he reached his teenage years, he was playing on a Reservation team as well as various Riverside teams against clubs from other reservations and towns. Late in life he remembered playing for the Santa Rosa team in games at Hemet and San Jacinto.[22]

As Meyers told the story, his first experience with baseball was as a pitcher, with his older brother Marion playing catcher. However, Marion was the better pitcher, so before long the two had traded positions and Jack was "behind the bat," as the position of catcher was then described. According to Jack, Marion was an excellent hurler. "But for an accident by which he lost an eye," he once said, "I believe my brother would have been a much better ball player than myself."[23]

By 1897 John Tortes Meyers was living with his mother (who never remarried), his brother, and his sister in a house Felicité had purchased on La Cadena Drive in Riverside.[24] Though he did not graduate from Riverside High School, a photograph, probably from the late nineteenth century, shows Meyers seated among a group of baseball players wearing Riverside High School uniforms.[25]

About this time Meyers played on a baseball team organized by the Santa Fe Railroad. As was common with teams sponsored by businesses, the players were given jobs. Most of his teammates were assigned light work, but the already muscular Meyers took a job in the railroad's shop that made and repaired boilers for the engines. He loved the work and attributed his ability to sustain the rigors of a full season's schedule as a catcher to the endurance he developed swinging a sledgehammer.[26]

One of the teams the Santa Fe club played was from Olinda in Orange County. The Olinda star was a teenage pitcher with a blazing fastball named Walter Johnson, who was on his way to becoming one of the greatest pitchers in the history of baseball. It was the first of a number of encounters Meyers would have with Johnson, tagged "Big Train" by famed sportswriter Grantland Rice for his size and speed. Meyers once said of Johnson, "[E]verybody knew what was coming, but still couldn't hit him. Walter's right arm was different than yours or mine. It was special, like Caruso's lungs or Einstein's brain."[27]

At some point during this period, while playing baseball in Riverside, Meyers took another job he later claimed also helped him develop his baseball skills. The story may very well be an example of the "sly wit" Meyers often displayed when talking to reporters. He was hired, he said, to bud citrus trees, and, while his back was turned, the foreman would simultaneously yell and throw an orange at him. At the sound, Meyers would spin around and impale the orange in flight on his budding knife.[28] It was, it could be said, good training for a "budding catcher."

By 1902 Meyers's baseball skills were already becoming sharply honed. That year he was tapped to play in a game by the Ontario, California, Athletic Club team. After losing the first game of a series against the Upland team, 36–12, the Ontario manager recruited Meyers as a "ringer" for the next contest. The moment Meyers entered the game, Ontario's fortunes changed. They went on to sweep the remaining four games in the series.[29]

Meyers called Hall of Fame pitcher Walter "Big Train" Johnson's right arm "different than yours or mine ... like Caruso's lungs or Einstein's brain." He both caught and batted against Johnson in California Winter League and barnstorming games (Library of Congress, Prints & Photographs Division, LC-DIG-hec-02661).

An article describing the Ontario–Upland game identified Meyers as a student at Sherman Institute in Riverside. While it is possible he attended the intertribal boarding school, as his nephews later did, he was 22 years old in 1902. It seems more likely that, if Meyers was associated with Sherman, he was on occasion "drafted" to play on the Institute's baseball team even though he was not formally a student.

Between 1902 and 1904 Meyers was playing on a variety of teams in southern California, while he worked on the Santa Fe Railroad. Even as he was continuing to play in the Riverside area, he also made appearances for semi-pro teams in San Diego, in both summer and winter leagues.

In 1903 Meyers had a tryout with the Los Angeles Nationals of the short-lived Pacific National League. Three catchers competed for a spot on the Nationals roster — Meyers, William Traeger, and a player named Hardy. Hardy won the position, and Meyers moved on.[30]

In an early indication of his willingness to take a stand for the rights of employees, Meyers refused to cross the picket line and left his railroad job when workers went on strike in 1904. He then began to pursue baseball opportunities beyond southern California. In his words he "roamed the 'sticks' of Arizona and New Mexico playing for eating money."[31] The teams he played for were, he said, "not in organized ball, you know, just bush-league, semipro, although I made a living of sorts at it."[32] He played with a team in Morenci, Arizona, and another in El Paso, Texas, where he also found work as a Spanish interpreter, since he spoke the language fluently.[33]

## Decision to Attend Dartmouth College (1905)

In the summer of 1905 John Tortes Meyers was playing for the Phelps-Dodge Copper Company semipro team in Clifton, Arizona, when he had his first big break. It came at the Southwestern Baseball Tournament, held each year in association with the Territorial Fair in Albuquerque, New Mexico. Teams traveled to the tournament from towns in New Mexico, Arizona, and Colorado to compete for a first prize of $1,000. In order to improve their chances teams sometimes recruited minor league players and even an occasional big leaguer. To draw bigger crowds in 1905 the tournament organizers hired heavyweight champion of the world Jim Jeffries as a "celebrity" umpire, though, as Meyers remembered, Jeffries did not do much umpiring.[34]

One of the entries in the 1905 tournament was the "Big Six" team from Trinidad, Colorado. The team derived its name not from the nickname by which New York Giants pitching star Christy Mathewson was already then known but from one of the team's sponsors, the "Big Six Bar and Grill." The owner of the team was Dr. Michael Beshoar, a Trinidad physician and baseball fan. His two sons, Ben and John, were its player-managers.

One of the pitchers for the Big Six team was Ralph Glaze, a Colorado native who had already earned a reputation playing baseball and football at Dartmouth College in Hanover, New Hampshire. Like other collegiate players at the time Glaze used a pseudonym (Ralph Pearce) at the tournament to hide the fact he was playing for money. If word reached Dartmouth he was accepting payment for playing baseball, Glaze could have lost his athletic scholarship and been expelled from the school.

Six decades after the tournament Glaze told the story of meeting Meyers and convincing the Cahuilla catcher to play baseball at Dartmouth.[35] Meyers impressed Glaze and his Trinidad teammates with his abilities as soon as they saw him. By 1905 Meyers was 5 feet 11 inches tall and weighed 194 pounds. According to Glaze, Meyers was using the name "John Tortes" in the tournament, "but if he was a tortoise he didn't run like one. He could peg that ball, and he could hit; and it didn't bother him at all when I conked him on the head with a wild pitch. He didn't want to take first base."

Meyers's use of his mother's Cahuilla clan name and not his father's name at the tournament raises interesting questions. In his twenties was he affirming his pride in his Cahuilla heritage by dropping his father's Euroamerican name for his mother's clan name? Unlike Glaze, at this point Meyers would probably not have been concerned about protecting his amateur status. He was simply trying to move up from the semipro ranks to full-scale professional baseball. That he would have the opportunity to play for a collegiate team and would therefore need to hide the fact he was playing for money was likely the furthest thing from his mind.

Meeting Meyers caused Glaze to recall that in its original charter Dartmouth College made a commitment to the education of Indians. Why not, Glaze thought, take "John Tortes" back to Dartmouth and have him apply for one of the scholarships reserved for Indians? Initially Glaze wanted the muscular catcher to play football at Dartmouth, but when Glaze suggested it, Meyers was not interested. "Where would I learn football on the reservation?" he asked. However, baseball was different. Glaze told Meyers he would become better known playing on the east coast and that could help him get into the big leagues. According to Glaze, Jim Jeffries joined in trying to convince "Tortes" to go Dartmouth. Glaze remembered the heavyweight champion was "generous with refreshments of a stimulating nature, and that helped our case."

Another version of the incident used a then common stereotype of Indian athletes as "fearsome warriors" to dramatize the tale.[36] The anonymous author described Meyers as a "big savage" who "was then so aboriginal in appearance that he threw a scare into the tenderfoot or buffalo that happened his way." According to this version Glaze decided to recruit the Indian to play at Dartmouth, but fearing "he might scare him clear off the reservation," Glaze approached Jim Jeffries, who arranged to have "the unwilling Indian" hoisted aboard an eastbound train.In contrast to this portrayal, Meyers himself always said that he gladly accepted Glaze's offer to enroll at Dartmouth. He willingly left the tournament to return with Glaze to Colorado and then travel east to New Hampshire.

In 1905, without a high school degree, Meyers would not be able to gain admission to Dartmouth as a regular applicant. However, his lack of a degree did not derail the plan for him to enroll in the college to play baseball and perhaps football also, if he could be convinced. According to Ralph Glaze, Trinidad team manager Ben Beshoar simply used a chemical to remove his own name from his high school diploma. For a reason Glaze never learned, instead of writing "John Tortes" in the space created by the erasure of his own name, Beshoar instead inserted "Ellis Williams," the name of the left fielder on the Clifton, Arizona, team on which Tortes had played. The Trinidad high school superintendent was convinced to write a letter of recommendation for "Williams," and several Dartmouth alumni in Denver were able to secure railroad passes for Glaze and "Tortes." "A good thing that was, too," Glaze remembered, "Chief Tortes ate me poor on the dining cars." "Indians need steak," Glaze quoted Meyers as saying.

For most of his life Meyers simply said he earned admission to Dartmouth by studying hard and passing the entrance examinations. For example, in 1947 he told Grantland Rice that only Indians who met academic requirements were admitted to Dartmouth, and "that's how I happened to enroll there."[37]

Meyers did not publicly reveal the truth about the circumstances of his admission to Dartmouth until late in life. As their friendship developed, he chose Lawrence Ritter as the one through whom a more accurate version of his admission to the Ivy League school would become public knowledge. The two were in New York together in 1966 to help promote the publication of *The Glory of Their Times*. One evening, after presenting a copy of the book to representatives from the College at the Dartmouth Club in New York, Meyers told Ritter the true story of his enrollment, not apologetically but with "a twinkle in his eye." Meyers said that in 1905, when Glaze approached him about going to Dartmouth, he had not even graduated from elementary school, adding, "Indians have never been encouraged to get a lot of education." The ruse was necessary for him to be able to win acceptance, but he told Ritter he was dubious it would work. The doctored diploma described "Ellis William" as being five feet six inches with red hair. He laughed and told Ritter, "I was six feet tall and my hair was coal black." However, Ralph Glaze had friends in the Admissions Office and they overlooked the discrepancy.[38]

Regardless of the circumstances, when he began the train ride east from Colorado to New Hampshire in September 1905, Meyers was embarking on a truly remarkable journey that would take him a continent away from his Cahuilla homeland into what he would come to call a "strange land." There he would reach the pinnacle of success and recognition in the white man's "national pastime," and be faced with the challenge of remaining rooted in his Cahuilla heritage while taking advantage of the amazing opportunities the dominant culture provided him.

## "Chief" Meyers

When was John Tortes Meyers first called "Chief"? Since the application of the stereotypical label to Native American athletes was already common by 1905, it is likely that beginning in his semipro days his teammates, opposing players, and fans all called him Chief. It is certain that by the time Meyers arrived at Dartmouth he was being called Chief, the nickname by which he was known at the College and for the rest of his life.

The first recorded use of the nickname that, in effect, functioned almost as a first name for Meyers, in lieu of John or Jack, provides an occasion for exploring the meanings of "Chief" when applied to Native American athletes, and what Meyers himself thought of the label.

Virtually every Native American ball player who played in the major leagues, beginning with Louis Sockalexis in the late nineteenth century and continuing into the 1950s, was tagged with the nickname "Chief." Like Meyers, Sockalexis, a Penobscot Indian from Maine, was recruited to play college baseball. In 1894 the captain of the Holy Cross team saw Sockalexis, an outfielder, playing in a summer league and convinced him to enroll in the Worcester, Massachusetts, school. His teammates at once began calling him "Chief." The label stuck with Sockalexis during his college days and brief major league career with the Cleveland Indians (1897–99), where the press dubbed him "Chief Sock-it-on-the nose" because of his powerful hitting. Cartoonists portrayed the college-educated Sockalexis as a warrior, wearing a Plains-style headdress and wielding a tomahawk. When he led his team to victory, the *Cleveland Plain Dealer* headlined, "The Indians Hung One Little Scalp on Their Belt." On another occasion, after a win, the paper described Socalexis and his teammates as "a tribe of Indians doing a scalp dance upon an expiring foe."[39]

The tradition of calling Native American major leaguers "Chief" continued throughout the first half of the twentieth century. In his groundbreaking study of the American Indian integration of baseball, Jeffrey P. Beck noted, "In addition to 'Chief' Charles Albert Bender and 'Chief' John Tortes Meyers, there were 'Chief' Moses Yellow Horse, 'Chief' George H. Johnson, 'Chief' Louis Leroy, 'Chief' Ike Kahdot, 'Chief' Euel Moore, 'Chief' Ben Tincup, 'Chief' Elon Hogsett, 'Chief' Pryor McBee, 'Chief' Emmett Bowles, 'Chief'

Jim Bluejacket, and 'Superchief' Allie Reynolds, among others."[40] Although his fame as an Olympian made him largely immune to the epithet as a major leaguer, when Jim Thorpe played summer baseball while a student at Carlisle Indian school in 1909, he was called "Big Chief" or "Big Chief Bullhead," and even took for a time to calling himself "Chief."[41]

Some historians have taken the position that "Chief" was not used derogatorily but was simply a benign means of identifying an Indian athlete.[42] They cite Indians who apparently enjoyed being called Chief. Charles Albert "Chief" Bender, Hall of Fame pitcher for the Philadelphia Athletics, "heard 'Chief' so often — and so often with affection — that he allowed the name to be etched into his tombstone. Marie, his wife, simply identified herself as 'Mrs. Chief Bender.'"[43]

Other historians state forcefully that while Native American players like Meyers may have grown accustomed to being called "Chief, to the point of acceptance, they knew it was in fact a caricature and racist slur, comparable to calling an African American man "Boy," as was also common at the time.[44] According to Beck, "the 'Chief' epithet was not meant to honor American Indian identity but to appropriate and cartoonize it as an 'Other' in the manner of the cigar-store Indian or the Wild West show Indian."[45]

For still others, the issue is more complex. Historian Joseph Oxendine, a member of the Lumbee tribe from North Carolina, is among those who note that in the early twentieth century Chief was not always used as an intentionally derogatory label. However, he also knew from personal experience that the nickname was most often a way to "define you and keep you in your place." Playing in baseball's minor leagues in the 1950s, Oxendine was often called Chief and came to the conclusion "[m]ost Indians do not want to be called 'Chief' because it demeans the significance of the [tribal] chief, and it's a constant reminder, like saying, 'Hey, Indian.' You don't mind being known as an Indian, but you don't want it to be your whole identity."[46]

What did Meyers think of being called Chief? As he began his rookie season in 1909, Meyers let it be known he preferred to be identified by his given name rather than the label "Chief."[47] However, the writer who noted Meyers's request ignored it in the same article, calling him "Chief." From then on Meyers must have known it was inevitable he would be tagged with the nickname. In his ninth decade, as he looked back over his life, he told a reporter with resignation, "Every Indian who ever goes into baseball is a 'chief.'"[48] In the view of some, despite his awareness of the inevitability of being called Chief, "as a man of dignity and intelligence," Meyers must have "loathed the nickname" because of its racist connotations.[49] It is noteworthy that, though he used "Chief" when talking about himself, he usually avoided the term when speaking about other Native American major leaguers.

However, Meyers was also aware Chief was not always intended as a pejorative. According to his grandniece Shanna Meyers, "being called 'Chief' didn't really bother him, because," as she put it, "that was just the accepted practice at the time."[50]

Ironically, John Tortes Meyers would come legitimately by the title of Chief years after his baseball career ended.

# Two

## *Cahuilla Roots*

### John Tortes Meyers and His Cahuilla Heritage

In 1912 Giants catcher John Tortes Meyers introduced himself in a *New York American* article to baseball fans who knew him only as "Chief" or "Big Chief":

> I was born and raised in Riverside, California, and hope to spend my days in that State. My people are Mission Indians. There are not many of these Indians left now, but it is one of the oldest tribes on the American Continent. A few are still gathered together on a Government reservation about sixty miles from Riverside, living under agency control and keeping their old customs; but the younger generation, for the most part, live in the towns, and have long since broken away from the traditions of their people.[1]

Meyers's reluctance to use the name "Cahuilla" was not because of a lack of pride in his own people. Members of the Meyers family who knew him all affirm he was intensely proud to be a Cahuilla and deeply valued his Cahuilla heritage.[2]

Meyers was also well aware the Cahuilla were quite distinct from the "Mission Indians." Nearly a century later the Bureau of Indian Affairs designation "Mission Indians" continues to be a nagging problem for the Cahuilla bands of southern California. As Meyers's grandniece Shanna Meyers puts it, "We are *not* 'Mission Indians.' The missions were on the coast and we're not there. We're still having trouble getting them to remove 'Mission' from our name."[3] By using this deceptive government label rather than the tribe's own self-designation, Meyers was subtly referencing the "agency control" under which the Cahuilla people were being forced to live.

As the 1912 article implies, Meyers also knew well the injustices the Cahuilla had suffered and were still enduring during his lifetime. By saying not many of his people remained, he was alluding to the steep decline in the Cahuilla population caused by the invasion of the Cahuilla homeland, the introduction of diseases like smallpox, and a history of abuse by Europeans and Euroamericans.

What happened on the reservation where some of Meyers's relatives lived and where he spent part of his youth reinforced his awareness of the injustices his people had suffered. Called Santa Rosa, because it is in the Santa Rosa Mountains about 60 miles from Riverside near the town of Anza, California, the small reservation is in a desolate mountainous area unsuited for growing crops. "They put us out in that pile of rocks," Meyers often said, "where they didn't think the property was worth anything."[4]

As Meyers acknowledged in the *New York American* article, while the traditional Cahuilla way of life was still followed on the Santa Rosa Reservation, he was among the "younger generation" who were leaving the old customs behind and moving away. It would have been tempting for him to turn his back on his heritage entirely, given the way the Cahuilla were viewed. In a 1913 article on Meyers and other Indian ballplayers, William Phelon distinguished the Giants catcher from others in his tribe, claiming the Cahuilla were "too indolent and goodhumored, too contented with their sunny clime, to get out and do any strenuous athletic stunts. Chief Meyers, who has more enterprise in his system than the rest of his tribesmen, is," Phelon concluded, "probably the only Mission Indian to make good at the game."[5]

Other Native American major leaguers chose to cope with the racism of the time by distancing themselves from their tribal roots. Meyers did not. As is evident in his use of his mother Felicité's clan name, Tortes, Meyers embraced his Cahuilla identity. As we will see, he sought to live by the principles implicit in the Cahuilla worldview. Even as he reached stardom in America's most beloved game, he wanted New Yorkers to know he planned to return to his homeland and his people after his playing days were over.

## Who Are the Cahuilla?

The name Cahuilla (pronounced *ka'-weeyu*) may come from the Cahuilla people's own word *ka'wiya*, which means "master" or perhaps "ruling one."[6] The Cahuilla speak often of power not just in the sense of physical ability but "mental and spiritual strength — strength of character."[7] Therefore, "Cahuilla" may mean one who is strong in mind and spirit. To live as a Cahuilla is to face life's challenges and overcome life's adversities.

According to archaeologists the Cahuilla first arrived in what is now southern California about 2,000 to 3,000 years ago, once occupying an area of about 2,400 square miles.[8] Cahuilla territory was bisected by a major trade route, the Coco-Maricopa Trail, which Meyers often cited as evidence of his people's economic sophistication.[9]

Traditional Cahuilla villages were established near springs (sometimes called "Indian wells") or streams in the mountains and desert canyons. Because of the scarcity of food, village boundaries and the areas in which the people of the village could hunt and gather food were carefully defined and protected.[10]

Most who have studied the Cahuilla cite three main groups: the Desert, Pass, and Mountain Cahuilla. Meyers's Santa Rosa Band was a part of the Mountain Cahuilla. When Cahuilla land was seized, the Mountain Cahuilla were forced into an isolated, rocky area "affording little encouragement to human occupation."[11] Or, as Meyers put it more vividly, the land upon which his people were made to live was "a pile of rocks."

Even though many younger Cahuilla turned away from old Cahuilla customs during Meyers's lifetime, the traditional way of life was still alive and remained so well into the twentieth century. In the 1950s about 25 percent of the Cahuilla still spoke their native language, and many more understood it. When a language remains alive, a culture retains its vibrancy. And when a culture remains in the same locale for long periods of time, memories persist because they are tied to place. So it was for the Cahuilla.[12]

## *Mukat's* Descendants: The Cahuilla Creation Story

Fundamental to the understanding of any culture is an appreciation of its unique story of origins. The traditional Cahuilla creation legend was still being recounted in conjunction with Cahuilla ceremonies in the late nineteenth and early twentieth centuries, and Meyers almost certainly heard one or more versions of it. The following is a summary of the beginning of the story as it was being recited in 1925.[13]

In the beginning there was only darkness. Red, white, blue, and brown all swirled together at one point, producing two embryos. They grew into children and made a hole in the sack of colors. When they emerged they named themselves *Mukat* and *Temayawut*. They made a center pole and also earth, the ocean and sky. From black mud *Mukat* made creatures. *Temayawut* made them from white mud. *Mukat* worked slowly to form a human being, with the fine body humans have now. *Temayawut* worked more quickly and made a body with a belly and eyes on both sides and hands like the paws of a dog. *Mukat* and *Temayawut* fought over whose bodies were better and how they should live and die. *Mukat* prevailed, so *Temayawut* took his creatures and left.

All of *Mukat's* creatures then came to life and the sun appeared. The creatures were frightened and chattered like blackbirds, in different languages. *Mukat* heard one human speak in Cahuilla and pressed him to his side. This one was the ancestor of the Cahuilla, who live in the abode of the sun, moon, and evening star. Only the Cahuilla speak their original language.

These earliest beings, called *nukatem,* were very large and had more *ʔivaʔa\** (power) than later humans would. Over time they turned into the moon, stars, rainbows and other natural beings. When Cahuilla look at the night sky, rainbows, or bodies of water they remember the first *nukatem.*

## The Traditional Cahuilla Worldview

The various Cahuilla bands have traditionally shared a common worldview, reflecting the story of origins.[14] As will become evident, Meyers took to heart many of the basic principles and values manifest in the distinctive Cahuilla way of looking at the world.

### The Creative Power *(ʔivaʔa)*

The Cahuilla call the creative force or energy present in all things *ʔivaʔa.* Nothing exists independently from *ʔivaʔa,* for all things were created through and by it. It is manifest in the special powers of Cahuilla people and in the actions of spirit beings. The force is neither good nor evil; rather, it is unstable and unpredictable. If treated respectfully, *ʔivaʔa* may be beneficial; however, if not treated properly, it may cause great harm.[15]

To cope with the uncertainty of *ʔivaʔa,* Cahuilla have sought to follow a clear set of values and rules for living. Meyers was certainly aware of the concept of *ʔivaʔa,* and he likely attributed his awesome power as a hitter to this force he knew to be present in the world. Instinctively, he would have recognized that only if he treated the power that gave him the ability to hit so well with respect would it remain with him and give him success. He also understood that to live fully and well he would have to observe the basic Cahuilla guidelines and principles outlined below.

### Authority

In Cahuilla culture tradition carries great weight and is the principal source of authority. Age is the second source of authority, and a basis for privilege, power, and honor. Elders are shown deference and respect in Cahuilla society, for their knowledge of the traditions is essential to being able to adapt to diverse and changing circumstances. Older people are also

---

*The "ʔ" sign represents a sound in the Cahuilla language, almost like a gulp.

believed to be "more cautious, precise, orderly, and [have] more creative power than [do] the younger people."[16]

Baseball, especially during the era when Meyers played, is the American sport most respectful of tradition and of the elders of the game. The deference Meyers learned as a Cahuilla for the authority of tradition and age served him well as a major league ballplayer.

## The Social Universe

In the Cahuilla worldview humans are not seen as rulers of the natural world. A traditional Cahuilla saying is that "I am related everywhere." Like all other beings humans have a responsibility to contribute to the harmony of all. This understanding helped Meyers adapt well to seeing himself as part of a whole when he left his Cahuilla homeland, whether as part of the Dartmouth College community or as a member of the New York Giants baseball team. He grasped, on the basis of his cultural heritage, that his purpose was not so much earning individual acclaim as contributing to the well-being of the group of which he was a part.

Traditional Cahuilla society was patrilineal, with identity determined by the clan of one's father. Each clan recognized a common male ancestor. There were at least seven, perhaps as many as 20 clans, until the influence of the system began to break down about the time Meyers was born. Because his father was not Cahuilla, Meyers took his clan name (Tortes) from his mother. The fact that he preferred his full name, John Tortes Meyers, throughout his life is a strong indication of the pride he had in his Cahuilla heritage and his clan identity.

When a Cahuilla child lost his or her father, the older brother's role was that of surrogate father to his younger siblings. Meyers's older brother Marion exercised that role after their father died when Jack was a boy, but when Marion passed away in the 1930s the "head of family" responsibilities would have passed to his younger brother. Meyers's awareness of that duty was certainly a factor in his decision to return to and remain in his Cahuilla homeland after his baseball career ended.

Ironic humor was used in traditional Cahuilla society to defuse tense situations and level social distinctions. Meyers skillfully used this kind of humor as a coping strategy at times when he felt intensely the sting of prejudice and the pressures of living between two worlds.

## Basic Cahuilla Values

In traditional Cahuilla society people were expected to live according to values established at the time of origins and transmitted by ritual leaders through songs.[17] Individuals who rebelled against these values were said to be "going against the song." Though the rituals and songs began to fade away during John Tortes Meyers's life, these values and their importance remained important to him. They clearly guided him as he made his way in the dominant culture.[18]

For the Cahuilla, industriousness is a valued characteristic in a person; to be lazy is disgraceful. This follows the example of *Mukat*, who used ingenuity to create the world and humans. As a rookie in 1909 Meyers quickly became aware that virtually all other players were faster on the basepaths, so he adapted by working hard to hone his skill as a power hitter and master the mental aspects of the game. He would be known for his strong work ethic and sharp intellect throughout his career.

Order, precision, and dependability are also traditional Cahuilla values. Just as *Mukat* was careful in creation (while *Temayawut* was careless) so must the Cahuilla people be. Things must be done "slowly, well, and deliberately." Actions have consequences not just for the individual but for the entire world system, so they must be thought through in all their implications. As we shall see, Meyers drew on these Cahuilla values in his careful, meticulous approach to the craft of hitting and catching, and in his overall approach to the game.

Moderation and personal control are other traditional Cahuilla values. Emotions are not to be displayed extravagantly, but with dignity and reserve. You should do your work without calling undue attention to yourself. While he was not always able to keep his temper in check on the ball field, Meyers did demonstrate incredible restraint during the constant barrage of racist baiting he experienced while playing. His strong sense of personal dignity was a quality often observed by teammates and opponents alike.

## The Cahuilla After the European and Euroamerican Invasion of Their Homeland

The first significant contact between the Cahuilla and Europeans came just over a century before John Tortes Meyers was born. In 1774 Spaniards from Mexico, led by Juan Bautista de Anza, arrived in the Cahuilla homeland. Anza and his men passed through the territory of a Cahuilla clan without seeking permission. According to a Cahuilla tradition passed through the generations, the warriors of the clan resisted the invasion, and the Spaniards were forced to withdraw.

At the time of first contact the Cahuilla population was perhaps as high as 10,000.[19] Because they were so far inland, isolated from the coastal missions established by the Spanish to control the native people and exploit their labor, the Cahuilla at first had few sustained interactions with the Spanish invaders.

By 1820, however, the Spanish had begun to move inland and mission outposts (*asistencia*) were established, including one among the Cahuilla at San Bernardino. Soon Mexican ranches sprang up on their land and the Cahuilla provided labor and often management. Spanish became and remained the second language spoken among the Cahuilla, until Euroamericans introduced English.

By 1830, a half-century before Meyers was born, some Cahuilla had converted to Catholicism and become dependent on European trade goods. Soon most Cahuilla were dressing in the style of the Mexicans and farming in the European manner. However, while they adopted European customs, most Cahuilla continued to practice their traditional ceremonies and abide by their own values.

During the next two decades a Mountain Cahuilla known by the Spanish name Juan Antonio served as an effective intermediary with the Mexicans. The willingness of Antonio and other Cahuilla leaders to adapt to European ways without surrendering their distinctive Cahuilla identity was a spirit Meyers would himself embrace.

When gold was discovered in 1849 Euroamericans began to flood Cahuilla lands on their way to the gold fields. Many stopped short of their destination and settled in Cahuilla territory. Relations were strained as the settlers took the most desirable lands. However, perhaps recognizing the inevitable, the Cahuilla adapted by charging for use of springs, working as wage laborers, and selling food to the newcomers.

In 1856 government officials named Juan Antonio "Principal-Chief" of the Cahuilla, though traditional Cahuilla society was and remained largely decentralized. With other Cahuilla leaders Antonio sent a letter to the Commissioner of Indian Affairs, outlining their grievances. "From time immemorial," the Cahuilla leaders stated, "we have lived upon and occupied [these] lands." However, they wrote, white settlers had forced the Cahuilla "to abandon portions of our improved lands greatly to the detriment and distress of our people." While other tribes had received aid and protection from the government, the Cahuilla had been completely neglected.[20]

Despite the ongoing mistreatment of the Cahuilla, in 1861 Antonio spoke eloquently of his people's sovereignty and willingness to cooperate with the government. Appearing before a U.S. judge in a dispute over jurisdiction in a criminal case, Antonio said, "I am an American — my people are all Americans, although we are Indians.... This is our country, and it is yours. We are your friends; we want you to be ours."[21]

In 1862 and 1863 a smallpox epidemic killed many Cahuilla, largely because they had not been offered the vaccinations that were then readily available in California. As a result, the Cahuilla population fell from as many as 10,000 at the time of initial contact with Europeans to about 1,200 less than a century later. The population continued to decline, dropping to about 1,000 at the time of the birth of John Tortes Meyers.

By 1880 some whites had become convinced that the Cahuilla and other California Indians would not survive if the government did not reserve at least some land for them. The first Cahuilla reservations were established by executive orders of the Grant and Hayes administrations in the 1870s. However, Euroamerican settlers went to court to challenge the orders. Vague descriptions of reservation borders were exploited and much of the reserved land was lost. Nevertheless, the reservations helped preserve relative Cahuilla isolation, creating enclaves where the traditional way of life was maintained and the Cahuilla could participate in Anglo-American culture only as necessary to survive.

Meyers was a toddler when the U.S. Congress established the Mission Indian (or Smiley) Commission to investigate why so many Cahuillas and other southern California Indians were being driven from their lands. It was motivated in part by Helen Hunt Jackson's 1881 exposé, *A Century of Dishonor,* which documented the theft of Indian land throughout the country. As a member of the Smiley Commission in 1883 Jackson wrote her own report to the Commissioner of Indian Affairs. The Cahuilla village she visited was high up in the San Jacinto Mountains, "a wild, barren, inaccessible spot." She attributed the independence of the Mountain Cahuilla she encountered in this village to their relative isolation from white settlements. "[T]he Cahuilla seemed a more clear-headed, more individual people than any other tribe we saw," Jackson wrote. "[They] are a particularly proud and spirited people." She demonstrated her point by telling the story of how despite lack of food due to crop failure they had refused to ask for help.[22]

An 1891 federal law formally established more reservations for the Cahuilla bands (including the Santa Rosa Reservation) and other southern California Indians. However, the Cahuilla were left with only two-thirds of the reduced land they had controlled before 1891.

The Tortes clan of Meyers's mother, Felicité, maintained traditional homes in the mountainous area that became the Santa Rosa Reservation. In addition, along with other Cahuilla they had temporary residences in "transient" villages established near Euroamerican towns. Felicité and others in her family lived for a time in such a community, called Spring Rancheria, located on the outskirts of early Riverside, California.[23]

During the first serious study of the Cahuilla on the Santa Rosa and other reservations in the 1890s and extending until another study in the late 1920s, researchers found commitment to traditional Cahuilla culture was still very

Spring Rancheria (shown here about 1890) was a small village on the edge of
Riverside, California, inhabited by "transient" Cahuilla Indians from various
reservations, including Meyers's mother Felicité Tortes and members of her
family (photograph by William Collier. Courtesy Riverside Metropolitan
Museum, Riverside, California).

strong and "ritual and worldview were very much as they had been prior to
European contact."[24] While John Tortes Meyers may not have had much direct
exposure to the traditional Cahuilla worldview and values at the temporary
village of Spring Rancheria, he certainly did while spending time as a youth
among his mother's many relatives on the Santa Rosa Reservation.

Nevertheless, with the establishment of reservations came increasing pressure for Cahuillas to be "civilized." As with other native nations, Cahuilla children, including Meyers when he was attending the government school at Santa
Rosa, were forced to speak English and trained to function in the dominant
culture, while being punished for speaking their own native languages and
practicing their traditional ways. Missionaries worked hard to convert Cahuilla
to Christianity, and Indian agents discouraged traditional ceremonies.

By the turn of the century, when Meyers was 20, the Bureau of Indian
Affairs agents controlled reservation life, appointing government agents,
judges and the police. As he wrote in his 1912 article, the people living on the
reservation where he had spent part of his youth, were "under agency control"
and "[t]he Government agent is the law."[25] Despite the discrimination they
experienced, many Cahuilla (including Meyers) served in the U.S. armed
forces during World War I.

The passage of the Indian Reorganization Act (1934) theoretically restored the right of the Cahuilla and other Indian nations to manage their own affairs, and some Cahuilla took advantage of this new freedom to buy back traditional lands and become successful cattle ranchers and business owners. Although most Cahuilla bands initially opposed the act, the tribal government structure with an elected council to oversee the affairs of the tribe was eventually adopted. After his baseball career, the new structure allowed Meyers to serve as an elected representative of the Santa Rosa Band for many years. As we will see, Meyers also benefitted from a new policy mandating the hiring of Native Americans for administrative positions in the Bureau of Indian Affairs.

During the Depression a number of Cahuilla returned to their small reservations where they could have at least a subsistence lifestyle and reconnect with their Cahuilla roots. Meyers was among them.

Although in declining numbers, some Cahuilla did their best to maintain the traditional ways during the 1930s and 1940s. In 1947 Francisco Patencio, who was one of the last Cahuilla traditional leaders *to* keep a ceremonial bundle and supervise rituals at a ceremonial house, died at the age of 91.[26] After his death, a few ceremonial houses remained, and his son performed the traditional songs he knew in them. In addition, bird songs and social dances were still performed, as they are to this day.

By the 1950s, according to one observer, the situation of the Cahuilla had become so "tangled and confused," because of the history of government mismanagement and incompetence, that "one is forced to admire the patience and skill of the few dedicated officials and Tribal Council members who have worked to bring some order out of the chaotic mess."[27] John Tortes Meyers, by now retired from baseball for three decades, was one of these leaders.

By the early 1970s, when Meyers died, there were about 900 people claiming Cahuilla descent, most enrolled members of one of the ten federally recognized Cahuilla bands (Agua Caliente, Augustine, Cabazon, Cahuilla, Los Coyotes, Morongo, Ramona, Santa Rosa, Soboba, and Torres-Martinez).

According to the 2000 census, of the 70 people living on the Santa Rosa Reservation 56 were Indians, most Cahuilla.[28]

A report on the Cahuilla released in 1996 summarized well the Cahuilla story:

> [It] is one of the great dramas of American Indian history, the story of a people determined to remain focused upon their best interests and the interests of their descendants. They were buttressed by a past preserved in their oral literature, passed on to them from generation to generation. Despite the outward symbols of cultural integration of the present and the appearance of passing into the mainstream of American culture, Cahuillas remain conscious of the persistent idea of Mukat's guiding his creations through time.[29]

# A Year at Dartmouth College and Three Years in the Minor Leagues (1905–1908)

## Dartmouth College and Indian Education

When "John Tortes" enrolled at Dartmouth College in the fall of 1905, the education of Native Americans was a largely unfulfilled promise the College had made at its founding. Granted by King George III of England in 1769, the Dartmouth Charter explicitly stated the College was established out of "the laudable and charitable design of spreading Christian knowledge among the savages of our American wilderness" and "for the education and instruction of youth of the Indian tribes in the land in reading, writing and all parts of learning which shall appear necessary and expedient for civilizing and Christianizing children of pagans as well as in all liberal arts and sciences, and also of English youth and any others."[1]

The College was founded by a missionary named Eleazar Wheelock who believed that if Indians were converted to Christianity and trained as missionaries, they would be more successful than non-natives in bringing the Christian gospel to their own people. In other words, Wheelock was an early promoter of the plan to assimilate Native Americans fully to the dominant, white society through evangelization and education. Over the years Meyers often told the story of Dartmouth's founding, always emphasizing that the Earl of Dartmouth, for whom the College is named, gave a large sum to Wheelock "with the stipulation that it was to be used only for the purpose of teaching any Indian who was qualified to matriculate at the school."[2]

To fulfill his objective Wheelock decided to locate the new college in "the Heart of the Indian country."[3] Originally, two schools opened in Hanover, New Hampshire, in 1769. Dartmouth College was reserved for the sons of Englishmen, hence its elitist tradition, while Moor's Charity School would be for Indians. The major fundraiser for Wheelock's project to educate Indians was the Reverend Samson Occom, a Mohegan Indian. Occom traveled to England and successfully raised money to support the mission to educate

Indians. However, Occom was not an uncritical supporter of the way Eleazar Wheelock was fulfilling the school's charter. He was upset when Wheelock placed increasing emphasis on the white students at Dartmouth after it effectively absorbed Moor's Charity School.[4]

By 1774 a hundred students attended Dartmouth, 21 of whom were Indians. With the advent of the American Revolution, the number of Native Americans at Dartmouth quickly declined. Reflecting the stereotypes of the time, a history of Dartmouth, written by an alumnus of the College several years after Meyers was on campus, noted the Indians in the early days had a penchant for "big beer." The author concluded that even if the Revolution had not occurred "the Indians would have been lost to Dartmouth, retreating into the forests before the white man's overwhelming civilization and refusing to come out."[5] Shortly before his death in 1779, Eleazar Wheelock lamented that although he had succeeded in teaching 40 Indians to read and write and had introduced them to the principles of Christianity, when they returned to their tribes, more than half "were sunk into as low, savage, and brutish a way of living as they were before and many of the most promising have fallen lowest."[6]

By 1829 the original commitment at Dartmouth to Native Americans was almost completely forgotten. Very few Indians were enrolled in the college. Foreign benefactors withdrew much of their support because their funding was contingent on the mission to educate Indians, but by then Dartmouth had acquired its own endowment and was able to survive without foreign donations.

The official version of the failure to keep the promise made in the Dartmouth Charter was that there were simply not enough qualified Indians for the college to recruit. It was the narrative Meyers himself apparently absorbed as a Dartmouth student, writing a few years after he left the school, "While there might be a lot of Indians who would like to have the advantage of a Dartmouth education, the trouble was they couldn't matriculate, couldn't pass the necessary entrance examinations."[7] Meyers's willingness to overlook Dartmouth's failure to follow through on the commitment of its charter and lay the blame where it more properly belonged — on the College's leaders — was undoubtedly shaped by the circumstances of his own admission and his affection for the school.

One Indian who did matriculate successfully at Dartmouth two decades before the arrival of "John Tortes" was Charles Eastman. Born in Minnesota in 1858 to a Dakota (Wahpeton Sioux) father, Many Lightnings, and a mixed-blood mother, Mary Eastman, he was given the name *Ohiyesa* ("Winner") early in life. Ohiyesa was raised in a traditional manner by his paternal grandmother in Canada and trained by male relatives as a hunter and warrior.

At the age of 14 Ohiyesa's father, who embraced Christianity while imprisoned for his role in the "Sioux Uprising" of 1862, reclaimed his son. Many Lightnings enrolled him in Santee Normal Training School in Flandreau, South Dakota, where the boy became immersed in the alien white culture. An excellent student, Ohiyesa took his mother's name, Eastman, and a new Christian name, Charles. Eastman went on to study for three years at Beloit College in Wisconsin, where he said he felt like a "stranger in a strange country,"[8] the same phrase Meyers would later apply to himself.

After a year at a prep school in New Hampshire, Eastman enrolled at Dartmouth College in 1883. In his autobiography, *From the Deep Woods to Civilization*, Eastman wrote with ambivalence and some irony of his years at Dartmouth. He knew at Dartmouth he would have the best hope of acquiring an education that would help him convince other Dakota to "accept civilization before it was too late." He felt his people were clinging too stubbornly to their old ways and needed "at once to take up the white man's way."[9]

Eastman's experiences at Dartmouth foreshadowed what Meyers would encounter at the College. The Dakota student felt that the president of Dartmouth as well as the College's faculty and staff, and virtually all students, accepted him warmly. However, Eastman also felt the sting of racism at Dartmouth. Though he considered his four years at the Ivy League school "rich and rewarding," he said he never felt at home there.[10]

As Meyers would later experience, when Eastman arrived at Dartmouth, it was assumed that as a "frontier warrior" he would excel at football. In his first "rush," he tackled a philosophy professor, mistaking him for a football player. The story was picked up and run by the Boston papers as an example of the "uncivilized" state Eastman was in when he came to Dartmouth.[11]

With such incidents in mind Eastman noted sarcastically that although the Indians of New England were gone, and could no longer attend Dartmouth, he "a warlike Sioux, like a wild fox," had found his way to the school from the "wild west." He ruefully observed, "It was [at Dartmouth] that I had most of my savage gentleness and native refinement knocked out of me. I do not complain, for I know that I gained more than their equivalent."[12]

After graduating from Dartmouth with honors in 1887 Eastman earned his medical degree at Boston University in 1890. Over the next several decades Eastman worked for the Bureau of Indian Affairs and published ten books and numerous articles, gaining fame as America's most distinguished Indian writer.[13] For many Native Americans facing the pressure of assimilation, Eastman's writings provided a bridge to self-respect by expressing the values of his own native tradition. Throughout his life he was an advocate for Indian rights, lecturing widely, and, in his own way, always promoting awareness of and respect for American Indian cultures.

Charles Eastman, renowned Dakota (Sioux) physician, author and defender of Indian rights, also attended Dartmouth College. Eastman sometimes appeared at events wearing traditional Native American dress, as in this photograph apparently taken during his senior year at Dartmouth (1887) (courtesy Dartmouth College Library).

For some of his lectures Eastman would wear, as he had on occasion while a student at Dartmouth and again in 1927 at the 40th anniversary of his Dartmouth graduation, "the full-dress costume of a Sioux chief," as one of his lecture advertisements put it. Wearing such attire seems to many observers today to manifest the stereotypes Eastman sought in his life's work to counter. In their view, by putting on such costumes he fell into the trap of "playing Indian." However, Eastman defended his wearing traditional Sioux dress as part of his educational mission to demonstrate visibly that being a sophisticated, cultured Indian did not mean divorcing himself from his tribal roots. In addition, by dressing in the costume that fulfilled the dominant culture's expectations of "Indianness," Eastman and other Native American professionals were able to get a hearing for the cause they were defending.[14] According to Colin Calloway, Professor of Native American Studies at Dartmouth today, "Eastman may have satisfied his classmates' expectations and fueled white stereotypes, but he also had his own agenda. Comfortable in starched collar and tie, he had no qualms about delivering a lecture wearing a war bonnet if it served his purposes and won points with his audience."[15]

John Tortes Meyers knew well the accomplishments of his predecessor at Dartmouth. In 1912 Meyers proudly wrote, "I was the first Indian to attend the college under the provisions of the fund since Dr. Charles Eastman, the great Indian author and lecturer, who has become one of the foremost men in the country."[16] Given his voracious reading Meyers likely encountered and was inspired by Eastman's accounts of succeeding while living as a "foreigner" in the white man's world. Here was another Indian professional willing to work hard, with skill, dedication, and tenacity, to become successful in the dominant society, but who also did not turn his back on his heritage and his people, despite the relentless pressure to do so.

Meyers would have questioned being compared so favorably to Charles Eastman. It bothered him that, unlike Eastman, he did not graduate from Dartmouth and make better use of the educational opportunities he had been given at the Ivy League school. He wrote in 1912, Dartmouth "offered me the same advantages that Eastman had, and I have many times since regretted not staying."[17]

However, even though they followed very different career paths, both Charles Eastman and John Tortes Meyers found the balance between their Native American roots and lives as successful professionals in the white man's world. Both adapted successfully to the dominant society, but neither lost sight of the places and people from whom they came. In different settings both Dartmouth men spoke out for Indian rights and worked on behalf of Indian people.

# "John Tortes" at Dartmouth (1905-06)

Between Eastman's graduation in 1887 and Meyers's enrollment in 1905, none of the five Native Americans who attended Dartmouth in the interim graduated. Despite the absence of Indian students, Dartmouth was continuing to make use of its own version of Indian symbols. The poet Robert Frost, who spent a year at Dartmouth in the 1890s, would remember, "Much of what I enjoyed at Dartmouth was acting like an Indian in a college founded for Indians."[18]

When the new Dartmouth Hall was dedicated in 1904 the sixth Earl of Dartmouth was present. He was greeted by students with the Dartmouth cheer — the "Indian chant" "Wah-Hoo-Hah!" Like other "Indian symbols" that became popular at Dartmouth over the years, the chant had been invented by whites. The full cheer (Wah-Hoo-Wah, Wah-Hoo-Wah, Da-di-di-Dartmouth, Wah-Hoo-Wah, Tiger-r-r-r) was the creation of a member of the class of 1879.[19]

Another "Indian symbol" popular when Meyers attended Dartmouth was a ceremony begun in 1854 at which graduating seniors gathered around the stump of an old pine tree linked to the college's origins to smoke and then break a "peace pipe." Three years before Meyers arrived at the College, the custom of carrying a cane topped with an Indian head to graduation began.[20]

When the train on which Ralph Glaze and "John Tortes" traveled from Colorado arrived at White River Junction, Vermont, in September 1905, Glaze recalled he "decided to do things in style, so I hired a rig there for the five-mile ride to Hanover, N.H., home of Dartmouth. Some of the boys were pretty surprised when I piled out of the fancy rig with this very big, very dark Indian."[21]

From the moment he set foot on the Dartmouth campus Meyers was known simply as "Chief" or "Big Chief," the "big, very dark Indian" Ralph Glaze brought from what most Dartmouth students still considered the "wild west."[22] However, his dress did not meet the students' expectations of what an Indian should be wearing that first day. "John Tortes" was still in the "glaring red" baseball uniform he wore during the Albuquerque tournament.[23]

As he would later tell Lawrence Ritter, Meyers had difficulty registering for classes since he carried two names— John Tortes and Ellis Williams. A Dartmouth Registration Certificate dated October 16, 1905, seems to have Tortes with Ellis Williams written over "John" to create the name "Ellis Williams Tortes." The Demming, Colorado, high school diploma carrying the name "Ellis Williams" had apparently arrived, and someone in the Admissions Office had decided to combine the two names. In a slightly different version of the story, Ernest Martin Hopkins, then assistant to Dartmouth President William Jewett Tucker, and later the College's president himself, recalled that Ellis Williams was the son of the superintendent of an Indian reservation in the west, who had been admitted to Cornell University. Williams decided not to attend and allowed his Cornell admissions papers to be used as part of Meyers's application to Dartmouth, saying, "He can take my papers perfectly well and take my name.... They name all these Indians ... give them Anglicized names and that's perfectly all right."[24] The Dartmouth certificate listed "Ellis Williams Tortes's" home address as Montezuma Valley, Colorado, with his place of birth Riverside, California. An additional year was shaved off Meyers's birthdate, which was listed as July 24, 1883. "John Tortes," whose occupation was described as "Hunter," was named as his parent. His "church preference" was identified as Catholic. "Williams'" room assignment was 6 H[allgarten] H[all].[25]

The obstacle of registering at Dartmouth overcome, Meyers signed up for Spanish since he could already speak it fluently. An alumnus who had been in the class with Meyers remembered that when the professor asked him to translate, "Big Chief" would say, "Spanish to English or English to Spanish. Which do you want?"[26] "Tortes" also took history, biology, graphics (mechanical drawing), and English during his first semester. English was apparently his hardest course. "We got him a 'pony,'" Glaze recalled, "to help him over Chaucer. We also provided a tutor for him, and all three of us, the tutor, the Chief and I roomed in Hell Gate Dormitory (the name the students gave to Hallgarten Hall)."[27]

"John Tortes" was so popular on campus he was soon invited to join Kappa Kappa Kappa, a Dartmouth fraternity. By 1905 Tri-Kap, as it was known, was considered by students to be one of the strongest fraternal societies at the school. One of the biggest obstacles to Tri-Kap membership for Meyers was the requirement to wear formal dress at fraternity banquets. At first, Glaze recalled, he had a "terrible time" getting his Cahuilla friend into a full-dress suit. Meyers balked at wearing a "plug hat," but when finally convinced, he looked in the mirror and said, "If that barkeep from Morenci saw me now, he'd never recognize me." After one banquet, Glaze found "Tortes" stuffing cigars and cigarettes into his pockets. "He was a prudent man, was John Tortes," Glaze observed.

While at Dartmouth Tortes smoked a huge Indian-head pipe given to him by one of his fellow students. Glaze remembered his friend strolling into another student's room, puffing on his empty pipe in vain. The student would tell him to help himself to some tobacco. Meyers would then stuff the bowl full, go back to his room and dump the tobacco into a container. According to Glaze, that was his system for keeping a ready supply.

Looking back on his experience at Dartmouth, Meyers believed he received special treatment, perhaps in equal measure as a result of his age and because of his status as the only Indian then at the school. "Even though I was but a freshman," he wrote, "I would wear my hat on the campus and smoke a pipe and that was quite a concession from the other students."[28] Contrary to what Glaze and others believed, in 1905 there was no money budgeted by the college to support Indians at Dartmouth. In Meyers's case President Tucker created a special fund of $500 to cover his expenses.[29]

According to Glaze, "Tortes" was "as popular with the townies as he was with the students, partly because of the Western stories." Meyers's yarns were not of his Cahuilla heritage and the traditional Cahuilla way of life, but of Indian braves in war bonnets, tipis on the open plains, and buffalo hunts. He was clearly telling the stories the students and residents of Hanover associated in their imaginations with Indians.

Glaze took "Tortes" to out-of-town football games, and remembered "he was interested in going to other places beside the saloons. I took him once to the Boston Public Library. There he saw that famous picture of Custer's Last Stand. 'That's the best break the Indians ever got,'" Glaze recalled his friend saying. It was a line Meyers would often use later in life.

According to Glaze, "Tortes" worked hard on his studies and passed everything except graphics his first semester. His favorite subject was history, in which he received his best grades. The second semester he had more trouble academically as his lack of formal schooling apparently caught up with him. His first New England winter also took a toll, though he adapted. In a display of Cahuilla ingenuity, in order not to have to take his hands out of his overcoat pockets to tip his hat to professors when passing them on campus, Meyers attached a string, which he kept in his pocket, to his hat. When he passed a professor he could pull the cord and lift his hat without getting his fingers cold.[30]

The plan Glaze championed to have "John Tortes" play baseball at Dartmouth did not materialize. According to Meyers, "I played a little baseball at Dartmouth, but naturally was ineligible for the regular team, on account of having played for money."[31] However, Meyers may have been recruited to play for some semi-pro teams near Dartmouth. Years later, one fan remembered seeing Chief Meyers while he was playing for a team in Franklin, New Hampshire.[32]

It was not baseball but the attempt to turn Meyers into a football player from the first day he arrived at Dartmouth that received the most attention on campus and beyond. The contemporary success and notoriety of the all–Indian football squad at the Carlisle Indian boarding school in Pennsylvania likely contributed to the expectation that Dartmouth's own Indian, "Big

Chief" Tortes, would be a great addition to the football team.[33] The assumption was that Indian men, who were "warlike by nature," would make good football players. Charles Eastman had encountered the same stereotype two decades earlier.

Meyers described his experience with football at Dartmouth succinctly: "I was out trying for the football squad, but I didn't last at that very long.

During his year at Dartmouth College (1905–1906), Meyers, shown here in a football uniform, was known on campus as "Big Chief" Tortes. Although he had never played football and had no interest in the sport, it was assumed that, as an Indian, he had the "savage instincts" necessary for the game. Dartmouth students prevailed upon him to try out for the team, but he never played in a game (courtesy Dartmouth College Library).

[The Boston papers] made much of the fact that I was out trying for the eleven. Bill Folsom, then the football coach, and now a lawyer in Boulder, Col., instructed me to tackle a fellow one day, and they said afterwards they thought I was charging a hostile tribe the way I went after him."[34] Ernest Hopkins remembered that Folsom lined "Tortes" up against two of the biggest linemen on the team, and Chief "brushed them aside as though they were flies on the wall."[35]

Meyers's ill-fated tryout with the Dartmouth football team soon became a popular story on campus. An article reporting the incident, apparently from an early fall 1905 edition of the student newspaper, *The Dartmouth*, appeared with the title "Dartmouth's Indian Chief," and began with a statement in bold: **"Stalwart Son of the Forest Hopes to 'Add a White Man's Mind to an Indian's Body' — He Knows Nothing of Football, but Thinks He Can Learn It."**[36]

The article shows that Meyers's Dartmouth classmates viewed him ambivalently in several ways. On the one hand, he was the stereotypical Indian: "Big Chief Tortes," "the son of the forest," who, in his mammoth frame, displayed physically the image of the Indian warrior. However, Tortes was also the archetype of the Indian fully committed to the goal of assimilation, desiring, like Dartmouth legend Samson Occom, "to add a white man's mind to an Indian's body." Yet what drew Dartmouth students to him was not to discover what he thought about issues of the day or even to learn about his heritage, but simply to see if this "flesh-and-blood Indian warrior" could adapt to the feigned combat of the white man's game of football. Indeed, it was his display of raw physical power that "won the hearts" of his classmates and made "Big Chief" a "big man on campus." The article's observation that "Tortes speaks excellent English" and "has a wealth of good humor" were two of the markers often given to show that a foreigner from a "primitive" culture was ready and willing to try to fit into the society that only welcomes the outsider on its own, stereotypical terms.

Soon word of "Big Chief" Tortes spread beyond the Dartmouth campus. According to Meyers, the Boston papers were picking up the stories of his football experience at the Hanover school, as they had Eastman's 20 years earlier. One such article, presumably from a New England paper, repeated many of the stereotypes of the campus reports but in an even more distorted and exaggerated fashion.[37] It then added a note about a telling incident:

> Just before the Brown game [on November 25, 1905], when it was announced at Hanover that Brown would bring a bear to Springfield [Massachusetts] as a mascot, the suggestion was made that a band of Indians be sent to represent Dartmouth with Tortes as chief. And the scalping of the Brown bear by the chief between the halves at Hampton Park was one of the features of the game.

A hand-painted sign celebrating Dartmouth's 24–6 victory over Brown shows a stereotypical Indian brave pulling a Brown bear to a teepee labeled "Hang-Over" and another Indian celebrating next to a large container of rum (representing the 500-gallon supply of rum claimed to have been present at Dartmouth's founding in a popular song written by a Dartmouth student in the 1880s).[38] The point was clear. Dartmouth students had made Meyers their own Indian mascot.

The stories of Meyers's football exploits at Dartmouth followed him into his major league baseball career, with the stereotypical themes amplified. An article titled "Chief Meyers Had Fine Time up at Dartmouth" appeared in the *Boston Herald* in December 1913.[39] The anonymous author chuckled when he thought of the now legendary incident on the Dartmouth football field eight years earlier. Nine hundred undergraduates turned out for the practice "and everyone was bug-eyed with wonder when the Goliath of an Indian shuffled out from the side line. He looked as tall as the Baptist church and as heavy as the town hall." No longer just a large man, "Big Chief Tortes" had become a mammoth, virtually mythic presence. In portraying Meyers as "the big grinning chief" who regarded "everything as a huge joke," the article was

A poster celebrating a 1905 Dartmouth College football victory over Brown University, with an image drawn from the legend popular at the College that the first Indians at Dartmouth enjoyed drinking from a barrel of rum. His Dartmouth classmates recruited Meyers to dress as the "Dartmouth Indian" and symbolically "scalp" Brown's mascot, a bear, at the game (courtesy Dartmouth College Library).

an early manifestation of the stereotype that would later give rise to the still-used "grinning chief" logo of the Cleveland Indians baseball team.

For several reasons, toward the end of his second semester at Dartmouth, Meyers decided to leave the college. It was a choice he would regret for the rest of his life. According to Ralph Glaze, when someone on the Dartmouth staff noticed that the high school transcript "Tortes" had presented described him as five feet six inches tall with red hair, President Tucker called the freshman in to explain. When he learned "Tortes" was not eligible to be a regular student, the Dartmouth president offered to get him into Andover Academy in order to better prepare for college. "That man," Glaze remembered Meyers saying of President Tucker, "has eyes like a tree full of owls."[40]

After the meeting with President Tucker, Meyers decided to forego the offer to attend a prep school.[41] At Andover he would have been with students fully ten or more years younger. It was clearly not an appealing idea. Instead, he decided to give professional baseball a try. From Dartmouth baseball coach Tom McCarthy, Meyers learned that Billy Hamilton, a former major leaguer now coaching in the Tri-State League at Harrisburg, Pennsylvania, was looking for players. According to Meyers, "Tom mentioned a sum that I could receive for playing professional ball, which was more money than I had ever seen in my life, and I couldn't resist."[42]

It is possible that the New York Giants were aware of Meyers's potential even before he left Dartmouth. Dartmouth administrator Ernest Hopkins remembered Chief Tortes coming to his office in the spring of 1906 with 15 hundred dollar bills. According to Hopkins, Tortes told him the Giants manager, John McGraw, had come to Dartmouth and given him $1,500 as a down payment for the Cahuilla catcher to commit to play for a minor league team in Minneapolis.[43]

Another, even more compelling, reason for Meyers's departure from Dartmouth in the spring of 1906 was a telegram received from his brother Marion telling him their mother Felicité was seriously ill in California, and he was needed at home.[44]

What are we to make of the year Meyers spent at Dartmouth? Seven years after leaving the college Meyers wrote glowingly of his Dartmouth experience: "I was made to feel not only at ease every moment of my college year, but they gave me consideration I had not received before or have not received since. Dartmouth is proud of its Indian traditions and it treated me as an honored guest."[45] Like Charles Eastman, John Tortes Meyers felt that the opportunity to obtain an education as good as any white man was receiving at the time, in a collegial atmosphere, outweighed the negatives of being so far from home in a much different climate and enduring the indignities of being the outsider.

Meyers told Lawrence Ritter, "You know, Dartmouth is just like the Giants: once a Giant, always a Giant. Mr. McGraw instilled a spirit there that never left you. And this is quoted from Chaucer: once a Dartmouth, always a Dartmouth."[46] Meyers never lost his sense of pride at being a "Dartmouth man," and remained connected to the College the rest of his life.

## Beginning a Career in Professional Baseball: Harrisburg and Lancaster, Pennsylvania (1906)

When Meyers left Dartmouth he was signed by Billy Hamilton, manager of the Harrisburg, Pennsylvania, Senators of the Tri-State League, to a contract paying him $250 a month for the summer of 1906.[47] A future Hall of Famer, "Sliding Billy" Hamilton, former Philadelphia Phillies outfielder, has one of the best lifetime steals record in the major leagues.

Meyers considered his days at Harrisburg "one of the hardest experiences of my life." The players were "old school" and refused even to speak to the rookie. However, Meyers recalled, "I made up my mind not to quit, no matter what they said or did."[48]

The turning point came on the Fourth of July when he was sent in to catch a pitcher who threw spitballs. Having no experience with the slippery pitch, the Cahuilla catcher allowed five passed balls in two innings, and Hamilton pulled him from the game. However, instead of returning quietly to the bench he yelled at his manager for having him catch a pitch he had never seen before. The astonished skipper admitted the rookie was right, and from then on Meyers was accepted by the veterans on the team.[49]

It was a story Meyers told often, always with some bitterness, because he knew he was being harassed not just because he was a rookie, but because he was an Indian. In describing his experience at Harrisburg to Lawrence Ritter, he said, "I don't like to say this, but in those days, when I was young, I was considered a foreigner. I didn't belong. I was an Indian."[50] However, he also took away the lesson that if he stepped forward to assert his rights he would be respected by his manager and teammates.[51] In this experience, as throughout his baseball career, Meyers was drawing on his Cahuilla heritage, recognizing that ?iva?a (power) properly respected will restore harmony and balance to any situation.

According to statistics compiled by Ray Nemec of the Society for American Baseball Research, Meyers played in 40 games for the Harrisburg club and briefly with a Lancaster, Pennsylvania, team in 1906. He had 132 at-bats, scored 16 runs, had 31 hits (with six doubles, one triple, and one home run), stole three bases and batted .235.[52]

## Playing in the Southern California Winter Leagues (1906-07)

At the end of the 1906 season Meyers considered returning to Dartmouth. He recalled six years later, "I had seen my mistake." However, his mother was still very sick, so he returned home to Riverside instead. In addition, as he described the situation, "I had no money, and I didn't like to tell them so at college."[53]

After returning to California Meyers was offered a tryout with the old Los Angeles Angels but did not make the team. The legendary Walter "Big Train" Johnson was also present and signed with the Angels.[54]

Instead of Los Angeles, Meyers played for the San Diego Pickwicks during the winter of 1906-1907. The Pickwicks, sponsored by a San Diego theater, began playing in the Southern California Winter League in December 1906. After being defeated by a team made up of major leaguers in an exhibition game on New Year's Day 1907, the Pickwicks started to win games. Meyers, remembered as "a rough and tumble character," was among the season's leading Pickwicks with a .390 batting average.[55]

In February 1907, the Pickwicks played a ragtag team from Anaheim they condescendingly described as "a bunch of farmers" because the Anaheim players wore three different types of uniforms. This "ragtag" team may have been the Los Angeles Angels, because pitching for the "farmers" was Walter Johnson, who led them to a 2–1 victory.[56]

In recounting his experience playing in the Southern California winter leagues, Meyers told a reporter six decades later he couldn't remember just what year it was, acknowledging, "My memory isn't good." Then with his characteristic wry grin he tapped his head and said, "Pardon my Shakespeare, but 'this distracted globe' doesn't do so good any more."[57]

After the end of the winter season Meyers thought about returning east to play once again in the Tri-State League. However, as he put it, "the Tri-State was an outlaw organization, the players had no contracts, and there was no such thing as a reserve rule."[58]

## Butte, Montana (1907) and the Southern California Winter League (1907-08)

Drawing on his connections with the Anaconda Copper Company from his days playing in Arizona, Meyers signed for the 1907 summer season with the Butte, Montana, Rustlers of the Northwestern League. Former major leaguer Russ Hall was manager of the Rustlers. In contrast to the Tri-State

In the winter of 1907–08 Meyers (third from left) caught Hall of Fame pitcher Walter Johnson (far left) when both played for the San Diego Pickwicks. In the center (not in uniform) is Pickwicks owner Bill Palmer (San Diego History Center).

League, the Northwestern League was legitimately professional. As Meyers recalled, when he signed with Butte, "I burned my bridges and became a professional player, putting all else behind me."[59] He said that in Butte he felt like an "old hand, because I had been with the Tri-State League one season, and I knocked the bushers around myself."[60]

Playing at Butte did not go as well as he hoped. "I didn't get much chance in Butte," he would recall, "because they had a wild fellow named William Roosevelt, a relative of Theodore, and just as strenuous as his relative. He was the wildest pitcher I ever saw. I don't know what became of him. He broke a finger for me in the opening game of the season and had me out for two weeks, and he pounded me with that baseball all the time I was with Butte."[61]

Meyers did improve his Harrisburg and Lancaster performances while playing for the Butte team. He appeared in 90 games, had 353 at-bats, scored 47 runs, tallied 91 hits (with six doubles, ten triples, and two home runs), stole nine bases, and batted .258.[62]

That fall Meyers returned to southern California and once again played in the winter leagues for the San Diego Pickwicks. In November 1907, the Pickwicks faced the Pacific Coast League champion Los Angeles Angels, also known by this time as the Loo Loos, in a five-game series for what was promoted as the "Coast Championship."

Without exclusive contracts the better players would rotate among teams, playing where the money was best. For the series against the Angels, San Diego manager Bill Palmer signed Walter Johnson to play with the Pickwicks. Johnson arrived in San Diego on the 2nd of November, just in time to have his picture taken with the Pickwicks in their new uniforms. He watched as they beat the Dyas club in the first of two warm-ups for the coming series. The victory was a good omen. According to one source, "Big Chief" Meyers, the Pickwicks' "superstitious catcher," told reporters it was the "first time I ever knew it to happen. Never played on a team before that was able to win the game after having its picture taken." But the "jinx" had only been postponed, as Johnson lost his last game as a teenager the next day, 4–2, with five Pickwicks errors contributing to the defeat.[63]

Several days later "Big Train" took to the mound in the opening game of the series with the Angels, with Meyers as his receiver. He struck out 16 and shut out the Los Angeles team, 1–0. Johnson even drove in the winning run with a sacrifice fly. Meyers, whom Palmer selected as captain of the team, collected three of the five Pickwicks hits, including a double. He also threw out three runners in the game.

In the second game of the series Meyers took a pitch on his fingertip, suffering a serious cut, and was unable to play in the remaining contests.

Johnson pitched in the deciding fifth game, but developed a sore arm and
had to lob the ball, allowing the Angels to win the game and the mythical
"Coast Championship" in a 9–3 rout.[64]

## St. Paul, Minnesota (1908)

In 1908 Meyers's baseball odyssey took him to St. Paul, Minnesota,
although, according to one report, "several other big teams were after him."[65]
"I was finally sold for $1,500 [by the Butte team] to [the] St. Paul [Apostles]
of the American Association," he recalled, "and reported there in the spring
of 1908. And then I did have my troubles. The manager was a famous ex–big
leaguer. He had it in for me for some reason. There were a number of old
heads on the club, and their idea seemed to be to have a great time."

The former major leaguer who managed St. Paul was Tim Flood, a second
baseman, who had more success as a player than as a manager. The old-timers
were Phil Geier, John Dunleavy, and Lefty Davis. Joe Laughlin shared the
catching duties with Meyers.

Meyers said he was so dissatisfied, "I wanted to get away from the St.
Paul club, and I figured I would be there a good while if I didn't stick pretty
close to my ballplaying." The team lost more than 100 games, but for Meyers
the season was not altogether unpleasant, because "it was there I met my wife,
and it was from there I came to New York."[66]

Meyers's wife, Anna, was an actress.[67] According to census data she was
born in Maryland and was a year older than her husband. The two were married in 1909 or 1910.[68] Jack and Anna moved to California when Meyers's professional baseball career ended in 1920, and were together well into the 1930s.
At some point they separated, and Meyers spent most of his retirement years
alone.

Only one source indicates Jack and Anna had any children. A brief article
published in December 1939 notes "Jay Meyers, 20-year-old son of Chief
Meyers, the baseball great, has been signed by Universal for a minor role in
the Mae West–W.C. Fields picture 'My Little Chickadee.'"[69] However, no "Jay
Meyers" is listed in the cast for the movie, and Meyers's grandnephew and
grandnieces say they were always told their Uncle Jack had no children.[70]

On July 20, 1908, the St. Paul Apostles (later called the Saints) sold the
rights to John Tortes Meyers to the New York Giants.[71] Giants manager John
McGraw paid the then hefty price of $6,000. The other premier manager of
the era, Connie Mack of the Philadelphia Athletics, also tried to sign Meyers,
reportedly offering the St. Paul Club "Catcher Schreck and $2,500 for the
Indian."[72]

According to Meyers, "I was hitting close to .300, never over ... and catching fairly well." For the season he played with the St. Paul team he appeared in 88 games and had 329 at-bats, scored 45 runs, had 96 hits (with 19 doubles, one triple, and one home run), stole four bases, and batted .292. His fielding average was .960.[73]

By the time the Cahuilla catcher was sold to the Giants, Mike Kelley had taken over as the St. Paul skipper. He had a reputation for sending more players to the majors than any other American Association owner or manager. Meyers is at the top of the list of Kelley's players who went on to have the most successful careers.[74] However, according to McGraw, after he had handed Kelley the $6,000 check to acquire Meyers, the St. Paul manager said, "The Indian is all right for this club, but he'll never make a Big Leaguer."[75]

# FOUR

# "Stranger in a Strange Land": First Seasons with the New York Giants (1908–1910)

## The Deadball Era (1901–1919)

John Tortes Meyers played major league baseball during the Deadball Era, the period from 1901 to 1919. It began with a rule change that took effect in the National League in 1901 and the American League in 1903. For the first time foul balls were counted as strikes until a batter had two strikes. The change shifted the balance to pitchers from batters, effectively ending the reign of .400 hitters.

Throughout the Deadball Era balls were left in play longer, and the disfigured spheres broke more sharply. Pitchers often called for fouls hit into the stands to be returned by fans so as to benefit from the irregularities in balls hit a number of times. It was not uncommon for balls to stay in play until the yarn with which their cowhide covers were sewn started to unravel. During this period the spitball was a legal pitch, and balls stained with licorice and other foreign substances remained in the game after they had been initially doctored.

Because of the dead ball the emphasis was on situational hitting. The style of play came to be known as "the inside game" or "scientific baseball." As Meyers's manager, John McGraw, the most accomplished practitioner of the inside game, put it, "I think the game far more interesting when the art of making scores lies in scientific work on the bases."[1]

Batters choked up and tried to slap balls through holes in the infield. "Choke and poke," the style was called, or "hitting 'em where they ain't" as "Wee Willie" Keeler of the Baltimore Orioles liked to say. Batters also tried to draw walks or get hit by pitches to reach base. The hit-and-run as well as the bunt were used to move runners into scoring position. Base stealing was also much more common. No other period of baseball has recorded more total steals. Though slow afoot, Meyers would become a remarkably adept base stealer by carefully studying pitchers' moves.

50

Home runs were not nearly as frequent as they later became in the major leagues and were often inside-the-park hits rather than over-the-fence drives. Most ballparks were much more spacious than modern stadiums. For example, at the West Side Grounds, home of the Chicago Cubs, it was 560 feet from home base to the center field fence. Between 1900 and 1920 there were 13 times when the major league leader had fewer than ten home runs for the season.

With speed on the base paths more highly valued and balls driven into outfield gaps going to the fence, triples were more common. In 1912, Owen "Chief" Wilson, who was not a Native American despite his nickname, had 36 triples, a one-season record that still stands.

During the Deadball Era games major league games were most often low-scoring affairs. When Meyers arrived in 1908 the average number of runs scored in a game was 3.38 per team. During his years in the major leagues, the average rose to 4.53 in 1912 and then fell to 3.56 in 1916. Batting averages were low. In 1908 the major league average was .239. It rose to .269 in 1912, then declined to .248 by 1916. On-base percentages and slugging percentages were also much lower than in later periods.

For the first half of the Deadball Era the ball used in major league games had a soft rubber core and did not travel as far as the cork-centered ball that replaced it. However, the new ball, first introduced during the 1910 season, elevated offensive statistics for only a brief period. Batting averages did start to climb, but not precipitously. Not surprisingly, Meyers's best years at the plate began in 1911. However, the trend did not continue, as batting averages (including Meyers's) began to fall after a few years.

The end of the Deadball Era was marked by several rule changes. The spitball was outlawed. When Ray Chapman died after being hit in the head by a pitch during the 1920 season, a new rule required that balls be removed from games when they became dirty. Intentional walks were banned for a time. As a result, between 1918 and 1921 the major league batting average for all players increased from .254 to .291. Since Meyers had left the major leagues before the Deadball Era ended, any fair assessment of his performance, in comparison with players of other periods, must take that into account.[2]

## Meyers and Mathewson: An Unusual Friendship

When John Tortes Meyers joined the New York Giants late in the 1908 season, major league baseball was still emerging from a period when "rowdiness" was common among players. As Meyers himself recalled, "Ballplayers were considered a rowdy bunch. We weren't admitted to hotels, that is first-class hotels. Like the sailors in Boston, on the Commons—'No Sailors Allowed.' We were in that class. We were just second-class citizens, even worse."[3]

Among those responsible for changing the tone of the game and increasing fan support were two of the most famous New York Giants of the era and legends of the game: pitcher Christy Mathewson and manager John J. McGraw. Grantland Rice described Mathewson as someone who "brought something to baseball no one else had ever given the game. He handed the game a certain touch of class, an indefinable lift in culture, brains, and personality."[4] Though remembered for his own rowdiness as a player and as a manager, John McGraw was also instrumental in improving the status and image of the game. Mathewson and McGraw were also the two New York Giants with whom John Tortes Meyers forged the closest relationships.

When he arrived in New York as the 1908 season was drawing to a close, the veterans on the Giants did not greet Meyers with much enthusiasm. Looking back at his arrival, he remembered, "[I]n those days, the veterans had no time for kids trying to break into the big league lineups, thus possibly taking their jobs. Why, at first, none of the pitchers, except Matthewson [sic] wanted to pitch to 'that big Indian kid.'"[5]

It is hard to overestimate the impact Christy Mathewson had on baseball and the esteem with which he was held during his playing years and after. "With his brains, demeanor, and attractive personality, plus his achievements on the field, he was the first authentic sports hero—certainly the first baseball hero." He was "a transcending presence" not only for baseball but for America in general.[6] "Matty," as everyone called him, spent almost his whole career with the Giants, finishing with 373 victories, tying him with Grover Cleveland Alexander for third place in total career wins among major league pitchers, behind only Cy Young and Walter Johnson. Only seven pitchers have won three World Series games in a single series. In 1905 Mathewson won three against the Philadelphia Athletics, all shutouts. He holds the modern National League records for wins in a season — 37, wins in a career — 373, and consecutive 20-win seasons — 12.

Already an established star by 1908, Mathewson was known to be aloof from his teammates. Giants center fielder Fred Snodgrass described Matty as "a reserved sort of fellow, a little hard to get too close to."[7] Why, then, did Mathewson choose to befriend the rookie Meyers and remain closer to the Cahuilla catcher than he was with any other Giant except John McGraw? Perhaps they hit it off because Meyers was a Dartmouth man who, like Mathewson (a graduate of Bucknell University), valued education and was interested in art and literature. Perhaps it was because "Big Six," as Mathewson was also known, sensed that in Meyers he had found his perfect battery mate, who was as calm and cool in tight situations as he was and with whom he could have great success. Or perhaps Mathewson, "the Christian gentleman," who by all accounts sought to live by his Christian values, recognized Meyers was being treated as a "foreigner" in the game and reached out to him. Maybe Matty recognized that Meyers lived by his own strict code of conduct, derived from his Cahuilla heritage. Or possibly, for all his success, Mathewson himself felt like an outsider among his teammates and understood better than other players what Meyers was experiencing.

Over the years Meyers talked more about Christy Mathewson than about any of his other Giants teammates. Meyers clearly admired Mathewson for his pitching genius but also for his intelligence and the way he handled himself off the ball field. Well into his eighties Meyers kept a portrait of his friend and battery mate above his bed.

"No question about the best pitcher. It was Matty." That was always how Meyers responded when asked to name the top hurler he caught during his career. "Hardly ever did he walk a man," the Cahuilla catcher would say. "He could put the ball precisely where he wanted it. And they didn't steal bases on Matty. If the count was two balls, no strikes, and the runner broke, Matty would see it out of the corner of his eye. He would quick-pitch out. Not only out, but the ball would arrive right up against my ear where I threw from, and we'd get the runner. You see, a 3-and-0 count meant nothing to Matty. He could throw three strikes on the corner any time."[8]

Mathewson once pitched 68 straight innings without allowing a walk, all with Meyers as his catcher. Matty knew how to pace himself, coasting when he was ahead and easing up on weak hitters, saving his best for tight situations. When a reporter reminded him that Mathewson never pitched on Sunday, to fulfill a promise to his mother who told him it would be a sin, Meyers added with a cagey grin, "Matty also thought it a sin to walk a batter."[9]

To illustrate Mathewson's accuracy Meyers described how Matty once won a bet from the writers Damon Runyon and Bozeman Bulger by stationing Meyers at home plate, hands on his hips, and throwing pitch after pitch through the crook of his catcher's elbow. Meyers said he never flinched. Matty would never miss. On another occasion, at a preseason game against a West Point team played at the academy field on the banks of the Hudson River in New York, the cadets bet Mathewson he could not throw 20 consecutive pitches to exactly the same spot. Meyers said he squatted, put his mitt on one knee and held it there while Mathewson hit it 20 straight times.[10]

Ring Lardner summed up Matty's nearly magical control succinctly: "he could shave you if he wanted to, if he had a razor blade to throw, instead of a ball."[11] Mathewson's manager and friend, John McGraw, said simply, in an oft-repeated phrase, "anybody can catch him in a rocking chair."[12]

What made Mathewson's control all the more remarkable was his array of pitches. By 1908 they included a fastball, with either an upward or inward movement at the finish; a slow ball; a drop curve; an out curve; an underhanded curve; and the celebrated fadeaway, or as Matty called it, the fallaway, which floated to the plate, then dropped off just as the batter was swinging at it.

Marveling at Mathewson's retentive memory, Meyers told reporters the pitcher memorized what every player could and couldn't hit. If a batter ever hit a hard one off Matty, he never saw the same pitch in the same place again. Meyers recalled how Mathewson used to strengthen his memory by playing checkers. He would regularly play his Giants teammates Buck Herzog, Larry Doyle and Fred Merkle in the locker room while dressing. Mathewson never looked at the checkerboard — he remembered all their moves, dictating his own. And he always won.

Meyers was often asked to compare Mathewson with the American League's most famous pitcher of the era, Walter ("Big Train") Johnson. His response in a 1947 interview was typical, reflecting his admiration for Matty's mastery of the mental aspects of the game. "I caught Walter out here in the West when he had all his stuff," Meyers said when asked if he had ever played with Johnson, and, if so, whether "Big Train" was a better pitcher than "Big Six." "And I caught him later on, too. But I'd still have to say Mathewson. From the start Christy had everything, dazzling speed, curves, everything. Walter didn't start throwing the other stuff until he lost his speed. He had an arm. Christy pitched with this," and, according to the reporter, Chief Meyers tapped his gray-haired head.[13]

Summing up his estimation of Mathewson in his interview with Lawrence Ritter for *The Glory of Their Times*, Meyers said, "How we loved to play for him! We'd break our necks for that guy. If you made an error behind him, or anything of that sort, he'd never get mad or sulk. He'd come over and pat you on the back. He had the sweetest, most gentle nature. Gentle in every way."[14]

Though Mathewson considered Meyers a friend and respected his abilities, he also demonstrated a lack of sensitivity when talking about his battery mate. In his ghostwritten book, *Pitching in a Pinch*, Matty explained why one catcher received for the same pitcher so regularly. He said a catcher gets to know just how much a pitcher's curve will drop when he calls for it. Such knowledge enables them to "work together harmoniously." "'Chief' Meyers, the big Indian catcher on the Giants, understands my style so well that in some games he hardly has to give a sign," the Giants ace told his ghostwriter.[15]

Despite his affection for Meyers, Matty seemed oblivious to how racially tinged remarks might increase the Cahuilla catcher's sense of isolation. He

The two Giants with whom Meyers was closest were his manager, John McGraw, and his battery mate, pitching legend Christy Mathewson. The two are wearing Giants sweaters in this 1914 photograph, with Matty holding a bat on his shoulder. Meyers is standing to McGraw's right (Library of Congress, Prints & Photographs Division, LC-DIG-ggbain-17200).

once told a sportswriter, "Meyers is naturally dark and when he becomes tanned, his skin is unusually so." Sometimes, Mathewson said he couldn't see whether Meyers was holding down one finger or two when his catcher was signaling pitches because the digits of the Indian were so dark, and he would cross up his catcher by throwing a different pitch than the one Meyers called for.[16]

## Meyers and McGraw: More Than a Manager

Meyers also had a unique and special relationship with renowned Giants manager John J. McGraw, who is rightly praised as the epitome of "what a baseball manager was supposed to be: smart, shrewd, pugnacious, tough and demanding with his players."[17] Upon learning McGraw had died, Baseball Commissioner Kenesaw Mountain Landis called the Giants manager "one of the greatest natural leaders any sport has ever known. Baseball to him was more than a game. It was a religion and war combined.... He was emblematic of the fire and dash that belongs to the national game. He knew ballplayers and he knew how to handle them."[18]

From 1902 to 1932 John McGraw led the New York Giants to ten National League pennants, three World Series championships, and 21 first- or second-place finishes. His teams finished out of the first division only four times in three decades. At this writing his 2,784 managerial victories are still second only to his rival Connie Mack's 3,731, but in 1927 Mack himself proclaimed, "There has been only one manager — and his name is McGraw."[19]

Called "Muggsy" and "Little Napoleon" (but never to his face, unless you were looking for a fight or were a fool!) McGraw developed his reputation for pugnaciousness as an infielder for the Baltimore Orioles and perfected it as a manager. As Arlie Latham, one of his coaches, said of McGraw's famous irate charges across the diamond to confront an umpire, "McGraw eats gunpowder every morning and washes it down with blood."[20] He was ejected from 118 contests as a manager and 14 as a player during his career, a record for total game ejections that stood until surpassed by Atlanta Braves manager Bobby Cox in 2007.

McGraw was known to keep such close tabs on players he would review hotel meal checks to see which of his players might be overeating. One of his heavier players, who may have well been John Tortes Meyers, who weighed around 200 pounds when he played for the Giants, once convinced a waiter to write down "asparagus" when he had ordered pie *a la mode.*[21]

At first many of McGraw's players were in awe of him, even afraid of him, but they grew to admire him. As Meyers's teammate Josh Devore said of their manager, "He was this gruff, angry guy sometimes, but the reputation was worse than the reality. How do you think he got so many different kinds of players to play so well for him through the years?"[22]

McGraw was, in Meyers's words, a "master of invective and irony."[23] "He couldn't stand a player telling him, 'I thought,'" Meyers informed sportswriters. To illustrate the point, he liked to tell the following story[24]:

> Mr. McGraw didn't have to use cuss words. He could cut you down without them. Like the time we were playing the Cubs and we had them whipped going into the ninth. Heine Zimmerman came up to bat and I called for a pitch high and outside. Heine reached out and hit it for a home run, to break up the game.
>
> When we got back to the bench Mr. McGraw said to me: "Jack, why did you pitch him that high one and outside." He actually spoke as if I had thrown the ball.
>
> I said, "I thought..." and before I could finish it he said with great scorn, "What with?"

Meyers sometimes got the better of his manager in these feisty exchanges. On one occasion the Giants catcher noticed how a Dodgers pitcher with a great pickoff move to first base was tipping the throw. Watching him carefully, Meyers saw that the pitcher would never throw to first after he dropped his eyes. On the bench Meyers asked his manager if he could steal second the next time he reached first. McGraw fumed, "Don't ever steal a base. That's not your job." Meyers said he just couldn't resist taking advantage of the opportunity and stole second on the pitcher anyway. McGraw fined him ten dollars for breaking his "no stealing" rule, but asked the slow-footed catcher how he was able to steal the base so easily. Meyers asked if the fine would stand if he told him. McGraw said, "No," so Meyers told him how he had figured out when to steal on the pitcher. "After that," Meyers remembered, "we ran the poor fellow out of the league."[25]

Another story Meyers liked to tell was that if the Giants had a four- or five-run lead, Christy Mathewson would lay the ball in so the batters could hit it because he "liked to see the outfielders run their legs off." The Giants manager would slide up and down the bench, "getting madder by the second." McGraw would get so steamed up, according to Meyers, "sometimes he'd take Christy out of the box — sometimes."[26]

Meyers credited McGraw with being instrumental in changing the way ballplayers were viewed and how they were paid. At a time when baseball players were all considered ruffians and second-class citizens, forced to stay in inferior hotels, Meyers claimed, "Mr. McGraw was the one who changed all that. He was the one who paid the price, and even more than the price, to get his ball team into the best hotels. Now, the ballplayer is respected."[27]

According to Meyers, McGraw's insistence upon respect was not only for members of his own team, but for other players as well. One day the Giants manager chewed out the fans during a game played in Pittsburg (the "h" was not added until later), shaming them for booing Pirates star Honus Wagner when he made a fielding error. Meyers told Grantland Rice years later, "McGraw stood up in front of the stands, held up his hands and gave those babies a piece of his mind. McGraw was a commanding figure, you know, and when he got through telling 'em about Wagner they were cheering instead of booing."[28]

What did McGraw think of his Cahuilla catcher? In a 1912 article, when Meyers was at his peak, McGraw called him "a vicious hitter," "the greatest natural hitter in the game." He also described him as "one of the best catchers in the National League," "a quick thinker," "a team leader," and "all around a very valuable man."[29] In 1934, McGraw included Rube Marquard and John Tortes Meyers on a short list of the best batteries in baseball history.[30]

On another occasion, after Meyers had caught George Wiltse in a one-hitter against the Pirates, the Giants manager gave his catcher nearly as much credit as he did to Wiltse, saying, "it was one of the greatest exhibitions of out-guessing skilled batters that [I] ever saw." In addition, according to McGraw,

Meyers "hits a baseball about as hard as any man in the world." He went on to note that "he is the only man that [I] ever saw who is more likely to hit the ball when a hit will bring in runs than he is when the bases are clear."[31]

All things considered, Meyer's relationship with McGraw was enigmatic. Like many other players and managers at the time, McGraw was a racist. He was the Baltimore Orioles third baseman in 1897 when Francis Sockalexis, one of the first Native Americans to play in the major leagues, signed with Cleveland. The first time Sockalexis appeared in Baltimore McGraw took the field before the game "wearing a war bonnet with feathers reaching down below the seat of his baggy pants" and chanted "war whoops." The crowd got the point. Every time Sockalexis came to the plate, ear-splitting war whoops erupted in the stands. Inspired by McGraw's example, for the next two games in the series many Baltimore fans wore feathered headdresses.[32]

Meyers's Native American teammate Jim Thorpe rebelled against McGraw's overt racism and abusive tactics while playing for the Giants. Once, after Thorpe had missed a sign, costing the Giants a run, McGraw yelled at him, "You dumb Indian!" It took half the team to restrain Thorpe from attacking his manager.[33] By contrast, although he was certainly aware of this side of his manager's character, Meyers seemed to appreciate that despite his prejudices, McGraw looked for talent regardless of the player's race.[34] He also recognized that in addition to imparting baseball knowledge and skills, McGraw cultivated in players willing to look beyond his bluster and bias "a professional attitude, maturity, and self-respect."[35] Although he was only seven years younger than his manager, John Tortes Meyers clearly considered John McGraw a mentor from whom he learned not only baseball knowledge but valuable life lessons as well.

According to Meyers's grandnephew, Colonel John V. Meyers, his Uncle Jack's most cherished possession was not the bat he received from Babe Ruth in a trade but rather a gold watch fob in the shape of a catcher's mitt given to him by John McGraw. The catcher's mitt had a diamond on the clasp, and a large pearl at the center of the mitt representing a baseball.[36]

Meyers summed up his attitude toward his manager in his 1964 interview with Lawrence Ritter for *The Glory of Their Times*: "What a wonderful man he was. Honest and forthright and charitable in the deepest sense of the word. We always called him Mr. McGraw. Never John or Mac. Always Mr. McGraw."[37]

## The 1908 Season: The View from the Bench

John Tortes Meyers began his major league career at an opportune time; 1908 was a good year to become a major league ballplayer. Fan interest in the game was on the rise. In 1907 total attendance at National League games was 2.5 million. A year later a million more fans were in the stands. Attendance would continue at three million or above for the next several years.[38] Beyond game attendance, millions more followed their favorite teams through the newspapers, reading reports by some of the best sports journalists of any era.

It was the impending trade of future Hall of Fame Giants catcher Roger Bresnahan that opened the door for Meyers. Bresnahan was one of three Baltimore players McGraw had brought with him to the Giants in 1902. "The Duke of Tralee," as he was known, had originally been a pitcher, but one day Bresnahan popped off to McGraw about the Orioles not having a good catcher, to which the manager responded, "If you are so smart, why don't you go in there and catch." He did, and it turned out to be one of McGraw's best managerial moves.

As a catcher Bresnahan was an innovator, the first ballplayer to experiment with a batting helmet and the first catcher to wear shin guards (adapted from cricket leg pads). Bresnahan contributed to the evolution of the image of the catcher from the "tough guy" who could withstand any degree of punishment to the "thinking man" who was the general of his team.[39]

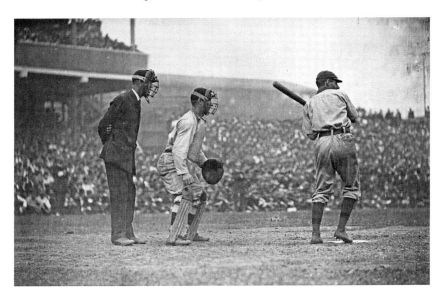

New York Giants Hall of Fame catcher Roger Bresnahan (center) was an innovator. He was the first major league catcher to protect himself with leg pads, as shown in this 1908 photograph. The Giants traded Bresnahan to the St. Louis Cardinals after Bresnahan assured Giants manager John McGraw that even though just a rookie, Chief Meyers was already a better ballplayer (Library of Congress, Prints & Photographs Division, LC-DIG-ppmsca-18473).

If Bresnahan was so valuable to the Giants, at a time when good catchers were particularly hard to find, why was McGraw willing to trade him? The most commonly heard explanation was to give the combative Bresnahan, who was one of McGraw's closest friends on the team and his clone on the field, an opportunity to manage. In addition, Bresnahan was nearly 30 in 1908 and was beginning to slow down, the time at which McGraw usually traded away his stars.

According to Meyers, McGraw was at first reluctant to consider letting his talented catcher go at the end of the 1908 season. However, Bresnahan had a ready response for the Giants manager. "The Indian over there," Bresnahan said to McGraw, pointing to Meyers, "is a finished ball player and he's better than I am." When McGraw still objected, Bresnahan continued, "He can hit better than I can, and can catch better. You don't have to tell him to hit to right or to hit behind the runner. What more do you want?"[40] That was quite a compliment from a player who was in his tenth season in the majors and would have a career batting average of .279, on-base percentage of .386, and slugging percentage of .377, and who, a year after his death in 1945, would be only the second catcher inducted into the National Baseball Hall of Fame.

Others in the Giants organization who saw both catchers play agreed with Bresnahan's assessment. One was long-time Giants secretary and McGraw confidante Eddie Brannick, who rated Meyers over Bresnahan in the list of all-time Giants greats he compiled in 1942.[41]

In return for Bresnahan the Giants received from the Cardinals catcher George "Admiral" Schlei, outfielder John "Red" Murray, and spitball pitcher Arthur "Bugs" Raymond. Raymond, who already had a well-deserved reputation for drinking too much and too often, would become one of McGraw's most infamous reclamation projects.

When McGraw brought players who had not yet played in the majors to the Giants he often held them out of games and sat them next to him on the bench for at least part of the season so they could learn by observation and from his comments on various situations on the field. That was the case in 1908 with Meyers, who had the opportunity to watch how the experienced Bresnahan handled pitchers and witness how McGraw dealt with players and umpires.[42]

Another rookie who joined the Giants during the 1908 season did appear in one game. Left-hander Richard "Rube" Marquard pitched five innings and suffered a loss. Marquard obtained his nickname in the minors, when it was said he was as good a pitcher as the famed "Rube" Waddell. Marquard and Meyers would team up as battery mates beginning the next year, for a total of seven seasons together with the Giants. The Brooklyn Dodgers picked up both, Marquard during the 1915 season and Meyers after the season.

When McGraw signed Marquard, enthusiastic writers dubbed him the "$11,000 Peach," reflecting the fact that the Giants manager had paid the then unheard-of sum of $11,000 to acquire him. It would take a few years (during which fickle writers began calling him the "$11,000 Lemon"), but Marquard, with Meyers as his catcher, would eventually rival Mathewson as the best pitcher on the Giants, winning over 20 games in three straight years, including a record 19 in a row in 1912.

Meyers's work with Marquard was critical to the lefty's success. According to Meyers, opponents quickly noticed Marquard was lifting his foot in his delivery. They would complain to the umpires, who would have Rube go through his motion to look for the illegal move. Once this "little one-act drama" was completed, Meyers said, Marquard wouldn't know whether he was pitching or shooting pool. To the amusement of his Giants teammates, Meyers would spend the mornings before the games Marquard pitched calming the pitcher's nerves and telling him to ignore the catcalls of opposing players and coaches.[43] The strategy worked, because Marquard went on to become one of the best pitchers in Giants history. He was inducted into the Baseball Hall of Fame in 1971 after being selected by the Veterans Committee.

Meyers was battery mate of Hall of Fame left-hander Richard "Rube" Marquard on both the Giants and Dodgers. On the left in this 1913 photograph is Giants infielder Art "Tillie" Shafer (Library of Congress, Prints & Photographs Division, LC-DIG-ggbain-11766).

The 1908 season was supposed to be a rebuilding year for the Giants. In the off-season McGraw acquired a group of players known as the "Kiddie Corps"—Pitcher Otis "Doc" Crandall (called "Doc" because he was, as sportswriter Damon Runyon is reputed to have said, "the healer of sick games") and infielders Fred Merkle, "Laughing Larry" Doyle (so-named for his ready smile and jubilant mood), Buck Herzog, and Al Bridwell. Also joining the Giants were veteran first baseman Fred Tenney, who attended Brown University, and "Turkey Mike" Donlin, who returned to the Giants after being away from baseball for a year. Other veterans on the 1908 Giants were Cy Seymour in the outfield, Art Devlin at third, and Bresnahan behind the plate. The rest of the pitching staff (Leon "Red" Ames, Joe "Iron Man" McGinnity, George "Hooks" Wiltse, and Luther "Dummy" Taylor) provided solid support for Mathewson.

After Meyers signed with the Giants in July 1908, the National League pennant race was a contest among the Cubs, Giants, and Pirates. By early September the three pennant contenders were virtually tied. On September 4, in a game between the Pirates and the Cubs in Pittsburg, with the score tied 0–0 in the bottom of the tenth, Honus Wagner singled to drive in the winning run. However, when the man on first failed to touch second base before turning toward the Pirates' outfield clubhouse, Cubs second baseman Johnny Evers tagged the base and yelled for umpire Hank O'Day to call the Pirates runner out.

According to Baseball Rule 59, the run should have been nullified if a force out took place on the play. O'Day was working alone that day and claimed not to have seen whether the Pirates runner tagged second base before leaving the field. He refused to disallow the run and the Pirates won, but he assured Evers in the future he would be attentive if a similar situation arose.

The Giants slumped in September. They dropped both ends of a doubleheader to the Cubs on the 22nd, and, while they were still in the lead when the day ended, the momentum was turning against them.[44]

The Giants–Cubs contest the next day, Wednesday, September 23, 1908, is remembered over a century later as perhaps the most famous single regular season major league game in baseball history. Known as "the Merkle game," it was certainly one of the most controversial. John Tortes Meyers had the best view in the stadium, sitting on the bench, next to John McGraw.[45]

In the bottom of the ninth, with the score tied, Fred Merkle, the Giants' rookie 19-year-old first baseman, committed one of the most famous mental mistakes in baseball history. With two outs and a strike away from sending a tied game into extra innings, Merkle stroked a single, moving Harry "Moose" McCormick from first to third. Al Bridwell then singled, and McCormick raced across the plate with what should have been the winning run. However, sure the game was over, Merkle broke for the outfield clubhouse before reaching second.

None of the Giants was thinking about what happened in the Cubs–Pirates game less than three weeks before. However, the Cubs' crafty second baseman, Johnny Evers, had not forgotten and called for center fielder Art "Solly" Hoffman to throw him the ball. As Evers knew well, according to Rule 59, Merkle was required to move up a base when Bridwell singled. If he didn't reach second and Evers had the ball and touched the bag, Merkle should be called out. The run would not count although the runner had already crossed the plate.

In the ensuing melee Giants pitcher "Ironman Joe" McGinnity, coaching at first, rushed over to intercept the ball and threw it into or at least toward the grandstands. However, Evers retrieved the errant ball (or more likely *a* ball thrown to him from the Cubs bench), stepped on second base, and screamed for Merkle to be called out.

Bob Emslie was closest to the play as field umpire, but refused to call Merkle out. He had almost been hit by Bridwell's single and claimed in diving out of the way he had not seen the play. As fate would have it, Hank O'Day made the call. Merkle was out, he ruled, and the game remained tied 1–1 at the end of regulation play. With the field overrun by "bugs" (as fans were then called), darkness descending, and the Giants in their clubhouse already celebrating the victory they were sure was theirs, the game could not continue, O'Day decided. From that day on, Fred Merkle had to live with the unflattering nickname "Bonehead Merkle" because of his costly mental error, and "to merkle" entered the language as a verb meaning "to not arrive."

The ruling was upheld and,

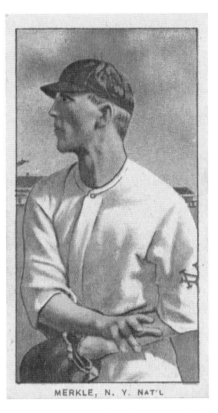

MERKLE, N. Y. NAT'L

New York Giants first baseman Fred Merkle is best known for his "bonehead" play in the 1908 World Series, but was highly respected by Meyers and his Giants teammates, and his manager, John McGraw, for his baseball skills and knowledge of the game. He is shown here in the famed American Tobacco T206 card series (1909–1911) (Library of Congress, Prints & Photographs Division, LC-DIG-bbc-0801f).

with the Giants and the Cubs tied at the end of the regular season, a make-up game was held on October 8, 1908. The Cubs won the game, 4–2, and went on to beat the Detroit Tigers and Ty Cobb in the 1908 World Series, their last Series win throughout the rest of the twentieth century and beyond.

Fred Merkle implored McGraw to fire him for the good of the team, but the Giants manager told the rookie, "Fire you? Why you're the kind of guy I've been lookin' for for many years. I could use a carload of you." He told him to get ready for the next season, that the writers would soon move on to other stories. Indeed, although the cry from opposing fans, "Touch second, Merkle!" would follow him for the rest of his career, Merkle did come back to the Giants the next season (with a raise) and played in the major leagues for another 18 years.

John Tortes Meyers called the "Merkle game" one of his most unforget-table experiences during his career with the Giants. He was also a staunch defender of his teammate, calling him "the smartest man on the club." John McGraw always went to Merkle to discuss strategy, never anyone else, Meyers pointed out. "The bonehead! What a misnomer! One of the smartest men in baseball, Fred Merkle. Isn't that something! It's the truth. It shows what the newspapers can do to you."[46]

## 1909 Season: A "Stranger in a Strange Land"

When John Tortes Meyers reported to the Giants' 1909 spring training camp in Marlin, Texas, with the pitchers and other catchers, he was eager to prove himself. A year earlier the Giants had moved spring training to this town of 4,000 in central Texas, about 160 miles south of Dallas, famous for its natural hot springs. They would train there for all the years Meyers was with the team. McGraw chose Marlin because it was alcohol-free and far from big city temptations, though close enough to Dallas, Houston, and San Antonio for weekend games. The Marlin civic leaders were ecstatic at the presence of the Giants and put on barbecues and fish fries for them at the Falls of the Brazos, a resort just outside town.[47]

Even before he reported to Marlin, Meyers was being touted in the national press. A February 1909 article contrasted the newly signed "full blooded Indian [who] looks like the goods" with "Indians of the imitation kind seen on the Polo Grounds in recent years," alluding to the Wild West shows popular at the time. Interestingly, the article identified the Giants rookie as "Jack Meyers," not "Chief Meyers." It cited his batting statistics at St. Paul in 1908 as evidence of his potential.[48]

Several years after his first spring training Meyers wrote of the experience, "I never saw so many ball players before in my life. They just flocked all over the field. There were eight catchers.... I took a look at that bunch and I saw they were all young and fast, and I said to myself, 'This is the biggest team of them all, and if you want to stick with it you'll have to figure to do it on something besides speed. You're not fast enough to complete with those kids.'

"I realize fully that I'm heavy on my feet," he acknowledged, "and for a time I was somewhat discouraged. Then I took my bat and went out and made an effort to do some hitting. I had luck. I made about thirty home runs that spring, and the newspaper boys with the Giants were boosting me to the skies."[49]

Another of Meyers's lasting memories of his first Giants spring training also deepened his resolve. It was a lecture McGraw, the master of motivation, gave to rookies. "Boys, baseball is a game of skill and chance," McGraw solemnly intoned. "Errors are a part of the game. Without them we wouldn't have any baseball. But don't make too many errors or you won't be here very long."[50]

Meyers was entering the major leagues at a time when the status of catchers was on the rise. As one writer at the time put it, "the great catcher must be a thinker, and inventor, a man who would make a success of any business calling for a level head."[51]

As spring training continued, New York writers began using the nickname by which Meyers had been known at Dartmouth and which would remain attached to him for the rest of his life. One titled his article "Meyers Breaks Up Game With His Bat" and reported, "Two men were on bases, when big Chief Meyers strode up to the plate. One run was needed to win. The Chief got one to his liking, swung his big stick, and the ball is going yet somewhere in the next county. He only gets credit for a single, but it was an awful wallop."[52]

In a series of articles he wrote for the New York Times, veteran Giants first baseman Fred Tenney described a 1909 exhibition game played in Waco before 1,500 fans: "Jack Meyers, the Indian catcher, made quite a hit with the Texas fans as well as with his own teammates. He was chock full of life and fun all during the game, and when the Texas rooters tried to rattle him he entered into the fray with zest and soon had the better of them in the battle of repartee."[53] The Waco fans were trying to throw Meyers off his game, most likely by chanting versions of the war whoops and name-calling that Meyers would hear throughout his major league career. "Go back to the reservation," "Dumb Indian," "Redskin," and "Heap big Injun" were common catcalls.[54]

The Giants traveled north in April, playing games along the way. They reached New York early one morning. One of the New York writers accompanying the Giants on the train described the scene in an article that received national circulation[55]:

> When the members of the New York National league club arrived in Jersey City on a cold morning just before the National league season began, after their long ride from the west, one of the first to leave the sleeping car which had brought the club over from Baltimore was Jack Myers [sic].

"Myers," the unnamed writer claimed, "isn't his right name and it is not half as euphonious as his right name, but he 'dubbed' himself 'Jack' Myers when he started to play professional baseball, and 'Jack' Myers he is likely to remain; he is not called 'Chief.'" However, later in the same article the writer ignored the Cahuilla catcher's stated preference and began using the nickname. "The 'Chief' had his baptism of fire," he noted, referring to the fact that McGraw played him against some of the toughest teams during the exhibition season.

The article demonstrates that at the beginning of his major league career Meyers was determined to define himself as an individual, not as a stereotype. It was a battle that would continue his whole life. He would always be seen through the objectifying filters of the white man's conception of him as an Indian.

The reporter's praise of Meyers in the article, that he is "the soul of good nature, a capital traveling companion, [and] a good conversationalist," rings rather hollow. For those who saw him only as "Chief," Meyers's ability to see the humor in situations arose because for them he was the "good Indian," the "happy Indian" who got along well among whites through always manifesting a light-hearted manner. As long as Indians like Meyers were willing to play the white man's game as they were expected to, figuratively as well as literally, they would be held up for admiration.

As he looked across the Hudson River to Manhattan, knowing it to be an island once the homeland of native people who had been deceived, swindled, and exiled, as his own Cahuilla tribe had been, Meyers said he felt like a "stranger in a strange land." The phrase is biblical. According to the Old Testament Book of Exodus, Moses spoke these words when he realized that though he had attained prominence and prestige by assimilating to Egyptian culture, he could never call Egypt his home. His people, the Hebrews, were persecuted aliens, and though he had adopted Egyptian ways, as a Hebrew he would always be a foreigner, a "stranger in a strange land."[56]

It seems legitimate to speculate that Meyers must also have sensed how much was at stake, not only for himself, but also because he would inevitably be seen as a representative of "the Indian," an exemplar of all Native Americans. John Tortes Meyers, and the handful of other Native Americans playing in the major leagues, would be virtually the only Indians most people who saw them play would know. He must have sensed on that April morning in 1909 how many would judge all Indians on the basis of his performance on the field and in the stories written about him. He also realized that what they saw and read would be inevitably distorted by the filter of stereotypes beyond his control. His opportunity to make a real difference for his people would be limited. He would have to pick his steps carefully. He must have wondered if he was up to the challenge.

In his first appearance at the Giants' home field, the Polo Grounds (ironically named for a sport never played there), in an exhibition game against the Yale University team, Meyers hit two home runs. The blows helped settle his nerves but raised expectations even further concerning the "big Indian" about to "go on the warpath" for the Giants.

On April 15, before a full house at the Polo Grounds, the Giants opened the 1909 season against the Brooklyn Superbas before a capacity crowd of 30,000.[57] "The Indian catcher Meyers seemed to be the most popular Giant present, though he is a new man," the New York Times noted. "His two home runs last week have boosted him high in notoriety. 'Hello Chief,' a thousand called. 'Get in the game and lift 'em over the fence.'"

McGraw started Schlei at catcher with Red Ames pitching. Meyers remained on the bench, watching a scoreless game go into extra innings. In the top of the 13th the Superbas scored three runs. In the bottom of the frame shouts went up from the bleachers: "Put in the Indian! Give us Meyers! He can hit a ball." The Cahuilla catcher did enter to pinch-hit, and singled, but as the Times put it, "the Indian did not get to the bat early enough." The Giants lost the game, 3–0.[58] The trend was established. Virtually each time Meyers was mentioned in the press, he would be "Chief," "the Indian," or "the Big Indian," whether or not any ethnic identifiers or nicknames were used for other players.

Two days later Meyers started his first game, catching Rube Marquard in the lefty's second appearance as a Giants starter. An additional 3,000 beyond the capacity of 30,000 were shoehorned into the Polo Grounds. The Giants won the game against Philadelphia 4 to 1 and the Times exuded, "$17,500 Battery Defeats Phillies," referring to Marquard's $11,500 price tag and the $6,000 McGraw paid to acquire Meyers.[59] The article on the game in the New York American claimed, "Chief Myers [sic] has been snapshotted so many times this season that he has acquired the camera habit.... T[eddy] Roosevelt used to be the most photographed man in America, but the former Great White Father never had anything on his sun-tanned ward."[60]

As the 1909 season continued, the new Giants catcher was attracting attention well beyond the New York papers. For example, Sporting Life noted Meyers was being touted as "another Sockalexis."[61]

The *Arizona-Journal Miner* reported that Meyers, who had played for several Arizona towns a few years earlier, was now "the sensation of the hour in New York baseball circles because of his wonderful hitting with the New York Giants." The *Miner* felt the need to add, "Nobody could ever take Meyers for anything but an Indian. He looks the part and furthermore is proud of his lineage. 'One name they can never hang on me,' is 'Big Chief Afraid of a Pitcher.' I believe that confidence at the plate is half the battle. I don't say that I can hit every kind of pitching, and doubtless I will have my troubles in the National league, but I'm not afraid of any of them."[62]

Once again Meyers's pride in his Cahuilla heritage is clear. In addition, his willingness to use ironic humor is evident in the article as he twists the "Big Chief" label into a joke through which he makes an important point. Even though he may be called "Big Chief," he would not be intimidated. He surely knew as long as he held fast to the Cahuilla values, he would remain strong.

Despite his potential Meyers was not at first the powerful hitter Giants fans expected. However, by mid–May he was beginning to fulfill the expectations of the New York writers and fans. In a game against the Cubs "Big Chief" Meyers proved he was a "big Indian" by sending 15,000 fans at the

**Meyers demonstrates his wide batting stance in this 1910 photograph taken at the Polo Grounds in New York (Library of Congress, Prints & Photographs Division, LC-DIG-ggbain-12464).**

Polo Grounds into "delirious joy" when he drove in the winning run in the bottom of the ninth.[63] On June 16 the Giants gave the Cardinals and their former catcher, Roger Bresnahan, now the player-manager of the St. Louis team, a 12 to 1 drubbing. "Indian Jack Meyers," the *New York Times* reported, "made a great showing, with a clout down the left field line which netted him three bases and sent Devlin and Bridwell home."[64]

While Meyers was becoming an important contributor, another Giants player was self-destructing. Bugs Raymond could not shake the demons that drove him to drink, and his performance suffered. In the second game of an August 24 doubleheader against the Pirates at the Polo Grounds, McGraw sent an inebriated Raymond to the mound. "The Entomologist" apparently begged his manager to take him out each inning after the fifth. McGraw, however, was giving the pitcher a lesson and made "the white and shaking twirler stay on the rubber to the bitter end."[65]

According to Meyers, "The one player McGraw never could handle was 'Bugs' Raymond, a great pitcher who never grew up. Raymond had a marvelous spitball. He could show it to Hans Wagner and then strike him out." Meyers remembered McGraw always sent Raymond's salary directly to his wife to keep the pitcher from drinking it up. However, Raymond found many ways to obtain alcohol. He would enter a bar when it was crowded, go to a wall phone, and say loudly into it, as Meyers recalled, "Yes, this is Raymond. Yea, BUGS Raymond. Yes, yes. BUGS RAYMOND OF THE GIANTS." The people in the bar would take notice and, when he hung up the receiver, buy him drink after drink.[66]

An incident with Bugs Raymond convinced McGraw that Meyers should not catch pitchers whose main delivery was the spitball. When a widely breaking spitter from Raymond split one of Meyers's fingers on his ungloved hand, the Giants manager told Meyers, "From now on you don't catch spitballers. You're the catcher for Mathewson and Rube and anybody who throws regular pitches."[67]

Hampered by a sore thumb during the latter months of the 1909 season, Meyers was steady if not outstanding. He typically had 1-for-3 and 1-for-4 games and was capable defensively. He even stole a few bases. On September 11 the rookie catcher collected his first major league home run, a grand slam, driving in all the runs in a 4 to 0 victory over the Brooklyn Superbas, with Mathewson on the mound.

However, the Giants faded late in the season, as did Meyers's performance. Though the Giants had a good record, 92–61, it was only good enough to finish 18½ games behind the sensational pennant-winning Pirates.

Meyers finished the 1909 season with appearances in 90 games, a .277 batting average and a .963 fielding average. Of his 61 hits in 220 at bats, ten

One of Meyers's more infamous Giants teammates was Arthur "Bugs" Raymond, a talented pitcher whose alcoholism cut short his career and his life (Library of Congress, Prints & Photographs Division, LC-DIG-ggbain-09151).

were doubles, five were triples, and one was a home run. He drove in 30 runs and stole three bases.[68] He also recorded eight pinch-hits in 24 at-bats, for the best average for a pinch-hitter (.333) in the National League.

Meyers acknowledged he slumped late in the 1909 season. "The fans and newspapers were panning me," he wrote several years later, "and I didn't know what to do. I just couldn't hit my stride." John McGraw took him aside and said, "Chief, you quit paying attention to what they're saying about you. Remember that you're playing baseball for me and for no one else. I know you can catch so you just get in there and do it and let me tell you when you're not going right." "That cheered me up," Meyers said, "and I soon struck my stride again. Do you wonder that I think McGraw is the best man in baseball?"[69]

## Speaking Out: Meyers and the Crazy Snake Movement (August 1909)

Though he was popular with fans, Meyers was still in a "try out" phase during the 1909 season. He could have been released at any time. This precarious situation made his decision to speak out forcefully on a controversial issue late in the 1909 season all the more impressive. He was a rookie, risking his own future, by violating the basic rule minority athletes have always sensed — don't be too political. The incident was not an anomaly. John Tortes Meyers was willing to take stands on issues of injustice. As his grandniece Shanna Meyers said of her Uncle Jack, "He wasn't afraid to speak out when he thought it would do some good."[70]

The situation that caused him to risk his career was the "Crazy Snake Movement" in Oklahoma led by a Creek Indian named Chitto Harjo (1846–1912). Known to whites as "Crazy Snake," Harjo was at the forefront of an effort by Creek traditionalists to retain tribal control over their lands rather than cooperating with the government's plan to divide the land into family allotments.[71]

Between 1901 and 1909 Harjo led a series of minor skirmishes against government forces. The state and national press sensationalized these encounters. One report in 1909 warned the "Oklahoma frontier [is] practically ablaze with the horrors of Indian massacre."

John Tortes Meyers could have avoided comment on Chitto Harjo and the Crazy Snake movement, but he did not. His response appeared in an August 1909 article written by J. W. McConaughy. In a piece announcing that McGraw was considering the rookie for the role of the Giants' "chief catcher," Meyers was quoted making a statement that could have jeopardized his popularity with the fans and his standing with the team[72]:

They say that the Indian has never shown a disposition to adopt the civilization of the white man, but he has

Chitto Harjo, a Creek Indian, was the leader of the so-called "Crazy Snake Movement" in Oklahoma that defended the rights of traditional Creeks. As a rookie in 1909 Meyers spoke out in defense of Harjo when the Creek leader was being vilified in the national press and the target of government authorities (Library of Congress, Prints & Photographs Division, LC-USZ62–111977. Copyright: Harrie D. Blake).

never had a chance. They are treated like irresponsible children. They are herded on reservations, and when some railroad or land company wants the reservation, they are driven off of it and onto a worse one. Poor old Crazy Snake, a weak old man, who didn't have even a butcher knife, was accused of an uprising and his land was taken away from him and he was driven into the cold. He never stirred a finger. But the white men who are robbing him and other Indians are believed by the public and not the Indian.

This statement reflects the perspective Meyers maintained throughout his life. Indians had always been treated and were continuing to be dealt with unjustly by whites, he believed. It was not that Native Americans were unwilling to adopt "the civilization of the white men." The Creeks and other relocated tribes from the east were called the "civilized tribes" because they had shown their willingness and ability to adapt in large measure to the white man's ways. Meyers knew, however, that willingness to assimilate does not mean full acceptance and respect for the human dignity of Indians.

The media image of Chitto Harjo was of a reincarnated Crazy Horse ready to lead a new Indian war. Meyers, who understood what it was like as an Indian to be caricatured in the media, knew that in 1909 Harjo was actually a broken old man who posed no threat. He knew the leader called "Crazy Snake" had paid a heavy personal price for trying to secure the justice his people deserved under the white man's own law. Yet, as Meyers knew from what had happened to the Cahuilla people, those who steal Indian lands are believed while Native Americans whose lands are seized and are willing to protest are treated like Chitto Harjo, the latest of Indian leaders seeking justice for his people.

There were apparently no repercussions for Meyers's forceful stance. His public statements were ignored. Baseball fans were neither interested in nor took very seriously the positions of players on political issues, much less Indian players on issues about which baseball fans had little concern after the sensationalism had worn off. The attempt of the press to inflame public passions with claims that the Crazy Snake Movement was evidence of a resurgence of violent Indian uprisings fell flat. When there were no bloody battles in Oklahoma, people soon lost interest. Why should anyone, much less baseball fans, care what Chief Meyers had to say about it? Besides, no other Native American athletes were being vocal on the issue. The only "warpath" most sports fans were interested in was the one the "redskin" Chief Meyers was on when he wickedly wielded his "war club" and drove balls over the Polo Grounds fence. The only war whoops they wanted to hear were those made from the stands when their very own Indian warrior stepped to the plate.

## The 1909-10 Off-Season: A Series with the Red Sox

After the 1909 regular season ended, the Giants played a best-of-seven exhibition series against the Boston Red Sox. The series was designed by owners to cash in on the bad feelings lingering from the Giants' refusal to play the Red Sox in a world series after the 1904 season. However, the series was a flop, with only 789 paid fans attending the fifth and deciding game (won by the Red Sox, who defeated the Giants four games to one). Players received only $125 each for the series.

Three years later John Tortes Meyers recalled the 1909 fiasco, commenting sarcastically, "[W]hen anyone asked [the players] what we were playing for, we said the championship of the New York, New Haven, and Harford Railroad, since it got most of the money."[73] His bitterness at injustices extended to the exploitation of major league baseball players by management.

Meyers and his wife Anna spent the rest of the off-season in southern California, with his mother, brother, and sister, and visiting his extended family on the Santa Rosa Reservation.

## The 1910 Season: The Giants' Regular Catcher

Once again, as they would throughout Meyers's years with the team, the Giants gathered in Marlin, Texas for spring training in 1910. The routine at Marlin was always the same, beginning with a mile walk from the Arlington Hotel where the team stayed, along the railroad tracks, to the practice field. McGraw threw batting practice and put the players through rigorous drills. He also liked to stage intersquad games between the "Yanigans" (rookies) and the regulars. As in the previous spring, Meyers demonstrated his power-

A 1910 photograph, taken by Paul Thompson, served as the basis for a drawing of Meyers that appeared on a variety of baseball cards (Library of Congress, Prints & Photographs Division, LC-DIG-ppmsca-13529).

hitting prowess. In the first exhibition game he slammed three home runs over the left field fence.

To show their appreciation for the hospitality shown to them, the Giants players put on a show for the townspeople before leaving Marlin. A quartet of Giants (including Meyers) sang several songs at a gathering of locals at the Opera House. The quartet repeated its performance at a dinner hosted by Dallas supporters.[74]

After playing exhibition games throughout Texas the Giants left Marlin in late March. They played a series of games in southern towns before heading north.

John Tortes Meyers was not the starting catcher as the 1910 season began, but he did see action early on, usually as a pinch-hitter. In games he did start he struggled. In a mid–May contest against the Cardinals McGraw pulled both Mathewson and Meyers in the second inning after Matty gave up eight runs.

The New York press, which had raved about the rookie catcher at the beginning of the 1909 season, was turning on him. In its report on a June 13 game against the Cubs, which the Giants lost 6 to 2, the *Times* observed, "The Indian backstopper had one of the worst days of his career. His two errors were costly, and he had two passed balls and a bad throw, all of which added to the gayety [sic] of the Chicago merry-go-round." Stereotypes of Native Americans proved useful in the bashing. One of the "Notes of the Game" in the *Times*' report read: "Discovered — the reason for Meyers's infirmities. Yesterday was the 13th, and the Redskins of old were always long on superstition."[75]

Meyers played again the next day, an indication of McGraw's willingness to stay with a player who was struggling in order to boost his confidence. The Cahuilla catcher started the game and his performance was markedly better. Meyers played errorless ball and was 1-for-3 at the plate. His hit came in the ninth inning when he lifted a drive to deep left for a double, missing a home run by "about an eighth of an inch."[76]

Though Meyers was 3-for-4, including a double, in a July 11 game against the Chicago Cubs, he continued to struggle defensively. Meyers had Frank Chance blocked at the plate, ready to tag the Cubs player/manager, but dropped the ball. The Cubs took advantage of the miscue, and, according to the *Times*, "through the door opened by the redskin they pulled not one but two runs."[77]

As the season wound down, Meyers's fortunes began to change. His play was strong enough for McGraw to make him the Giants' lead catcher. Several games in late August and early September show how important he was becoming to the Giants' offense. In a game against the Cubs Meyers went 3-for-3 with a double and a stolen base. The next day he was 2-for-6 and scored two runs. He played in both games of an August 29 doubleheader in Pittsburg, recording 3 hits in 4 at-bats in the first game and going 1-for-3 in the second with a double. He was again 1-for-3 in a September 6 victory over the Boston Doves. He missed a three-run home run by a foot on a long drive into the left field bleachers.

The 1910 season ended with the Giants holding on to second place behind the Cubs in the National League race. Meyers played in 127 games, with 365 at-bats, 25 runs, 104 hits (including 18 doubles and one home run), 125 total bases, 62 RBI, and 5 stolen bases. His batting average was .285. He was one of only four major league catchers to catch more than 100 games during the season.[78]

A wrap-up article on the 1910 season noted, incorrectly, "John T. Meyers, the stalwart catcher of the New York National League team" is "the only full blooded Indian playing baseball in the major leagues." Though neither Meyers nor he were "full-blooded," the As pitcher Albert Bender was, by 1910, also a major league star. It identified Meyers as "a fine, stalwart fellow of swarthy complexion and dark eyes." According to the article, though he did some "horrible pegging" early in the season, his throwing improved and he had become "a magnificent receiver, comparing indeed with the best men in the big leagues."[79]

## The 1910-11 Off-Season: A Crosstown Series and a Vaudeville Tour with Matty

After the 1910 season, the Giants reversed their policy of ignoring their crosstown rivals, the American League New York Highlanders, later to become the Yankees. Since both New York teams finished second in their respective leagues during the season, the cry to determine the city champion was irresistible. The promised financial payoff for both teams was also a key factor. McGraw and the Giants agreed to a best-of-seven-games series. Beginning at the Polo Grounds, with 25,000 present for an October 13 game, the series lived up to fans' expectations. McGraw showcased his style of play with the Giants stealing bases almost at will on the Highlanders, and the Giants won the seven-game series. Total attendance surpassed 100,000, and each Giant received $1,110 for the victory, while the Highlanders players were awarded $706 each.[80]

When the series ended, Meyers joined Christy Mathewson in a vaudeville skit entitled "Curves," written by *New York Evening World* sportswriter Bozeman Bulger.[81] A young actress, May Tully, who appeared alongside the two ballplayers, produced the half-hour sketch. During the routine Meyers portrayed a stereotypical "bad Indian" who threatened Tully, a "forlorn maiden." Transformed into a stereotypical cowboy in a white hat, Mathewson rode in to rescue Tully from the "redskin" by hitting Meyers on the head with a baseball.[82]

After closing a two-week run at New York's Victoria Theater in late October, "Curves" opened as the headlining act at the Alhambra.[83] The reviews for the sketch were apparently not very good. A week later Matty and Meyers moved on to the Orpheum in Brooklyn, where they took second billing to "Baldina and Kosloff and their dancers."[84]

After shows at the Colonial Theater in New York, Mathewson and Meyers took their act on the road. In all "Curves" had a 17-week run. For both of the Giants players it would be their only vaudeville appearance. Mathewson was paid $1,000 a week, far more than he made as the highest paid major league pitcher ($10,000 a season). Matty demonstrated his Protestant frugality by taking the streetcar to the performances. Though he received considerably less, Meyers rode to the shows in a cab.[85]

Matty, who once commented, "Repartee is not my line," said he could not morally justify taking so much money for doing something at which he was so unqualified.[86] He assuaged his feelings of guilt over his performance by instructing theater managers to allow the boys who gathered at the stage door in hopes of seeing their idol free admission to the show.[87]

Meyers gained additional national exposure after the 1910 Season when Hassan Cork Tip Cig-

MYERS, N. Y. NAT'L

One of the Meyers (misspelled Myers) cards in the famed American Tobacco T206 series (1909–1911). A rare Honus Wagner card in the same T206 set sold for $2.8 million in 2007 (Library of Congress, Prints & Photographs Division, LC-DIG-bbc-0804f [front] and LC-US Z62-134594 [back]).

Meyers and his Giants friend and battery mate Christy Mathewson were featured in one of the Hassan Tobacco Triple Folder (T202) card series (1912) (Library of Congress, Prints & Photographs Division, LC-DIG-bbc-1985f [front] and LC-DIG-bbc-1985b [back]).

arettes (The Oriental Smoke) produced a series of baseball cards. The Hassan card was just one of many items on which Meyers's likeness appeared throughout his career. In the years he was with the Giants he was featured "on several dozen items such as cards, silks, art stamps, pins, pennants, discs, blankets, and card games, most available as giveaways or premiums to buyers of cigarettes, cigars, confectionery products, bakery goods, clothing, and sports magazines or newspapers." Best known today is the American Tobacco T-206 series. Meyers appeared in three poses in the over 500 different cards in the series made famous by a rare Honus Wagner card that in 2007 garnered $2.8 million in a memorabilia auction.[88]

# FIVE

# Becoming a Star: The
# 1911 Season and World Series

## 1911 Spring Training: A Brawl in Atlanta

As spring training for the 1911 season approached, John Tortes Meyers and Christy Mathewson were wrapping up their vaudeville tour with a week's run in Cincinnati. Neither Matty nor Meyers would appear in another vaudeville show. As one reporter observed, Mathewson "had a great year in theatricals, but ... he enjoys himself a lot more making money when he knows that he earns it."[1] Meyers likely agreed. In late February they met Mathewson's wife Jane and son Christy Jr. in Indianapolis for the trip south to the Giants' spring training camp in Marlin, Texas.

McGraw felt he had a winner when the Giants gathered in Marlin. The team might not have been as skilled as his earlier league champion teams, but with Fred Merkle, Larry Doyle, Al Bridwell, and Art Devlin in the infield; Red Murray, Fred Snodgrass, and Josh Devore in the outfield; and a jackrabbit named Beals Becker on the bench, they were younger and faster. Meyers was not a speedster but he was a "thumping hitter." Mathewson was still the most effective pitcher in the league. Although he struggled in his first two years, Rube Marquard would blossom on the mound during the 1911 season. Doc Crandall, "Hooks" Wiltse, and Red Ames were the other hurlers.[2]

The early weeks of spring training were uneventful. McGraw followed his routine of dividing the team into two squads so that players would have more game experience. He emphasized the fundamentals he knew were the keys to victory, including situational hitting, bunting, and base stealing. Because of the importance he placed on the theft of bases, all the players, pitchers included, practiced sliding in specially designed pits.

When the Giants left Marlin, they once again played a series of games across the south, arriving in Atlanta, Georgia, on the frigid morning of March 29, 1911. The Giants won the first game of the planned four-game series 10 to 3, with Bugs Raymond on the mound. Meyers was 3-for-3, with three singles.

On March 30 the Giants routed the Atlanta team, known locally as the Crackers, 11 to 0. In the first inning New York captain Larry Doyle (famous for saying, "It's great to be young and a Giant!") hit the longest home run ever seen in Atlanta, and the Giants coasted to victory behind the one-hit shutout pitching of Red Ames and Charles "Jeff" Tesreau.

Meyers did not play during the game on the 30th, but he was very much at the center of the action. According to the *New York Times,* an Atlanta rooter named Erskine Brewster had "called [Meyers] a negro" during the game on the 29th. Though a fan, Brewster had been recruited by the short-handed Atlanta team to play. On the 30th, when McGraw said something to Brewster about his comment to Meyers the day before, the Atlanta fan responded sarcastically. At that point a fight began. Christy Mathewson grabbed Brewster from behind, and the burly Atlanta rooter threw him over his head. When Meyers entered the fray, Brewster knocked him to the ground. After some more jawing the Atlanta fan started after McGraw. Al Bridwell came to his manager's defense, exchanging blows with Brewster, who got the best of the diminutive Giants shortstop, causing him to bleed profusely from the mouth. Matty then grabbed Brewster again and began to choke him. Al O'Dell, the Atlanta third baseman, responded by picking up a bat and threatening to kill Mathewson. He was about to take a swing at Matty with the bat when McGraw and the Atlanta manager intervened to end the fight.

On the same day the *Times* story was running, the *Atlanta Constitution* placed on its front page an article entitled, "Giants Mopped By Atlanta Fan." It claimed, "One Atlanta fan, Erskine Brewster ... had come near licking the entire Giant team." The article noted that the day before Brewster had merely raised "the Indian whoop." It also included a statement made by McGraw that, "This big fellow, Brewster, made several personal remarks to Mathewson and Meyers yesterday, to Mathewson about his wife, and to Meyers asking if he had his squaw with him. This afternoon Meyers and Mathewson saw him on the field, and asked him what he meant by his remarks." In McGraw's version Brewster was afraid to mix it up with Mathewson and Meyers, picking instead on the smaller Bridwell.

The altercation was a national story. If it had occurred today, ESPN undoubtedly would have featured the incident on SportsCenter. In 1911 other papers around the country covered the fight. The *Chicago Daily Tribune* ran the story under the headline "Giants in a Row; Given Beating." The *Portsmouth [New Hampshire] Daily Times* suggested the insults hurled at Mathewson and Chief Meyers were "entirely too personal," and justified the Giants' pugnacious response.

The *Atlanta Constitution's* claim that Erskine Brewster merely "raised the Indian war whoop" seems unlikely. Meyers had heard such yells at virtually every game he played since joining the Giants. He probably would not have reacted so strongly to what he had already become accustomed to enduring from fans.

The version in the *New York Times*, that Meyers's ire was aroused when Brewster called him a "negro," is more plausible. A decade earlier John McGraw, then managing the Baltimore Orioles, signed Charlie Grant, a Negro star player, claiming Grant was a full-blood Cherokee Indian and calling him Charlie Tokahoma (probably a play on "poke a homer"). Grant joined the Orioles in April 1902, but his cover was soon blown when White Sox owner Charles Comiskey recognized Grant as a player on Chicago Negro teams. Comiskey threatened to "get a Chinaman and put him on third" and said Grant was a "Negro fixed up with war paint and a bunch of feathers." When Comiskey complained, American League owners demanded Grant's dismissal and he never played in the majors.[3]

The story of Charlie Grant entered baseball lore and was likely known to Erskine Brewster. Meyers, whose complexion was dark, had previously been called "negro" by fans.[4] What set Meyers off was likely not just that Brewster called him a "negro," as the *Times* put it, but that the Atlanta fan used a more racially charged epithet and supplemented it with other insults. If this version is accurate, then Mathewson came to Meyers's defense because of a racist slur against his battery mate.

McGraw's version of what happened to spark the fight with Brewster also has a ring of truth. McGraw contended that Mathewson and Meyers responded violently because of the Atlanta fan's comments about their wives.

Mathewson generally avoided confrontations with fans. According to his teammate Larry Doyle, Matty "was always courteous when fans pestered him."[5] However, if Brewster did, as McGraw contended, insult Mathewson's wife Jane, the Giants pitcher would likely have attacked him.

In addition, though he generally avoided fights, this was not the only time Mathewson became involved in a brawl. On a more infamous occasion, during an April 1905 game in Philadelphia, he punched a boy selling lemonade when the youngster ran onto the field and made a remark about another New York player. Matty split the boy's lip and loosened some of his teeth. A dismayed *Sporting News* writer at the time suggested Matty's association with McGraw and "the old Baltimore crowd had made a hoodlum out of [him]."[6] Mathewson would also show his support for his manager. In May 1905, when McGraw had been thrown out of a game in Pittsburg after he baited one of the Pirates' pitchers, Mathewson was tossed for striking a fighting posture in front of the Pirates' bench.[7]

If, as McGraw described the incident, Brewster taunted Meyers by asking the Cahuilla catcher if he "had his squaw with him," Meyers's uncharacteristically violent reaction is understandable. Long before this incident, "squaw" had come to be used in a derogatory manner by whites speaking to or about Indian women of all tribes. Labeling an Indian woman a "squaw" was roughly the equivalent of calling a black man "boy" or, when the intention was derogatory, a Native American man "chief."

While Meyers and most of the rest of the Giants were focused on the seething hostility with the Atlanta team and their fans, their teammate Bugs Raymond had other concerns. While in Atlanta, as one writer observed, "Raymond deserted his place on the front seat of the buttermilk buggy and consorted again with Demon Rum, likewise with the beverage that made Milwaukee famous."[8]

Damon Runyon reported it was in Atlanta that Raymond acquired the nickname "Bugs." Raymond told him how one day he was pitching in Atlanta and "a whole flock of these big fat grasshoppers and lightning bugs came swooping down upon the diamond. I got a broom and swept 'em all back of first base and went on pitching, and ever since that they've called me 'Bugs.'"[9]

Waiting for John Tortes Meyers when he arrived in New York just before the start of the 1911 season was a questionnaire from Charles Emerson, Dean of Dartmouth College, requesting information for an alumni catalog. Even though he had spent only a year at the College, Meyers was and always would be considered a Dartmouth alumnus. In response to "Name in Full," Meyers wrote simply "Tortes," the name by which he was known at Dartmouth. He left most of the other questions blank. For his "Permanent Address" he wrote, "R. F. D. #2, Riverside, California." By 1911 he and his wife Anna were spending winters on the farm he had purchased outside Riverside. For "Present Occupation," he entered "Baseball — N. Y. "Giants." Under "General Information," he wrote, "Dear Dr. Emerson: You know my connection with the College and can fill out anything that I have omitted, as I do not know the exact date of entering or leaving College. Resp. yours. J. Tortes-Meyers."[10]

## The 1911 Season: Becoming a Star

On opening day, Thursday, April 13, 1911, 30,000 excited Giants fans gathered at the Polo Grounds. The wooden grandstand was bedecked in red, white, and blue bunting. As usual, the vaudevillian George Cohan was there, and he was joined by trainloads of Wall Street workers. A brass band played "East Side, West Side," and John McGraw was presented with a floral horseshoe for good luck. As he typically did at the beginning of seasons, the Giants manager held Mathewson for the Saturday game, pitching Red Ames instead.

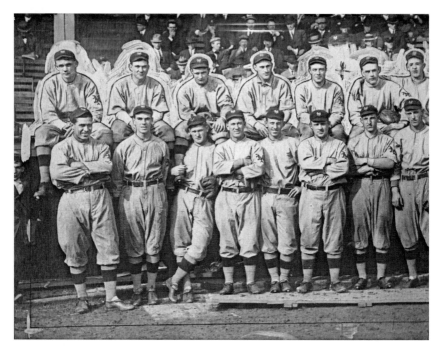

The 1911 New York Giants. Top row (left to right): Rube Marquard, Larry Doyle, Josh Devore, Art Fletcher, George Burns, Art Wilson, Red Ames. Bottom row: Meyers, Fred Snodgrass, Red Murray, Arlie Latham, Beals Becker, John McGraw, Buck Herzog, Fred Merkle (Library of Congress, Prints & Photographs Division, LC-DIG-ggbain-10918].

Ames was good, but lost to Philadelphia, 2–1. It would be the last game played in the old stadium.[11]

The wooden Polo Grounds burned down during the night after the first game. The actual cause was never determined, though the best guess is that a cigarette tossed from the car of the elevated train that ran above the stadium started the conflagration. Rumors spread that the Chicago Cubs were somehow responsible, or, reflecting the international political situation, that Russian Bolsheviks set the fire.

The idea to have the Giants play night games in Brooklyn's Washington Park stadium was floated, but the American League New York Highlanders graciously invited the Giants to share their small Hilltop Park until a new Polo Grounds could be built. The Giants owner called his Highlanders counterpart "a real white man" for responding to the Giants' need.

A new double-decker steel-and-concrete Polo Grounds accommodating 38,000 (the most of any park in baseball at the time) was built in an unbelievable ten weeks and ready for games by June 28, 1911. The new stadium was christened a basilica by the press, because of the ornate frieze decorating its upper and lower decks and a flock of steel eagles atop the roof. Wedged against Coogan's Bluff and shaped like a horseshoe, the new Polo Grounds was only 257 feet down the line in right field and 277 in left, but 433 feet in dead center. Foul territory on the first- and third-base sides was huge.[12]

Playing in the Highlanders' home park turned out to be good luck for the Giants. During the first two months of the 1911 season they vied with the Cubs, Pirates, and Phillies (who were riding the success of rookie pitcher Grover Cleveland Alexander) for the lead in the National League. As the season progressed, the contributions of John Tortes Meyers to the Giants' success were evident. He was becoming a *bona fide* major league star.

While Meyers's reputation was rapidly growing, another Giant was attempting a comeback. McGraw's "reformation" of Bugs Raymond officially began on April 17, 1911, as the spitballer took over after "Hooks" Wiltse was hurt in the second inning. Raymond pitched well, holding Brooklyn scoreless until the ninth, and the Giants won, 3 to 1. He had, a writer noted, resumed "the true pitching form he used to show before he left the straight and narrow path." Demonstrating the mastery of the "inside game" their manager taught them, the Giants stole five bases. Even the slow-footed Meyers stole a base, showing that good base running is not just a matter of speed.[13]

McGraw's managerial magic was evident in a May 20 win over Honus Wagner and the Pirates at Hilltop Stadium. With the score tied 1 to 1 in the bottom of the ninth, after Devlin singled, McGraw stopped the game to insert Fletcher as a pinch-runner. The pause so rattled the Pirates pitcher he uncorked a wild pitch. Meyers then rolled an easy grounder that was promptly booted by the second baseman. McGraw once again signaled time out and put in Beals Becker to run for Meyers. Becker promptly stole second. As Drucke walked to the plate, McGraw waved him back and called for pitcher Doc Crandall to hit. Crandall delivered the winning blow.

The outcome could have been different. Honus Wagner's mighty blast to right field in the first inning missed being a home run because it bounced into the crowd ringing the outfield for a ground rule double. In the fifth Meyers was hit in the ribs, loading the bases. However, when Drucke shot a hard ground ball toward short, it was "devoured by the huge hands of Wagner, who also planted his right pedal on second in time to get the Indian Meyers at that base." Meyers allowed a passed ball in the seventh, but then saved a run when he tagged out Bobby Byrne, who was trying to score from second on an infield hit.[14]

In a mid-season analysis of the 1911 National League pennant race, W. A. Phelon defended "the big Injun, Meyers" against critics who claimed Meyers was too weak defensively to be considered a top major league catcher. The clinching argument for Phelon was that Christy Mathewson preferred having Meyers as his catcher and "[w]ith the standing Matty has in the New York team, with the pull he doubtless has with McGraw and [Giants owner] Brush, it's a baked cinch, that Matty would only have to say: 'This Indian will not do—get me another catcher.'"[15]

With a five-run spurt in the fifth, the Giants defeated the Pirates in Pittsburg, the June 7 win lifting New York into first place. In the decisive fifth Meyers reached on an error and later scored.

During another game two days later, in which the Giants won their third straight game in Pittsburgh's home park, Meyers objected to umpire Bill Klem's strike calls when the Giants catcher was at bat. As the *New York Times* described the scene, "[A]fter a run-in with Umpire Klem the Indian was forced to retire in favor of Wilson." The Pirates fans responded by jeering Klem. Meyers was popular in the city in part because he and Matty had sold Red Cross Christmas stamps in the city during their recent off-season vaudeville tour.[16]

In his ghostwritten book *Pitching in a Pinch,* Christy Mathewson described how, in one of the games against the Pirates during the 1911 season, the Giants were able to benefit from stealing the Pirates' signs. "Hooks" Wiltse noticed that Pirates player/manager Fred Clarke was signing a hit-and-run by tapping the plate with his bat. The next time up, Wiltse yelled, "Make him put them over, Chief," which, translated, meant, "Order a pitchout, Chief. He just gave Byrne the hit-and-run sign." Meyers signed for a pitchout, and Byrne was caught ten feet from second.[17]

The new Polo Grounds was ready, and the Giants played their first game in the stadium on June 28, 1911. They won that contest, and the magnificent new surroundings seemed to give the slumping team the boost needed to propel them toward the league championship.

Meyers contributed to the team's success. He homered in the first inning of a 9 to 4 victory over the Pirates in a July 13 match up at the Polo Grounds, a game that lifted the Giants into a tie for the National League lead with the Philadelphia club. However, the pennant race remained a four-team free-for-all.

McGraw and most of his players attributed the surge of the Giants not so much to their new stadium but to the arrival of Charles Victor Faust. Faust was a 30-year-old Kansan who convinced himself, on the basis of a prediction by a fortune-teller, that he would become a pitcher for the New York Giants and help them win the 1911 pennant. He was so certain of his fate he showed up at the hotel where the Giants were staying in St. Louis during a late–July series with the Cardinals. Seeing a publicity opportunity, the superstitious

McGraw put the lanky, 6-foot-2, 180-pound Faust through a mock workout and seated him on the bench in a Giants uniform. With Faust "on the team," the Giants took the final three games of the four-game set.

Meyers may have benefitted from the presence of Faust. He was 2-for-3 in 3–2 win over the Cardinals in the last game of the series. Marquard pitched the complete game victory on one day's rest. In the second inning, after Herzog singled, stole second, and took third on a ground out, Cardinals player/manager Roger Bresnahan called for Meyers to be walked, and the Giants catcher stole second. Marquard made Bresnahan and the Cardinals pay by driving home Herzog. Snodgrass then singled and Meyers scored. The Giants continued their wild base running with five base thefts in the game.

When the Giants left St. Louis they did not bring Faust along, and the Giants lost four of their next six games on the road. Determined to fulfill his fate, the eager Kansan was waiting for the team when they arrived back in New York ten days later, and the Giants players convinced McGraw to let Faust suit up and sit on the bench. The naïve Faust actually believed he was a member of the team and McGraw would some day tap him to pitch. To the Giants players, Faust, whom sportswriters dubbed "Victory," was a good luck charm whose presence was directly related to the team's success on the field.

During the Deadball Era the Giants were not the only team with a "mascot" like "Victory" Faust. Connie Mack and the Athletics had adopted a small hunchbacked man named Louis Van Zelst several years earlier and were also winning.[18]

Rube Marquard was on his way to a spectacular year after a mid-season hot streak. He would end the 1911 season with 24 wins and only seven losses. Mathewson gave all the credit to Wilbert Robinson's work with Marquard, saying the Giants coach had turned Rube into "the premier pitcher in the league." Robinson was a catcher himself, a teammate of McGraw on the Baltimore Orioles, whom the Giants manager called upon for special projects such as helping Marquard reach his full potential. According to Matty, the old catcher's work with the youngster showed why catchers "can always have the best influence on pitchers."[19] The catcher behind the bat for both Mathewson and Marquard, who also deserved some credit for their phenomenal success, was John Tortes Meyers.

In the stretch run during the 1911 season Meyers was dominating offensively hitting in 17 straight games. He was rapidly becoming known as one of the best hitters in the National League. For example, in an August 9 game played in Chicago he was 3-for-3 with a triple and drove in three runs in a 16 to 5 Giants rout of the Cubs. Two weeks later Meyers doubled and scored a decisive run in a 3 to 2 Giants victory over the Pirates at the new Polo Grounds. In a mid–September game against the Braves, Meyers stroked a double off "grizzled veteran" "Grandpa" Cy Young, who had just joined the Boston team and was in the final season of his storied 22-year career.[20]

By August 1911, John Tortes Meyers was climbing rapidly toward the pinnacle of success on the baseball field, and sportswriters and fans were heralding his ability to adapt his instincts as a "warrior" to his batting prowess. At the same time another California Native American, in a much different context, was the focus of national attention. On August 29, 1911, near Oroville, California, an emaciated man, soon dubbed "Ishi, the last of the Yahi," emerged from the wilderness and became an instant curiosity. Ishi was a member of a northern California tribe known as the Yahi that had been decimated since the arrival of Euroamericans. Almost immediately the press labeled Ishi "the most uncontaminated aborigine in the known world."[21] Anthropologist A. L. Kroeber rescued Ishi from being put on display in circuses as "California's last wild Indian," and took him under the care of the University of California's Museum of Anthropology, hoping to salvage information from him about Yahi culture before allowing contact with modern civilization.

The "last Yahi" did provide valuable knowledge of his native language and worldview, but Kroeber could not resist the pressure to put him on public display. Ishi soon became part of the museum's exhibits, visited by thousands who eagerly watched him acting out his "primitive way of life." With no immunity to the diseases carried by Euroamericans, Ishi was often ill and died of tuberculosis in 1916. His brain was taken to the Smithsonian Institution for study.[22]

While the discovery of Ishi was dominating the national news, Meyers was reflecting on what he had to endure as an Indian in order to become a successful major league ballplayer. In September 1911, Meyers told a reporter, "I'm here yet, ... so I must have something. But I have had a hard time making good. Some day I am going to write a book and call it 'How I Made Good in the Big League.' When I first started every one was out to get me, and all the crabs playing ball would come into me spikes first and call me all the names that they had been accustomed to apply to the umpires. I couldn't get back, for what chance has an Indian? What chance has one ever had?"[23]

While a constant barrage of racist slurs continued to greet Meyers from the stands and opposing benches, he *was* being recognized in the New York papers for his baseball knowledge. After a September 16 game in which "'Chief' Meyers was "[t]he Giant who first solved the mystery of [Pirates pitcher Marty] O'Toole's remarkable curves," the *Times* noted Meyers "has become the deepest student of batting on the team."[24]

As a team the 1911 Giants were on a roll that would take them to the National League pennant. During a September 18 contest with the Pirates the

Giants stole home three times, a record for a single game that still stands a century later. The next day the Giants won their 11th straight road victory in another game against Pittsburg. Meyers was 1-for-3. Two days later the Giants took two from the Cardinals as Meyers went 3-for-7. He was now well ahead of his nearest rivals, Honus Wagner and Fred Clarke, in the race for the National League batting title. "The Indian has been gaining at a steady clip for weeks and now threatens to carry off the honors," the *Times* observed.[25] In a September 30 game against the Cubs, Meyers went 3-for-3 in a win. Meyers also shone defensively. He bluffed a throw to second on an attempted double steal and nailed the runner trying to score from third. The next day he threw out two Cubs trying to steal.

With the pennant cinched, McGraw finally inserted the Giants' "good-luck charm," Charles "Victory" Faust, into an October 7 game. With the cooperation of the Boston Rustlers, Faust pitched the top of the ninth inning, allowing one run and batted in the bottom of the inning, though there were already three outs. Five days later McGraw once again let Faust pitch against the Superbas. Brooklyn even allowed Faust to score, to the amusement of the Giants' fans. The fact that the Giants were 36–2 during the 1911 season when Faust was in uniform was convincing evidence for many he had indeed brought good fortune to the New Yorkers.[26]

For the 1911 season the Giants compiled a record of 99 wins and 54 losses, finishing 7½ games ahead of the Cubs and 14½ in front of the third-place Pirates. New York stole 347 bases, a season total for a team not exceeded since the 1890s. The Giants won by playing McGraw's brand of "inside baseball" to perfection, not only stealing bases but bunting to advance runners, going for the extra base, catching the opposing team asleep whenever possible. By contrast, home runs were not important. In 1911 the Giants had only 41 as a team. However, the Giants were dragging at the end of the season and McGraw called his old buddy Wilbert Robinson up from Baltimore to raise the team's spirits.[27]

In 1911 Meyers was third in the National League batting race, finishing with a .332 average, behind only Honus Wagner (.334) and Roy Oscar (Doc) Miller of Boston (.333).[28]

Meyers appeared in 133 games during the 1911 season; only in 1914 did he play in more (134). His 391 at-bats were his most for a season. His 130 hits included 18 doubles, nine triples and one home run. He stole seven bases, one less than his career best the next year. His 61 RBI were one below his career best of 62 in 1910, while his total bases (169) were exceeded only in 1912 when he had 177.[29] Despite the continuing criticism that he was not as good a fielder as other backstops, in 1915 Meyers led the catchers of the league in fielding percentage.[30]

His overall record during the 1911 season earned John Tortes Meyers tenth place in the new Chalmers Most Valuable Player Award, voted on by one baseball writer from each National League city. The Chalmers Award (presented between 1911 and 1914) was named after Hugh Chalmers, an automobile manufacturer who presented the winner in the National and American Leagues with a Chalmers Touring Car. Meyers would finish third in the Chalmers MVP balloting the next year and fifth in 1913.

Based on a careful analysis of an array of data, the modern sports statistics company, STATS, Inc., (an acronym for "Sports Team Analysis and Tracking Systems") has named John Tortes Meyers to its National League All-Star Line-Up for 1911, along with his Giants teammates Mathewson, Marquard and Doyle. Indeed, Meyers is included on the STATS National League All-Star team each subsequent year through 1914. Only Hall of Famer Roger Bresnahan is named as catcher on as many teams during the Deadball Era. Meyers and Bresnahan are the only two catchers named by STATS to their National League All-Star Team for the entire Deadball Era (1901–1919).[31]

## Contrasting Responses to Assimilation

On October 12, 1911—Columbus Day—a new reform group, the Society of American Indians (SAI), met for the first time in Columbus, Ohio. The gathering was in response to a call by six Indian activists and intellectuals, including Charles Eastman, John Tortes Meyers's predecessor at Dartmouth College. In their call, the six wrote, "[T]he time has come when the American Indian should take the initiative in the struggle for his race betterment, and to answer in his own way some of the vital questions that confront him."[32]

Called "Red Progressives," SAI members were largely boarding school or university-educated Indians. While there were a number of other progressive organizations, like the Indian Rights Association, seeking to work for the betterment of Indians, the SAI was unique as an organization led by Indians rather than whites. While whites could be associate members, only Indians were admitted to full SAI membership.

The two themes put forward by the SAI were pan–Indianism, the belief that Indians should cooperate together across tribal boundaries on a common political and social agenda, and assimilation of Indians to the culture and lifestyle of the dominant society while they retained pride in their own Indian identities.[33]

On October 14, 1911, with the SAI organizational meeting still in session, Charles Albert "Chief" Bender took the mound against the New York Giants in the first game of the 1911 World Series. Although Bender would win two decisive victories in the series and give up only five runs, on that day he lost the game when Giants catcher John Tortes "Chief" Meyers scored the winning run.

Both events represent responses to the profound changes through which Native Americans were passing in the first decades of the twentieth century. According to Philip Deloria, the SAI provided a context in which Indians were able to approach assimilation on their own terms. By contrast, Bender and Meyers and other Indian athletes at the time were expected to display the traits whites associated with Indians in their "primitive" state before they were affected by their contact with "civilization."[34]

However, the distinction should not be overemphasized, especially when taking into account the perspectives of these two Indian athletes themselves. Despite the racial epithets others used to define them, Bender and Meyers certainly did not see themselves as enacting primitive stereotypes. In their own distinct ways, they fought to rise above such expectations.

Meyers called Bender, a Chippewa Indian who grew up on the White Earth Reservation in Minnesota, "one of the nicest people you'd ever meet."[35] The great A's pitcher "Rube" Bressler, who roomed with Bender, described him as "one of the kindest and finest men who ever lived."[36] Bender's father was of German ancestry; his mother was Chippewa.[37]

Bender was a graduate of the Carlisle Indian Boarding School in Pennsylvania and spent time at Dickinson College. Meyers was impressed his friend "didn't go to the minors at all. Straight to the Big Leagues."[38]

A lanky (6'2"), 185-pound right-hander, Bender signed a contract with legendary Philadelphia Athletics manager Connie Mack in 1902. Mack never used the label "Chief" when talking to Bender. Instead, the A's manager called Bender by his middle name "Albert," the name by which he signed his contract with the A's. However, Mack *would* sometimes call Bender "Chief" when talking to others about him.[39] Mack once said, "If I had all the men I've ever handled, and they were in their prime, and there was one game I wanted to win above all others, Albert would be my man."[40]

Bender spent 12 productive seasons with the A's. His best year statistically was 1910 when he led the American League in winning percentage with an impressive 23–5 record and a 1.58 ERA. In 1911 and 1913 he was 17–5 and 21–10. For his major league career, Bender had a record of 212 wins against 127 losses, with 1,711 strikeouts and a 2.46 ERA. Christy Mathewson said in 1919, "Bender is a student of baseball and a deeper student than many fans and writers are willing to admit. His presence on the bench or coaching lines would naturally mean much to a ball club, for I have never met a player who could grasp situations as quickly as the Indian."[41] The crafty right-hander had a devastating fastball and a sharp curve, and delivered pitches overhand, sidearm, and even underhand in a "submarine" motion.

After retiring from the major leagues Bender remained active in baseball, nearly teaming up with his friend Jack Meyers in the minor leagues. Connie Mack hired him as a scout for the Athletics in 1939, a position he held for the rest of his life.

Charles Albert Bender was elected to the Baseball Hall of Fame at the first meeting of the reorganized Veterans Committee in 1953. In the Hall of Fame yearbook, he is identified simply as "Chief Bender." His plaque in the museum is titled Charles Albert Bender ("Chief") and begins "Famous Chippewa Indian," before listing his on-field achievements.

In his biography of Bender, Tom Swift noted:

> Charles Albert Bender played every game of his career while managing a type of pressure few players ever face. Most must bend their minds just to begin to understand an ounce of it. It's true he was afforded acclaim and privilege other American Indians of the time were not. Bigotry sometimes makes exceptions. But that is altogether different than saying he dodged its calloused hand.[42]

Before the second game of the 1905 World Series against the Giants, New York manager John McGraw taunted Bender, shouting, "It'll be off the warpath for you today, Chief." Bender pitched magnificently to earn a 3–0 shutout. However, Charles Dryden of the *Chicago Examiner* could not resist racist stereotypes in describing the A's pitcher's performance. Bender was "the dusky child of the forest" who "had won a new turkey feather for his head piece, and then for a wind-up came within half an inch of letting the champions scalp him."[43]

When asked if his Chippewa background was the reason for his amazing poise on the pitching mound that day, Bender said, "I want to be known as a pitcher, not an Indian." However, a cartoon in the *Philadelphia Inquirer* the next day showed him dressed as a warrior using an "Indian sign" to hypnotize Giants batters. Other epithets Bender heard from Giants fans and players throughout the 1905 Series included "Back to the reservation!" and "Giants grab heap big wampum!"[44]

Charlie Bender and John Tortes Meyers handled the bias they experienced differently. As we have seen, Meyers acknowledged he felt like a foreigner and was willing to speak up against injustices against Indian people. He did not, except for the rare occasion, retaliate physically when insulted, but he did sometimes respond, choosing ironic humor as his weapon.

On occasion, like Meyers, Bender made comments that revealed the constant pressure he was under as a Native American major leaguer. For example, he said, "I wouldn't advise any of the students at Carlisle to become a professional baseball player. It is a hard road to travel."[45] One day, when he was having a rough outing, and fans were doing their typical war whoop heckling,

Bender walked over to the third base stands and yelled, "You ill-bred ignorant foreigners; if you don't like what I'm doing here, why don't you go back where you came from?"[46]

However, such overt responses were not typical. On most occasions when he was being heckled viciously, Bender would "just smile, sometimes tip his cap, in some ways anticipating what *New York Times* sports reporter William C. Rhoden would call the accommodating, 'tying oneself in knots' behavior of Jackie Robinson."[47]

Bender would even deny he was the victim of prejudice. On October 10, 1909, for example, he told a *Chicago Daily News* reporter, "There has been scarcely a trace of sentiment against me on account of birth. I have been treated the same as other men."[48] Of course, Bender made this comment during the prime of his career when "making waves would have only made his life all that more uncomfortable."[49]

On the whole, Bender, unlike Meyers, chose denial, withdrawal, and stoic silence as his coping mechanisms. Bender entered baseball because it offered him the best opportunity both for money and advancement. Meyers too saw baseball as his road to financial success. However, while Bender largely and purposefully tried to leave his Indian identity behind, choosing to integrate fully into white society as much as possible during and after his playing days, Meyers remained connected to his Indian heritage and Cahuilla homeland during and after his baseball career, willingly involving himself in the affairs of his people. In contrast, after leaving the White Earth Reservation where he was born, Bender never lived in Indian country again, only going back for occasional visits. He chose instead to live in Pennsylvania when he signed with the Athletics in 1902. After his baseball career ended, Bender remained in the state for the rest of his life.

Bender, Meyers, and other Native American players in the early history of baseball experienced a catch-22. If they released the tension and frustration they felt as a result of the treatment they experienced outwardly, they risked being labeled "savage Indians." If they kept it in, it was assumed they were displaying the "naturally impassive and unfeeling" nature of all primitive people.[50]

The difference between Bender and Meyers was that while Meyers found ways to express rather than bottle up his frustration, Bender was more inclined to keep his hostility inside, and, as biographer William Kashatus put it, "pursued a major league career to distance himself from his Indian heritage." Kashatus concluded, "[I]t was a decision that haunted him the rest of his life." Late in his career Bender struggled with abuse of alcohol. On one occasion, a writer reported Connie Mack confronted his star pitcher at the team hotel "when Chief Bender blew in after a somewhat prolonged dalliance with the fire water which the soul of the red man craveth."[51] Although Bender attained greater lasting financial success than Meyers, the "tragic legacy of his life" was, according to another Bender biographer, "the abandonment of [his] native culture to chase after the white man's American Dream, a dream that proved to be a personal nightmare."[52]

## The 1911 World Series: "Indian Versus Indian"

Although the World Series (then known as the world's series) had been the most popular sporting event in the nation since its inception in 1903, in 1911 the Fall Classic rose to an even higher level. Pitting the New York Giants against the Philadelphia Athletics, it was the first series played in the new steel-and-concrete stadiums, with fans restricted from crowding onto the field and constricting the playing surface.

With the 1911 Series the "media circus" was also born. Hundreds of photographers swarmed the field before each game, snapping every conceivable shot. Before the first game the Giants' batboy/mascot Dick Hennessey was

Meyers and his manager and mentor, New York Giants Manager John McGraw, shown together at the 1911 World Series that pitted the Giants against Connie Mack's Philadelphia Athletics (Library of Congress, Prints & Photographs Division, LC-DIG-ggbain-10327).

even photographed shaking hands with the A's mascot, Louis Van Zelst, like two prizefighters ready to go at each other.[53]

The Series was the first to be covered by a large national and even international press corps. In the press box for the 1911 series was an immensely talented group of sportswriters including Damon Runyan, Heywood Broun, Grantland Rice, Sam Crane, Fred Lieb, Bozeman Bulger, Sid Mercer, and Ring Lardner.

Alongside were 50 telegraphers ready to flash the game action, play by play, to sites from Havana to Los Angeles. After each game a summary was sent to Tokyo. Throughout the nation thousands would follow the games on various types of public scoreboards, including new electronic models. The U.S. Supreme Court justices had clerks slip them inning-by-inning reports, and the proceedings of the houses of Congress were interrupted when there was a change in the score.

It was also the first World Series when daily reports, ghostwritten by sportswriters, appeared under the names of ballplayers in the series. For example, John N. Wheeler of the *New York Herald* paid Christy Mathewson $500 to allow him to write a daily column under Matty's name.

The 1910 World Series had been the first to be recorded by motion picture cameras. When the Giants and A's players heard the 1911 Series would also be filmed and the three-member National Commission (composed of the National and American League Presidents and the Reds owner) had already sold the movie rights for $3,500, they naturally wanted a share of the fee. The A's picked Harry Davis to speak for them. The Giants selected John Tortes Meyers, an indication that his teammates clearly recognized the Cahuilla catcher's intellectual ability and persuasive skills. Davis and Meyers petitioned the Commission for 60 percent of the $3,500 paid for the filming, but they were turned down.[54]

To repeat the appearance of the storied 1905 New York Giants team which had beaten the A's, McGraw had his players dress in all-black broadcloth uniforms trimmed in white. However, the A's were a much stronger team than in 1905. In addition to their ace, Albert Bender, the A's pitching staff included Jack Coombs, who had won 59 games the past two seasons, and Eddie Plank. Eddie Collins was the best second baseman in baseball, and J. Franklin Baker was the hard-hitting third baseman.[55]

Fred Snodgrass remembered that, before the first game of the 1911 series, McGraw had the team go onto the field first to wait for the A's to pass by. As they did, each Giant had a shoe off and was sharpening his spikes with a file. The idea was to spook the A's, letting them know the Giants would be running the bases hard. In particular, third baseman Frank Baker was believed to be a "spike-shy" fielder who would get out of the way when a Giants player slid into third.[56]

Meyers and Philadelphia Athletics star pitcher Charles Albert "Chief" Bender pose before the first game of the 1911 World Series, dubbed by sportswriters at the time as the "Indian versus Indian" series (Library of Congress, Prints & Photographs Division, LC-DIG-ggbain-09861).

In his assessment of the two teams in the 1911 Series, W. A. Phelon countered critics who claimed Meyers could not throw out runners. If you checked game statistics, Phelon noted, you would find that "the son of the forest" had thrown out many runners attempting to steal during the season. He concluded, "the Injun [has] educated his throwing wing till it will nip anybody the Athletics can send up."[57] Phelon's analysis turned out to be prophetic.

Before the first game of the Series John Tortes Meyers and Charles Albert Bender posed for a photograph. They were, as the press made sure was widely known, the game's two greatest American Indian players. Writers soon dubbed it the "Indian versus Indian" series. One reporter at the time wrote, "[W]hen the Pilgrims landed on Plymouth Rock they first fell upon their knees, and then fell upon the aborigines. Things have changed. The aborigines now fall upon the whites and make short work of them."[58]

## First Game (Saturday, October 14)

For the opening game of the 1911 World Series nearly 40,000 fans, many struggling for vantage points, witnessed "the sort of ball one likes to see on a real hard-cider day," as the *New York Times* described the scene. Inspired by the two Native Americans in the game, the *Times* article overflowed with Indian images. Playing up the heritage Bender was trying to escape, the *Times* writer couldn't resist showing off his "knowledge" of various tribal religions:

> During four innings [Bender] had the Indian sign on McGraw's scouts. Yes, Bender was there with all the aboriginal sign language of all the separate tribes. He possessed the Apache omen, the Mandan magic, the Sioux sorcery, the Arapahoe evil eye, and even the Siwash shibboleth. (Say it fast and you get a gold tooth free.) Then the Giants boiled some snake root, rubbed it in their hair, and discovered his secret. They told on Mr. Bender. The news spread and his incantations and exorcisms became powerless to affect them.

When Meyers faced Bender for the first time in the third inning it was not the Giants' power-hitting catcher against the A's best pitcher, but "Chief Meyers, the Mission Indian, fac[ing] Chief Bender, the Chippewa." In another "anthropological" comment, replete with an attempt at a humorous twist on General Philip Sheridan's famous comment, *Times* writer W. J. Lampton observed in his notes on the game:

> the ethnology of the game was interesting at that point when Bender was sending them in hot to Meyers at the bat, ... with Mathewson and Thomas in their places, Bender and Meyers being redskins and the other two palefaces. Somebody has said that the only good Indian is a dead Indian, but whoever he was, he never saw Bender and Meyers play ball.

In the seventh inning, it was once again "Indian against Indian." When "Big Chief Meyers" doubled, the *Times* employed yet another allusion to a distorted version of Native American religions, suggesting that "it required only Devore's timely hit over third base to score the Witch Doctor and win the game." In describing the scene, the *Times* writer offered, "Perhaps the mind of these two Redmen went far back to the barren, arid plains. (Sounds poetical, doesn't it?) Maybe they wished they had tomahawks in their hands instead of a bat and a baseball." When Meyers reached second, he was "blowing like a hunted deer."

According to a syndicated article on the game ghostwritten for Meyers, the Cahuilla catcher ostensibly engaged in banter with Bender before stroking the seventh-inning double. Bender, whom "Meyers" in the article calls "my redskin friend Albert," warned the Giants hitter, "Good night for you, Chief." When Meyers blasted the ball to the wall, he made a sarcastic comment to Bender, who shook his fist at his friend. To show there were no hard feelings, "Meyers" concluded by saying, "Albert Bender is a wonderful pitcher.... I am glad to belong to the same race as that big fellow."[59]

Meyers and Bender were not accomplished major league ball players as much as they were "primitives" acting out their warlike instincts in the guise of a baseball game. Never mind that Bender was pitching magnificently or that Meyers's blast in the seventh missed being a home run by a foot; the burning question for the *New York Times* was, "Now who's the best Indian — the Mission or the Chippewa?"

As though bewitched by Bender, Mathewson, the *Times* article asserted, had his own "Redskin wizardry" and "set the fans to ghost dancing." "He was the big Shaman, the Wizard, the Warlock.... All in all, Matty's necromancy had it on Bender's by a slight margin, due no doubt to his coming from another tribe."[60]

The *New York Herald* praised Mathewson's performance in a doggerel that included a racist reference to Bender[61]:

> You punched the Mack men full of holes;
> you spiked their biggest gun;
> You tore the scalplock off the Chief;
> you put 'em on the run.

In fact, the game was a classic pitchers duel between two outstanding hurlers at their peaks. The A's scored in the second inning, ending Mathewson's streak of 28 scoreless innings in World Series play begun in 1905. McGraw believed the A's hunchback mascot, Louis Van Zelst, was stealing Meyers's signs when Van Zelst retrieved the bat of the previous hitter because he was "near the ground." McGraw argued that Van Zelst would then relay the signs to the Athletics coach at third base who would tip off the hitter. To thwart the theft McGraw had Matty and Meyers change signals in the third inning, and the A's did not score again. Matty credited McGraw, saying, "Every play made by a Giant has been ordered by McGraw."[62] In this instance, the wily McGraw may have outsmarted himself. It wasn't that the Athletics were stealing the Giants' signs as much as it was the A's bench picking up moves Mathewson was making that tipped his pitches.[63]

The first game of the 1911 Series was also another demonstration of McGraw's patented "inside baseball." In the fourth inning Fred Snodgrass was on second when McGraw called a hit-and-run. "Snow," as his teammates called him, made it halfway to third before Herzog drove the ball to Collins. When Collins fumbled it, Snodgrass scooted home. However, not all the writers in attendance considered this brand of baseball entertaining. "Maybe a scientific game of ball is worthy of the high esteem in which it seems to be held by numerous fans," one observed, "but to a man of untrained perception it is about as interesting as to watch a mathematician work out a problem in differential equations on a blackboard."[64]

The 2–1 victory was Matty's fourth in a row over the A's, during which he had given up only one run in 36 innings. In the four games he had allowed only one walk and had thrown only 92 pitches per outing.

After the game players on both teams discovered that Giants President John Brush was swindling them by undercounting the gate. Brush reported attendance of 38,281 but a standing-room only crowd was present. At least 40,000 and probably more fans were stuffed into the Polo Grounds. Since bonus shares were based on a percentage of the gate, the players felt they were being cheated. John Tortes Meyers stepped forward to protest Brush's action. He convened "a committee of Giants and A's players, including Bender, and met with the National Commission to discuss the matter."[65] Their charge was dismissed, but the incident clearly shows again that Meyers was willing to take the lead in challenging an injustice. It was the second time in the 1911 Series Meyers assumed leadership in arguing that the players were not being treated fairly.

It was not the first run-in Meyers had with the famously tight Giants owner. At the height of their success on the field Meyers and Mathewson decided to put up a united front against Brush. When they entered the owner's office, Meyers recalled, "He was in a wheel chair, Mr. Brush was, and he said to us, 'What is the purpose of this visit?' Well, he knew darn well what we came in for, and Matty told him we wanted a raise. Well, he couldn't walk, but he got out of that wheel chair and pounded his fist, and said, 'It don't come in at the gate! Now get out of my office.'" They didn't get raises.[66]

In the stands for the first game of the 1911 Series were about a thousand women, at least some of whom were there to demonstrate their support of the right-to-vote for women. One writer commented, "The ladies don't care who plays baseball if they can play politics. Which shows that women are not men's equals.... Lady bleachers are known as bleacherettes. Lady fans are fannies."[67]

## Second Game (Monday, October 16)

After a day off for the Sabbath (as required by state laws at the time) the 1911 Series moved to Philadelphia. Shibe Park, with a capacity of 33,000, was sold out and enterprising neighbors had built grandstands on their rooftops, accommodating an estimated 5,000 more. Hundreds of thousands gathered in New York, at the Polo Grounds, Madison Square Garden, and in the streets, to follow the game on giant electric scoreboards.

Rube Marquard took the mound against Eddie Plank, the future Hall of Fame southpaw. In his ghostwritten review of the game, "Marquard" acknowledged he was nervous in his first appearance in a championship series. He also said the Giants were overconfident after their victory in the first game.[68]

When Josh Devore opened the game by striking out, the A's fans responded by pounding tom-tom drums they had brought to the game to try to rattle Meyers. When Marquard had trouble with his control in the bottom of the first, allowing a run on a wild pitch, Meyers, one writer observed, "went out to the box to talk to him in a fatherly way."[69] The wild pitch came, "Marquard" claimed, when Meyers called for a high fastball to Eddie Collins, but Rube thought his catcher had asked for an "incurve." Marquard's ghostwriter, Frank Menke, explained, "I tried to change after I had begun my serving, and the result was a passed ball, on which ["Bris"] Lord scored."

In the second inning, Meyers singled, driving in a run. In the bottom of the inning the Giants catcher made a good defensive play, throwing out Plank on an attempted bunt. The score remained tied 1–1 until the sixth, when A's slugger Frank Baker, who had led the league with 11 home runs during the regular season, came to the plate with a man on. Meyers again went to the mound to calm the Giants pitcher, but, with his adrenaline pumping, Marquard tried to blow a high fastball by Baker, who promptly sent the pitch over the right field fence. "Marquard" noted, "I thought to cross him by sending a fast high straight ball, the kind I knew he liked. Meyers had called for a curve, but I could not see it [because he was blinded by the sun, he said] and signaled a high fast ball." The two runs gave the A's the lead and the win, 3 to 1.

Christy Mathewson's ghostwriter, John Wheeler, attacked Marquard under Mathewson's byline. Although Matty had not approved or even seen the article, readers thought their idol had accused a teammate of throwing a chin high fastball and costing the Giants the game after McGraw had explicitly warned him before the game not to give in to Baker's strength. However, Matty refused to blame Wheeler and took responsibility for what appeared in print under his name. Marquard was understandably upset and Connie Mack posted the column in the A's clubhouse at the Polo Grounds before the next game.[70]

## Third Game (Tuesday, October 17)

Because the two cities were so close, games in the 1911 Series alternated parks. The third game was played in drizzling rain at the Polo Grounds. Mathewson again took the mound for the Giants, and Jack "Iron Man" Coombs pitched for the A's.

McGraw was still convinced the A's mascot was stealing Meyers's signs by looking over Meyers's knee when retrieving a bat. Therefore, the Giants went to a system in which Mathewson gave his catcher the signs instead of Meyers giving them to the pitcher.[71]

It was actually Bender who took the lead in reading the motions of pitchers rather than anyone on the A's stealing signs.[72] For example, Mathewson would tip his fastball by holding the ball in his right hand, with his arm hanging loosely to his side. One writer gave a racial explanation for Bender's reading pitchers' motions, saying the Chippewa pitcher was displaying "the cunning characteristic of his race" by seeing things that "escape the eye of the Caucasian."[73]

The game remained scoreless until the third inning, when Meyers singled on a hard-hit ground ball. He took third on a single by Mathewson and scored on a grounder by Devore. In the fifth Meyers kept the Giants in the lead by blocking the plate and tagging out A's runner Danny Murphy, who was trying to score on a slow roller to Matty. With the score still 1–0 in the eighth inning, Meyers once again held the A's scoreless by blocking the plate and tagging out another A's player. When the ninth inning began, with the Giants still leading by a run, New York fans began to leave in anticipation that Matty would shut down the A's once again. However, Baker homered to right, tying the game at one run each. Meyers and Mathewson always maintained they had struck out Baker on the pitch before he hit the home run. In a 1939 interview with Grantland Rice, Meyers said, "The third strike cut the plate by three or four inches—and they called it a ball."[74]

In his ghostwritten reflection on the game, "Marquard" claimed Mathewson told him on returning to the bench in the ninth, "I gave Baker a high, fast one. I have been in the business a long time and have no excuse."

In the Giants' tenth, Snodgrass reached on a walk, moved to second on a sacrifice, and started for third when the A's catcher, Jack Lapp, dropped a pitch. However, Lapp quickly recovered and pegged the ball to Baker at third. Seeing he was nailed, Snow jumped into the air and landed on Baker with his sharpened spikes. Baker held the ball but only after being cut by Snodgrass. This was the second time Snow had spiked Baker in the Series, and the A's fans in attendance responded with catcalls. Even a hometown writer concluded, "The endangering of Baker by such a move seemed unsportsmanlike and out of place."[75]

Later in the day an erroneous report went out on the wires that a rabid fan had shot Snodgrass and he had been taken to the hospital in critical condition. His parents in California heard he had been killed, and it was several hours before a retraction reached them.[76]

The game went to the 11th inning still tied, but the A's took the lead by playing their own version of "inside baseball." "Rube" Oldring grounded out, and Collins lined a single to left. Baker singled and went to second, with Collins advancing to third on a throwing error by Buck Herzog. Collins scored when third baseman Art Fletcher fumbled Murphy's grounder, and Baker scored when Harry Davis singled to right.

The Giants mounted a comeback in the bottom of the inning, scoring one run, but the game ended with the A's clinging to a 3–2 lead. Meyers had yet another opportunity to win the game for the Giants, when he came to bat in the 11th, with Herzog on second. The *Times* reported, "War whoops, yells, Indian talk, filled the air as [Giants fans] pleaded, begged, yes, implored the Redman to tear the cover off the ball and drive it to the wilderness and win the game."[77] The A's pitcher, Jack Coombs, remembered after Herzog had doubled, "The Chief almost did to me what Baker did to Mathewson. He sent a long drive into the left field bleachers. The ball started fair, but the wind blew it back and sent it into foul territory by only a few inches. After the Chief gave us that big scare, he rolled out to Collins, Herzog taking third."[78]

## Fourth Game (Tuesday, October 24)

A huge storm caused a week's delay between the third and fourth games of the 1911 Series. When play finally resumed on October 24, 1911, in Shibe Park, Matty again pitched, and Bender took the mound for the A's.

In the first inning Devore reached base when he tapped a roller toward the mound. According to the account in the *New York Times,* "The Indian threw up his hand, deflecting the ball to Barry, but Joshua was too fleet and beat out the throw easily."[79] Devore scored on Doyle's triple, and Snodgrass, who was greeted with cries of derision from the A's fans, drove in Doyle. Bender then settled down and held the Giants scoreless for the rest of the game.

A two-run lead was ordinarily all Matty needed, but this would not be his day. "Home Run" Baker, as he was now being called in Philadelphia and would be known for the rest of his career, doubled to start a three-run rally in the fourth. He followed with another double in the fifth. Matty allowed ten hits and was pulled for a pinch-hitter in the eighth. One writer said Marquard, who was warming up to replace Mathewson, had a "sardonic grin." It would be Matty's last appearance for the season.

In his 2005 book, *The Old Ball Game: How John McGraw, Christy Mathewson, and the New York Giants Created Modern Baseball,* Frank DeFord demonstrated that twenty-first century writers are still capable of employing stereotypical descriptions of Native American ballplayers when he wrote that the "celebrated medicine man, Chief Bender" allowed no more runs and the A's won, 4–2.[80] Matty said simply, "I have no excuse to make."

In the game Meyers reached on a fielder's choice in the second inning, but was stranded. In the fifth he doubled, but was thrown out while trying to advance on a wild pitch. According to the *Times,* "Manager McGraw was coaching at third, and he and the Indian looked at each other, sharing the deep disappointment of the blighted play."[81] Meyers grounded out in the seventh and again in the ninth for the final out of the game.

## Fifth Game (Wednesday, October 25)

Back at the Polo Grounds, before 34,000 enthusiastic fans, the Giants came back to win the fifth game, with Marquard and Coombs starting. When Snodgrass walked to the plate in the first inning, he was greeted with thunderous applause from the home crowd.

The A's tallied three runs in the third inning after an error by Giants captain Larry Doyle preceded a three-run blast by the A's Rube Oldring. In the Giants' third Meyers punched a "red-hot" grounder into left for a single. When Beals Becker, pinch-hitting for Marquard, lined out, Jack Barry almost doubled Meyers off first. However, as the *Times* put it, Meyers's "existence in this vale of joys and sorrows was prolonged a bit." Soon, Meyers was thrown out trying to steal.

Red Ames took over for Marquard. He held the A's scoreless until he was relieved in the eighth by Doc Crandall. Meyers drove in the first Giants run on a sacrifice fly in the seventh. The stands were rapidly emptying in the ninth when the Giants came to bat, trailing 3 to 1. Herzog and Meyers obliged by grounding out, and little hope remained. However, Fletcher kept the game alive, dumping a Texas Leaguer to short left. Crandall's ringing double to right center drove in a run, and he tied the game himself, scoring on a hit by Devore. The *Times* jubilantly observed, "Men and women who were perfect strangers suddenly became acquainted and slapped each other on the back with hilarious abandon."

The Giants broke the tie and won the game in the bottom of the tenth on a sacrifice fly by Merkle that curved over the foul line. The ball would probably have landed foul, but it was caught and Doyle raced home from third. If the Athletics had protested, Bill Klem, who was the home plate umpire, said he would have had to call Doyle out because he missed the plate by six inches on his slide. However, neither Connie Mack nor his players protested.

A chart accompanying the *Times* article on the game listed the height, weight, and ages of the Giants and A's players. At 195, Meyers was the heaviest on both teams, followed by Mathewson at 190. Meyers's date of birth was listed, incorrectly, as 1882.[82]

## Sixth Game (Thursday, October 26)

Connie Mack surprised observers by bringing Albert Bender back to the mound for the sixth game in Philadelphia on only one day's rest. McGraw held Mathewson out for an anticipated seventh game and sent Red Ames to the mound instead.

The game began when Bender, called "the Redman" in press coverage, speared a drive by Devore "with his bare hand" and threw the Giants' leadoff man out at first. Doyle bounced a long drive "off the top of the right field stockade" for a double, and scored on an error with two out. The A's tied the game in the third and went ahead for good in the fourth, scoring four runs.[83]

In the fifth, Meyers rocketed a single to center, but was stranded. "Hooks" Wiltse entered the game and "had all the magic of an East Indian conjurer hidden in his south paw."[84] With the "red boy," as the *Times* now called Bender, doubling up its racist labeling, still pitching, the A's continued their dominance. The Philadelphia team scored once more in the sixth.

Meyers struck out in the seventh and the Giants were scoreless. With the A's pouring it on in the bottom of the inning, McGraw "hooked Hooks" and brought in Marquard. The *Times* couldn't resist, offering that Rube dropped his pen and made for the mound, and then reported that on his first pitch Marquard was "as wild as a hungry Zulu and chuck[ed] a lurid heave, which Meyers didn't even touch on its savage flight to the grandstand." On a roll, the *Times* suggested the Giants might have been better off playing Charley Faust, who was still on the bench, to bring them better luck.[85] When the bombardment ended, the A's led 13 to 2. The game mercifully concluded when Art Wilson, who replaced Meyers behind the bat in the top half of the ninth, grounded out.

After the game the Giants manager walked over to the A's bench and offered his congratulations to Connie Mack. McGraw had genuine affection for the A's manager despite their nearly opposite temperaments. "You have one of the greatest teams I've ever seen," he told Mack. "It must be. I have a great team, too, but you beat us."[86]

Meyers played in all six games of the 1911 Series and had 20 at-bats. With six hits, his average was .300, second only to Doyle's seven hits and .304 average among Giants regulars. Defensively, by throwing out 12 runners, including six runners trying to steal, in the six-game 1911 Series, Meyers set a major league record that still stands a century later.

The Giants did not have a single home run for the Series, and only one triple. The A's "Home Run" Baker was the hitting star, with nine hits, including two home runs, and a .375 average. The Giants could manage only three stolen bases over the six games. A's catcher Jack Lapp squelched four New York attempts in the third game alone. As a team the Giants batted only .175.

Forty years later, Ty Cobb, who was present for the 1911 Series, remembered how Albert Bender, in what he called "the greatest bit of brainwork I ever saw in a ballgame," famously tricked Meyers. The Athletics pitcher made the Giants catcher think he was going to throw him a curve by motioning his outfielders to move, and then threw the fastball-hitting Meyers a heater straight down the middle, striking him out.[87]

The 1911 Series set an attendance record with 179,891 paid admissions. The winning A's players each received $3,654.50, while the losing Giants' full share was $2,436.39. The loser's share was a record by over a thousand dollars.

## The 1911-12 Off-Season: On the Farm in Riverside

Although exhausted, the Giants players voted to accept the invitation of Cuban promoters to go to the island after the 1911 World Series for a 12-game exhibition trip. Meyers, however, passed up the $500 paid to each player and returned home to California in order to "give his personal attention to his fruit farm at Riverside, and to enjoy a much needed rest from the diamond."[88]

On November 13, citizens of Riverside presented Meyers a loving cup. According to the *New York Times* report on the occasion, "the 'Chief' was urged by the fans in attendance at his reception to make a speech of the home run variety, but he struck out."[89]

An article, apparently published after the 1911 season, was one of the few written during John Tortes Meyers's entire major league career to challenge directly the stereotypes through which he was commonly viewed[90]:

One of the most intelligent men playing baseball today is Meyers, the big Indian who catches so brilliantly for the Giants. Mr. Meyers spends all his spare time reading, but when dragged into a conversation talks entertainingly on current events, ancient and modern history, literature and art. There is not a more learned man in the baseball profession, but the fans who give the Indian war cry every time they see Mr. Meyers in action know not their man.

# Six

# An MVP Year: The 1912 Season and World Series

## 1912 Spring Training: The "Complete Tribe"

McGraw began the Giants' spring training in 1912 by telling players that anyone not angry at the Giants' loss in the 1911 Series could "find another Goddamned nine to play for."[1] Then he promptly lightened the mood by having his charges play handball and tennis.

"The tribe will be complete when Meyers arrives," was how the *New York Times* began its coverage of the Giants' 1912 spring training.[2] Eager to put to rest a rumor that he had added weight during the winter and was out of shape, Meyers arrived in Marlin ready to play. In a March 16 game against local Texas Leaguers he homered twice. He also chased a runner down between second and third, making the tag himself.[3]

By this point in his career Meyers was taking advantage of his success on the baseball diamond to earn extra money through endorsements. In the March 1912 issue of *Boys' Life* he was listed alongside Christy Mathewson and several other "world famous players" in an ad for Goldsmith baseball gloves. The popular magazine promised readers portraits of stars like Ty Cobb, Christy Mathewson, Rube Marquard and Chief Meyers if they ordered a mitt.[4]

Fred Merkle had regained his confidence and held out for $4,000, with the Giants offering only $3,000. Once he signed (settling for a raise of $500), Merkle joined Meyers (who had signed a three-year contract), Snodgrass, and Murray as the team's best batsmen. Proven hurlers Mathewson and Marquard would again have stellar performances in 1912, and rookie Charles "Jeff" Tesreau would pitch very well.

At 6'2", Tesreau, who heralded from the Ozarks mountains of Missouri, was often described in the New York press as "a bear of a man" or simply "the bear hunter of the Ozarks." A right-handed spitballer, he had "speed like lightning" and a devastating curve ball that bent "like barrel hoops." Sportswriters ironically dubbed Tesreau "Jeff," after the half-pint cartoon character in the popular "Mutt and Jeff" strip. Tesreau had been acquired from the St. Louis Browns in 1910 and played in the minor leagues until joining the Giants for the 1912 season. He remained with the team, playing a key role in the Giants' success, until an argument with McGraw during the 1918 season caused him to quit the team and not return. After leaving the majors Tesreau, who was often portrayed in the press as an ignorant hillbilly, took a position as baseball coach at Meyers's *alma mater,* Dartmouth College, where he remained until his death in 1946.

As a spokesman for players' rights Meyers was interested in an ongoing investigation into the control of the national game by a "baseball trust." According to Illinois congressman Thomas Gallagher the trust "enslaved" the players, forcing them to accept salaries or be barred permanently from the game. However, Meyers and other players would be disappointed in the eventual outcome when baseball owners succeeded in quashing the inquiry.[5]

## The 1912 Season: A "Hall of Fame" Year

No one was thinking much about baseball by the late afternoon of April 15, 1912, after Christy Mathewson opened his 13th year in a New York Giants uniform with a loss to Boston. Word was spreading that the White Star Line's luxury ship the *Titanic* had hit an iceberg in the North Atlantic and was sinking on its maiden voyage from England to the United States. The next day headlines announced over 1,200 drowned. Across the country, attendance at baseball games dropped off for a few days.[6]

The period of widespread mourning was short-lived, and enthusiasm for the national pastime soon returned. In an April 20 game played at the Polo Grounds before 20,000 boisterous fans, the Giants rallied to beat the Dodgers, 4 to 3. The hero for the Giants was not John Tortes Meyers, who was embarking on his best year in the majors, but Art Wilson, who won the game with a walk-off two-run homer in the bottom of the ninth. Wilson replaced Meyers after the Cahuilla catcher was ejected in the top of the inning. According to the report in the *Times,* "the redman was chased out of the game" by home plate umpire Charles Rigler after disputing a call. After replacing Meyers, Wilson allowed two runs to score when he made a wild throw in a rundown. However, Wilson redeemed himself with the game-winning blast. Before being ejected from the game Meyers was the star for the Giants. According to the *Times,* "It was the Indian's trusty club that drove in the two runs which the Giants had culled up to that time."[7]

Within a few weeks of the start of the 1912 season Meyers was being acclaimed as one of the top players in the major leagues. He was batting at a

.600 pace, with four doubles and a home run. Even though McGraw "had to fork over a stiff sum for the slugging redskin" in 1908, one writer commented, "the 'Big Chief'" was "now worth about ten times the amount John J. paid for him."[8]

By the end of May the Giants had run off three strings of nine straight victories for a 28–6 record. With Charles "Victory" Faust once again allowed on the bench, though not in a Giants uniform, many fans and players believed his magical powers were at work. For the less credulous the Giants' wins had more to do with a combination of good pitching, hitting, fielding, and base running. The Giants were firing on all cylinders with John J. McGraw in the driver's seat in his patented "inside baseball" style.

During this period Damon Runyon chronicled the Giants' success for the *New York American*. Runyon often featured Meyers in articles. For example, although the Giants lost to Roger Bresnahan's Cardinals 5 to 1 in a May 31 game, Runyon reported that Meyers was striking fear into the hearts of opposing managers after a homer the writer called a "terrific wallop."[9]

Runyon also shared the Cahuilla catcher's wry wit. During a game against the Boston Braves Meyers overheard the Boston catcher say to the Braves' left fielder, after the fielder dropped a fly ball allowing three Giants to score, "You bush bastard, now you've spilled the beans." Meyers laughed, not at the left fielder's error, but at the irony of the Boston catcher's saying, "spilling the beans" in the city called Beantown. When Runyon later asked Meyers why he laughed, the Giants receiver told him, and the writer turned the incident into a hilarious story.[10]

Mathewson was having yet another excellent season, but the pitching star for the 1912 Giants was Rube Marquard. With Meyers as his battery mate, Marquard was winning every game he pitched. In a June 3 contest Meyers propelled Marquard, his "sensational battery bunkie" as Damon Runyon described the left-hander, to an 8 to 3 victory over the Cardinals with a grand slam home run.[11]

Meyers's powerful hitting was one of the principal reasons for the Giants' success. He drove in three runs to propel the Giants and Mathewson to a June 7 win, 7 to 6, over the Cincinnati Reds. The next day Marquard won his 12th game in a row, beating the Reds 6 to 2. Just three days later Marquard won again and the Giants had a 34 and 7 record, well ahead of the second-place Cubs.

At a packed Polo Grounds Meyers hit for the cycle against four Cubs pitchers in another Giants victory, recording a single, double, triple, and home run. He was the first major leaguer to accomplish the feat during the 1912 season, and only the second Giant to complete the cycle since the origin of the club. Only 11 Giants accomplished the feat the entire time the club was

The New York Giants at the Polo Grounds near the end of the 1912 season. Meyers is second from the right in the top row. His battery mate Christy Mathewson is on the far right. In the middle, on the far left (crouching), is Giants coach Wilbert Robinson, who was later Meyers's manager when he played for the Brooklyn Dodgers. Others in the photograph, according to the Pictorial History Committee of the Society for American Baseball Research, are, in the top row (left to right): Doc Crandall, Fred Merkle, unidentified player, Red Murray, Hooks Wiltse, Larry Doyle, unidentified player, Al Demaree; middle (crouching, on the right): unidentified player, Beals Becker; bottom row, seated (left to right): Moose McCormick, Josh Devore, unidentified player, Art Fletcher, George Burns, Ted Goulait, Buck Herzog. Seated in front is team mascot Dick Hennessy (Library of Congress, Prints & Photographs Division, LC-DIG-ggbain-11997).

in New York, and through 2010 only 14 major league catchers had hit for the cycle in a game.

Marquard's unbroken streak of wins nearly ended when he left the June 12 game for a pinch hitter in the eighth inning with the Giants trailing. However, when the Giants rallied in the bottom of the inning to win the game over the Cubs, 3 to 2, the official scorer credited Marquard with the victory. Not only was Meyers contributing with his bat, he was making big plays defensively as well. In the eighth inning the Cubs' Lew Richie was sliding into home with his spikes high. Meyers, who was 2-for-3 in the game, stood his ground and tagged the Cubs runner hard. Richie was so shaken up he had to leave the game.[12]

The next day, in another Mathewson win, Meyers was 2-for-2 in a 3 to 2 victory over the Cubs. But Meyers and the Giants cooled off, losing to Pittsburg in a June 14 contest. Meyers went hitless, and when the Giants catcher left the game, Runyon described his departure by writing, "Chief Meyers went to his tepee."[13]

An article entitled "'Chief' Meyers Tells His Life Story to American Readers; Hardy Indian Overcomes Many Obstacles in Meteoric Rise," appeared in the *New York American* on June 16, 1912, with the byline "By 'Chief' Meyers." The theme, repeated elsewhere by Meyers, was that he had, as the subtitle for the article put it, "'booted' life's chance by choosing [a] diamond career."[14]

Despite using all the well-worn clichés that fixated on Meyers "the Indian," Damon Runyon did show his appreciation for the catcher's talents as a ballplayer and his intelligence. In an inset published with Meyers's article, Runyon wrote:

> The accompanying article is the life story of John Tortes Meyers, the great Indian catcher of the New York Giants, written by himself, for the New York American. Meyers is recognized as one of the greatest natural hitters that ever broke into the game.... Meyers is a Dartmouth man, and one of the best educated ball players in the country.

However, in one of the drawings accompanying the article, an illustrator displayed Meyers in a Plains Indian headdress, breastplate, and buckskin. Another portrayed him dancing while menacingly holding a "war club."

In a surprising statement for a star in the nation's most beloved sport, Meyers began the article by admitting, "If I had it to do all over again, knowing what I know now, and offered the same opportunity that I once had, I probably wouldn't be a professional ball player." It was not, Meyers wrote, that "I don't consider ball playing as clean and honorable and as desirable as any other profession in the world," but since walking away from Dartmouth after only one year at the College he had come to realize that he had made an error far greater than "booting" a baseball.

Meyers acknowledged, "Baseball has been mighty good to me. Any man who has had over a year on a championship club, with a world's series thrown in, as I have had, is lucky. I am proud of my profession." He also loved being a New York Giant, saying he had "lived some of the most pleasant hours of my life" as a Giant. "It is something to have been a friend and companion to the men who make up the New York National League Club." It was a conviction that never left him. As he would tell Lawrence Ritter more than a half-century later, Meyers believed "once a Giant, always a Giant."[15]

Meyers went on to let his readers know he would advise any young man with the natural ability to adopt baseball as a career. "Still, if I was back in

1906, and know what I know now," he added, "I don't believe you would have ever heard of 'Chief' Meyers of the Giants."

Why was Meyers ambiguous about becoming a professional ballplayer? In part, it was the prejudice he had endured. In contrast to Albert Bender, who said to a reporter in 1909 that he had never experienced racism in the game, Meyers told the *American's* readers that as a ballplayer he had been through "both pleasant and unpleasant experiences." Surely he had in mind the overt racial insults and baiting he so often experienced.

If Meyers had completed his Dartmouth education and pursued a career in engineering, as he planned, he would not have had to endure the constant public harassment based solely on his identity as an Indian. However, from the platform of the visible arena he chose, he was able to transcend the racially biased expectations surrounding him and prove an Indian could excel at the white man's most valued game. In addition, he could be both highly cultured in the terms the dominant society recognized and remain committed to his heritage and his people. It was a delicate balancing act, but one John Tortes Meyers performed well, better than any other Native American ball player of the era. While Meyers may have regretted his whole life not finishing his education at Dartmouth and pursuing professional baseball instead, it can be persuasively argued he was able to have a more significant impact in the long struggle for the rights and dignity of Indian people by taking the path he did.

On June 17, 1912, with Meyers behind the bat, the "Marquis-de-Marquard," as Damon Runyon called the Giants pitcher, won his 14th straight game, equaling the modern record jointly held by Ed Reulbach, who pitched for the Cubs from 1905 through 1912, and Jack Chesbro, who pitched for the Pirates and Highlanders between 1899 and 1908. Two days later Rube won his 15th. Relieving, he only pitched three of the ten innings in the game against Boston but was credited with the victory.

A week later Marquard collected his 16th straight win by beating the Philadelphia Phillies in a squeaker, 2 to 1, with Grover Cleveland Alexander pitching for the Philadelphia club. The Phillies ace held Meyers hitless in two plate appearances. During the 1912 season Meyers struck out only 20 times; three of the whiffs were by Alexander. Late in life Meyers would remember Grover Alexander as the guy who got him each time because he "was fast and had a peculiar hitch that fooled a batter."[16]

More typically during this period Meyers was wielding a hot bat. He delivered the decisive blow, homering in the eighth inning of a comeback June 27 win against the Phillies. The next day the Giants took both ends of a doubleheader against Boston. In the first game Meyers was 2-for-3, with a triple. In the second game he was also 2-for-3, with a double.

By the end of June the Giants had won 50 games and lost only 11 for the season. An editorial in the *New York Times* suggested that people disgusted by the "disgraceful exhibitions of malice and rowdyism" in the political conventions under way at the time were finding relief "in the decent and inspiring game of baseball." The editorial pointed out that ten times more people were standing before the baseball scoreboards in New York cheering Mathewson, Marquard, and Meyers than were reading the bulletins concerning the Democratic National Convention in Baltimore where William Jennings Bryan was a featured speaker and Woodrow Wilson was nominated as the Democratic candidate for President of the United States on the 46th ballot.[17]

On July 3, 1912, Rube Marquard completed his consecutive victories streak with his 19th straight win since the beginning of the season (a record he still holds), also his 20th straight in regular season play. Meyers always maintained his friend had been cheated by one game. "The record books say he won 19 straight games in 1912," he told Lawrence Ritter, "but they're wrong. He actually won 20 straight, but they didn't give him credit for one of them." Meyers was correct. Marquard had relieved Jeff Tesreau with the Giants trailing 3–2 in an April 20 game. The Giants rallied to win, 4–3, but the official scorer awarded the victory to Tesreau rather than Marquard. Meyers proudly said, "I caught just about every one of those 20 games. And do you know that of those 20 straight wins, 16 or 17 were complete games?"[18] The streak, broken with a loss to the Cubs on July 8, 1912, helped propel the Giants to a 16-game lead in the National League by Independence Day.

In mid–July the second of the series of articles Meyers wrote for the *New York American* appeared, this one entitled "Chief Meyers Tells of 'The Job of a Catcher.'"[19] Meyers began by vividly describing the occupational hazards associated with his position. They included being loaded down with equipment, even on a hot summer's day; blocking the plate when a runner is sliding in spikes first; getting hit by a swung bat; taking foul tips off your fingers; and, all in all, having the toughest job next to the pitcher, but going out each and every day while the pitcher took the mound only every fourth or fifth day.

Despite the difficulties of the position Meyers wanted readers to know, "I wouldn't trade my job as a catcher for any other I know of, at that. To my mind, it's the most interesting, most exciting of all. You see more, know more, [and] learn more about the game than in any other position. And the game is still the big thing to me."

Next, the Giants star provided an "insider's" look at the catcher's job. During the morning of game day he reviewed the batters on the opposing team with the starting pitcher. It was the catcher's job, Meyers explained, to study each batter to determine his strengths and weaknesses. "Once in a while," he acknowledged, "I have gotten tips on batters' weaknesses from friendly mask men of other clubs, but not often. Nearly always it is a matter of close study."

Meyers obviously enjoyed the intellectual challenge of the catcher's role. From his perspective, "the theoretical part of the game comes first. It's like a general laying his plans before the battle. How these plans are going to work out is the big question that only the game itself can settle."

After relating the plotting of strategy with his pitcher, Meyers described his handling of different types of hitters and what happened when they reached base. In an era when base stealing was common, he wanted it understood that "[t]he successful catcher is the one who learns to pick out the genuine attempt to steal from some little foot or body movement of a runner, and to know these characteristics of each opponent, and to remember them."

Meyers claimed, perhaps deceptively, that he had "very few" signs for pitchers. The only three he regularly used, or at least would acknowledge in print, were for the fastball, curve, and pitch-out. With veteran pitchers he typically only used the sign for the pitch-out, because hurlers like Mathewson knew what to throw to a given hitter in a particular situation. Meyers also asserted, "I have never known any of our signs to be stolen, either by a batter looking around, by a coach, or by a runner on second base. If ever we think the other boys are getting wise to us we can shift signs in a second."

Meyers concluded his description of his vocation as a catcher by saying a receiver "doesn't get the glory a pitcher does, though he's getting more credit than he used to and the fans are coming to realize that he must be a pretty responsible and capable sort of a fellow."

About the same time that Meyers's thoughtful article on the science and art of catching appeared in the *New York American,* Ed Goewey devoted a portion of one of his popular "The Old Fan" columns in *Leslie's Illustrated Weekly* to the Giants catcher. Focusing on his perception of Meyers's Indian identity, Goewey called the Cahuilla catcher "our husky friend ... whose name will be remembered long after those of Sitting Bull and Chief Joseph have passed into oblivion." Goewey mistakenly claimed Meyers was a "full-blooded Indian," then explained the California Indian had benefited from a white man's education academically and in sports. He is a "big, good-natured, affable boy, well learned and a gentleman," Goewey noted. He added that Meyers had avoided the "taste for firewater" that ended the career of his "redskin predecessor, Sockalexis." Goewey lauded Meyers as a favorite of fans and players and one of major league baseball's most feared hitters. A cartoon accompanying the column displayed a darkened ball player, wearing a feather in his hair and leaning on a bat.

The title of the article ("The Old Fan Says That the Case of Chief Myers [sic] Proves That the Live Redskin Can be a Good Indian") demonstrates that

Goewey was drawing on the stereotype of the "good Indian" widely held during this period. Famous Indians like Sitting Bull and Chief Joseph were "bad Indians," because they were mean-spirited and resisted assimilation to white society. Chief Sockalexis would have been a "good Indian," but he had fallen victim to the lure of "firewater." By contrast, Meyers was an Indian who deserved to be included in the category "good," because he was "good-natured and affable" and had immersed himself in the white man's ways.[20]

As the 1912 season moved into its second half the Giants continued their winning ways. By the third week of July they were being called the prospective pennant winners, after a 12 to 6 victory over Cincinnati in which Meyers was 3-for-5.

The Giants mounted a near comeback from a five-run deficit against the Cubs in a July 27 match up before 38,000 at the Polo Grounds. During a tumultuous eighth inning Meyers came to bat. "Peril was marked all over the situation for the Cubs," the *New York Times* exulted. "Wasn't Chief Meyers at the bat with his war club, and isn't that enough to inject a little scare into any team?"[21] Meyers launched a drive toward left that appeared headed for the bleachers, and the crowd was delirious. However, the left fielder crashed into the fence, made the play, and the Giants' rally was halted one run short of tying the game, which the Cubs won 7 to 6.

In August the Giants lost ground. After his consecutive wins streak ended, Marquard lost more games than he won, and the Giants' once seemingly insurmountable lead over the Cubs in the pennant race closed to five games. However, Meyers was doing his part to keep the Giants in the lead. In an August 16 game with the Cubs in Chicago he was 3-for-4, and the Giants won 7 to 4.

The Giants were now six games ahead, but in an 11-inning thriller the next day fell to the Cubs, 6 to 5, with Mathewson taking the loss. Meyers was 2-for-4 and scored two runs. The contest attracted 30,000 fans, the largest crowd ever to squeeze into Chicago's West Side Park. So many New Yorkers crowded around the electronic scoreboard in Times Square that streets were blocked and streetcars had difficulty getting through.

In an August 22 doubleheader Pittsburgh (now with the "h" at the end) won the opener 3 to 2 and the Giants captured the second game, 8 to 6. For the day Honus Wagner had a total of seven hits, with two doubles, a triple, and a home run in nine at bats; he scored five runs in the two games and hit for the cycle against Mathewson.

Christy Mathewson was the best pitcher he had ever seen, Meyers often said, and Honus Wagner was the greatest hitter.[22] "Honus could hit any ball he could reach," Meyers once told Grantland Rice. "Inside or outside were just the same to him as over the plate. High or low meant nothing."[23] When asked by a young pitcher to name Wagner's weakness as a hitter, Meyers responded wryly, "a base on balls."[24]

Meyers praised Wagner not only for his hitting but also as an all-around player, calling "The Flying Dutchman" the greatest baseball player he had ever seen. "Wagner was an artist," he told the reporter. "He had such know-how and did things that were just amazing. He's the only player I ever saw who could stop the other team cold just in fielding practice. When he came out to warm up, the pepper game would stop and all eyes were on Wagner. He was a classic in the field. And a great, great hitter."[25]

However, on this day Meyers was Wagner's equal. He figured in all eight Giants' runs in the second game, driving in five runs, scoring two, and contributing to another.[26]

Meyers had two hits in three plate appearances in an

During several seasons Meyers dueled with Pittsburgh Pirates Hall of Fame shortstop Honus Wagner for the honor of the top batting average in the National League. Meyers considered Wagner the best hitter he ever witnessed (Library of Congress, Prints & Photographs Division, LC-DIG-ppmsca-18464).

August 29 squeaker, won by New York, 4 to 3, over Brooklyn at the Polo Grounds. "The huge Ozark bear hunter" Tesreau was on the mound for the Giants. Meyers was hitting so well McGraw made an exception to his rule that Meyers did not catch the spitballer.

Although the Cubs could not overtake the Giants, they did win 13 of the 22 match-ups between the two bitter rivals during the 1912 season, closing to within 3½ games by early September. In a September 17 contest the Cubs bounced Marquard, described in the *Times* game report as being "as wild as a cannibal," from the pitching box after scoring all their runs in the first three innings. A hobbled Meyers was 0-for-2 in the losing effort, but did score a run before being relieved by Wilson.[27]

Their backs against the wall, the Giants rallied with a string of victories and clinched the pennant. The New Yorkers finished the 1912 season ten games ahead of the Pirates and 11½ games ahead of the Cubs. They won 103 and lost only 48. During the Deadball Era, the franchise's .682 winning percentage in 1912 was exceeded only by their pennant-winning years in 1904 (.693) and 1905 (.686).

Charley Faust, once again in a Giants uniform, was allowed to sit with the Giants in their 1912 team photograph, but his tenure with the team had come to an end. His bizarre behavior was wearing thin with McGraw, if not the writers on the 13 New York daily newspapers, for whom Faust was a constant source of good copy. In July, the Giants players convinced "Victory" his imaginary sweetheart "Lulu" wanted him to return to Kansas. Three years later Charles Victor Faust died of tuberculosis after being committed to a mental hospital by his brother.

Drawing on the popular notion that as "primitives" Indians were by nature superstitious, sportswriter John B. Sheridan contended the real reason for Faust's presence with the Giants for much of two seasons was his effect on Meyers. Sheridan said that early in his tenure with the Giants, Faust was sitting next to Chief Meyers before a game and told the Giants catcher he would have a single and a double that day. In the game the Giants catcher did have a single and a double. The next day Faust told Meyers he would have two singles and a home run and on the next afternoon go hitless. When Victory's predictions again came true, Sheridan claimed the Cahuilla catcher went to McGraw "and asked him to retain Faust as (the Chief's) own individual ouija board." Because Meyers was such a valuable member of the team, the Giants manager agreed to the request. Thereafter, Sheridan explained, "Each day while sitting on the bench Meyers would ask Faust what he was going to get at the plate that game, and the mascot seldom missed in his guess." While Sheridan appeared to be convinced of the veracity of the story, it sounds like the kind of trick Meyers might may well have played on a gullible sportswriter in his trickster role, exploiting the popular image of the "superstitious primitive."[28]

On September 7, 1912, as the Giants were closing in on the pennant, Arthur "Bugs" Raymond, who remained under contract with the Giants, but had not been with the team during the season, died of a fractured skull after a fight in a pickup ballgame. He was thirty years old.

Rave reviews for John Tortes Meyers's performance flooded the national press during and after the 1912 season. One reporter compared his hitting to the slugging of Hans Wagner. "[Meyers's] big bat is feared more than that of any slugger in the National [League], not even excepting 'Hans' Wagner," Ed Goewey wrote, "for when he connects with the ball it is sure to travel some.

This stick work of the big redskin has caused him to become a record-breaker of a novel kind. To date the various pitchers facing him have openly confessed their fear of his batting prowess by deliberately giving him free passage to first base considerably more than twenty times."[29]

Meyers finished the 1912 season with his career-best batting average — .358, second only to Heinie Zimmerman, who batted .372. Meyers's 1912 average was the record by a catcher in the National League for a season until Mike Piazza batted .362 in 1997. Meyers led the National League in on-base percentage with a .441 mark and drove in 54 runs. He frequently drew intentional walks in an era when they were relatively rare. Meyers played in 126 games, had 371 at-bats and reached career highs not only in batting average, but also runs (60), hits (133), total bases (177), home runs (6), and stolen bases (8). He had 16 doubles and five triples. As noted previously, he also hit for the cycle in a game during the season, one of only 14 catchers in major league history to accomplish that feat.[30]

Despite his stellar performance Meyers was not chosen as the most valuable player in the National League in 1912. That honor went to Giants second baseman Larry Doyle, who batted .330 for the season, had an on-base percentage of .391, and drove in 90 runs. As the League's MVP Doyle received a Chalmers Touring Car. Honus Wagner, who batted .324, had an OBP of .395, and drove in 102 runs, finished second. Meyers was third.

In the era before the National Baseball Hall of Fame was created, one of the highest honors for a major leaguer was to be named to the annual Spalding Baseball Guide Hall of Fame. Meyers was chosen for the 1913 edition in recognition of his performance in the 1912 season. According to the 1913 Guide, "Meyers is an instance of the greatest improvement on the part of a catcher of any member of the major leagues."[31]

Meyers was also named to the Grand National All-America Baseball Team in 1912. To be eligible a player must have been on a team that won a pennant in a season after 1871 and appeared in at least 50 games (or 25 for pitchers) during the season. The player at each position who had the highest combined fielding and batting average (or winning percentage for pitchers) was named to the team. In 1912 Meyers's 122 games qualified him, and his .973 fielding average and .358 batting average were easily the best for a catcher in the past 41 years.[32]

In yet another recognition of his outstanding performance during the 1912 season Meyers was profiled in the 1912 Reach Guide, sponsored by the Reach Sporting Goods Company. The biography in the Reach Guide identified him as "Catcher 'Jack' Myers [sic] of the New York team." According to the Guide, "Myers" is "a good-natured aborigine from the sequestered people of his tribe. At the Pala reservation [sic], in California, the notable backstop is

known to the mission Indians as 'Tortes.'" Like other baseball sources it gave
his birthdate incorrectly as July 29, 1882. The Guide went on to say, "As a boy
he played with his little white brothers of the town." The biography concluded
by observing, "Myers is a bright fellow, despite his native reserve. When he
warms to enthusiasm he can discourse on almost any topic intelligently."[33]

As the Reach Guide demonstrates, commentators were still having trouble properly identifying the Giants catcher. His last name was frequently
spelled "Myers," and one article written at the end of the 1912 season called
the New York Giants star "Chief Tortoise Meyers."[34]

Finally, STATS, Inc., the modern sports statistics company, again has
named Meyers to its All-Star team in 1912. Also named to the 1912 STATS,
Inc. team from the Giants are Mathewson, Marquard, and Doyle.[35]

## The 1912 World Series: Eight Games and a "Muff"

The 1912 World Series matched a New York Giants team with 103 wins
against an equally dominant Boston Red Sox club with 105 victories. It would
be remembered a century later as "the greatest World Series ever played — so
great, in fact, that in all future years, both words would be permanently cap-
italized."[36]

Anticipation was heightened by the fact that in 1904, John McGraw,
whose Giants were the National League victors, refused to let his team play
the Boston team, which had won the 1903 world's series, saying the American
League played at an "inferior" and "haphazard" level. The 1904 world's series
was cancelled, and, eight years later, the Red Sox and their fans were more
than ready to prove McGraw wrong.

The Red Sox, called the "Speed Boys" by the Boston press, were led by
player/manager Jake Stahl and featured talented center fielder Tris Speaker,
known as the "Grey Eagle" (for his prematurely graying hair). "Spoke," as he
was called by his teammates, was third in the American League in 1912 with
a .383 batting average. The other Red Sox star that season was 22-year-old
Howard "Smoky Joe" Wood, a right-handed pitcher who won 34 games, ten
by shutout, and lost only five during the 1912 season. He struck out 258 and
finished with a 1.91 ERA. A Boston sportswriter gave Wood the nickname
Smoky Joe for his blazing fastball.

For the Giants, Rube Marquard finished the season with 26 wins. Christy
Mathewson notched 23 victories and the rookie Jeff Tesreau was victorious
in 17 games while leading the National League with an ERA of 1.96. In addition
to Meyers's and Doyle's hot bats, Fred Merkle hit at a .309 pace and led the
team with 11 home runs.

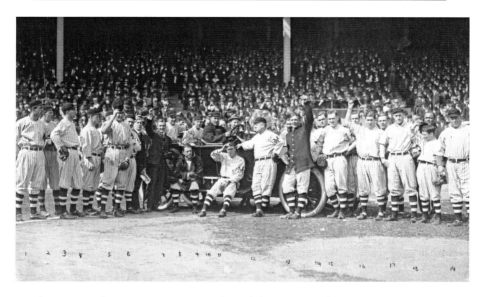

The New York Giants on opening day of the 1912 World Series. Larry Doyle (No. 10 in the picture) is being awarded a Chalmers Touring Car as the National League's most valuable player. Meyers, who finished third in the MVP balloting, is standing behind Christy Mathewson (number 13 in the picture, wearing a sweater). Others identified by the Pictorial History Committee of the Society for American Baseball Research, in the picture are, by number: (4) Red Murray, (5) Ferdie Schupp, (7) Rube Marquard, (9) Buck Herzog, (10) Larry Doyle, (11) George Burns, (12) John McGraw, (14) Jeff Tesreau, (18) Art Fletcher, (trainer in background) Ed Mackall, (19) Wilbert Robinson (Library of Congress, Prints & Photographs Division, LC-DIG-ggbain-11754).

The 1912 Series set a record for media attention. Three hundred reporters covered the games, and telegraph lines carried updates to cities throughout the country within seconds. Thirteen players and John McGraw signed to let their names be used in ghostwritten columns during the Series.

## Game One (Tuesday, October 8)

The atmosphere in New York was electric for the first game in the 1912 Series. Nearly 38,000 assembled at the Polo Grounds. The throng included a contingent of Red Sox supporters from Boston known as the "Royal Rooters." After a long parade from their hotel, 300 "Rooters" snaked into the stadium behind a band playing their trademark song, "Tessie." The song's inane lyrics ("Tessie, you make me feel so badly. Why don't you turn around? Tessie, you know I love you sadly, babe. My heart weighs a pound.") had nothing to do with baseball, but the Rooters would often alter the lyrics to fit members of the opposing teams in order to rattle them. Boston mayor John "Honey Fitz" Fitzgerald (grandfather of President John Fitzgerald Kennedy) then led a boisterously sung "Sweet Adeline." The mayor, ever the self-promoting politician, continued strutting around the field until forced to take his seat.[37]

Tickets for the 3:00 P.M. game included seats in the bleachers for $1 and in the grandstand for $2 (both prices up from 50 cents during the regular season). The seats with the best view of the field in the Polo Grounds were in the upper tier and went for $3 a game (the equivalent of $65 a century later). Tickets went on sale Monday morning at 8:00 A.M., and the only way most fans could get close enough to the Polo Grounds box office to purchase them was by bribing one of the New York policemen ostensibly keeping order.[38]

Mathewson and Marquard were not pleased with the starting lineup, because McGraw had decided to pitch his rookie spitballer Jeff Tesreau against Smoky Joe Wood in the opening game. McGraw's rationale was to save Mathewson for Boston's Fenway Park because he knew the veteran could handle the pressure. He did not say why he passed over Marquard.

For five innings the Giants' "Bear Hunter of the Ozarks" made his manager look like a genius by holding the Red Sox not only scoreless but also hitless. The Giants scored twice in the third, and the Red Sox finally broke up Tesreau's no-hitter by tallying a run in the sixth after a triple by Speaker. They scored three runs in the seventh, aided by Meyers's failure to catch a high pop foul, to take a 4–2 lead.

The Giants rallied in the bottom of the ninth. With one out, Merkle and Herzog both singled, and Meyers drove a line drive into the gap in right field. Merkle scored, but McGraw, coaching at third, held up Herzog when Red Sox center fielder Harry Hooper was able to cut the ball off. With Herzog at third and the fleet-footed Beals Becker replacing Meyers at second, the Giants could have won the game with another single. However, Art Fletcher struck out, and Doc Crandall, who had replaced Tesreau in the eighth, also fanned. The game was over, and the Red Sox drew first blood. Smoky Joe was dominant, striking out 11.

The 25,000 Giants fans packed into Times Square to watch a play-by-play report of the game on the new 17-foot-long electric scoreboard quietly dispersed. Twice that number gathered in Boston Commons roared when they heard the final score.[39]

Meyers was 1-for-3 in the game and also reached base after being hit by a Wood fastball in the sixth. Defensively, he threw the Boston player/manager Stahl out on a steal attempt at second. McGraw, however, blamed Meyers for the loss. In his ghostwritten article the Giants manager asserted his catcher should have caught the pop foul in the seventh to end the inning. In addition,

McGraw said, in the two hits that followed, Meyers's judgment was more at fault than Tesreau's pitching. When Mathewson told his battery mate about the article the next morning at the team hotel, the Giants pitcher had to physically restrain Meyers from leaving the room to find McGraw and punch him in the mouth.[40] It would be an episode Meyers preferred to forget in later years when reflecting on his relationship with his manager, and he never mentioned it to reporters or to family members.

## Game Two (Wednesday, October 9)

The second game of the historic 1912 Series was played in Boston's Fenway Park before a crowd of 30,148 on a chilly, rainy day. It was the first postseason game in the now famous Fenway, which had opened at the beginning of the 1912 season and remains the Red Sox home a century later. Ticket prices were between 50 cents and five dollars, with stands added to the stadium after the end of the regular season to accommodate more spectators.

Mathewson started the game but was not particularly sharp, due in part to the fact the Giants did not arrive in Boston until 2:30 A.M. as the result of an accident that delayed their train. With the game scheduled to start at 2:00 P.M., Matty and the other Giants got only a few hours sleep. However, Big Six showed his battling instinct and would have won the game except for five errors by his tired teammates.

Despite the miscues the Giants clawed their way to a 6–5 lead in the top of the tenth inning before the Grey Eagle rifled a line drive over the head of Beals Becker in the bottom of the inning. The gutsy Speaker, though hobbled earlier in the game after trying to slide into first, scored on the play. The Grey Eagle would have been out at the plate, but Art Wilson, who entered the contest as catcher after McGraw lifted Meyers for a pinch runner in the top of the inning, dropped the throw home.[41] After stomping on home with his injured foot for emphasis, Speaker rushed toward Buck Herzog, the Giants third baseman, who had tried to trip him rounding third. McGraw restrained Herzog, who was ready to fight, but then went after Speaker himself when the Red Sox center fielder screamed the epithet the Giants manager hated: "Muggsy!" However, before McGraw could reach Speaker, Giants coach Wilbert Robinson stepped between them, ending the incident before either was thrown out of the game.

The game, now almost four hours old, was tied 6–6 after 11 innings when it was called because of darkness. Matty's gutsy 11-inning performance against three Boston pitchers, during which he allowed no walks and no earned runs, was wasted as the umpires decided that a full make-up game would be played the next day.

Before leaving the game Meyers was 2-for-4 with an RBI. He also received an intentional pass in the tenth. His RBI in the second, a liner that nearly took third baseman Larry Gardner's head off and drove in Herzog, impressed his manager, who commented, "Meyers certainly leaned against that ball. I played third base for a good many years when there were some terrific hitters in the league, but I don't think any of them could hook a ball down that left field foul line harder than the Indian. He is a natural hitter, and has the weight to drive a ball."[42]

Meyers's defense was also strong, as he tagged out Harry Hooper at home in the first and caught him again later trying to steal second.

The players on both teams were losers when the National Commission decided not to give them a portion of the proceeds from the extra game that would need to be played. Meyers and his Giants teammates chose Christy Mathewson to represent them at a meeting of the Commission on the morning of the October 10 make-up game. Matty eloquently argued that the Commission was making decisions affecting the players financially without consulting them or considering their interests. In his words, "the National Commission is liable to find itself left flat without a club to play in some future world's series if they refuse to take up our grievances and give us fair treatment." Smoky Joe Wood, speaking for the Red Sox, joined Mathewson in the protest. The Commission listened politely, deliberated for three minutes, and then announced that the rule limiting players' compensation to 60 percent of the receipts of the first four games played, regardless of whether one of the games ended in a tie, would stand.[43]

## Game Three (Thursday, October 10)

Rube Marquard pitched one of the best games of his career in the replayed match up at Fenway Park on October 10 before a packed crowd of 34,624, the largest in Boston history at the time. Before the game Marquard announced to all who would listen, "I will be shoving them over at these alleged swatters of Boston so fast that they won't be able to see the ball."[44] Rube was, it turned out, not blowing smoke. Although his fastball was not as overpowering as Wood's in the first game, it was still effective. Through six innings he allowed only four singles, and only one Red Sox player reached second base. In the seventh he pitched out of trouble after Stahl doubled.

Red Sox rookie Buck O'Brien's curve was breaking, but the Giants got to him for two runs and were leading 2–0 into the ninth inning. With one out in the top half, Meyers singled solidly to center. Art Fletcher lined another shot to center; Meyers was already lumbering around second when the hobbling Speaker made an impossible grab of Fletcher's fly and doubled the Giants catcher off first.

In the bottom of the ninth Boston rallied with a run and had men on second and third with two outs. A hit would win the game. Hick Cady drove a ball deep into right center, and right fielder Josh Devore gave chase "like a frightened terrier." Darkness was once again descending, and with it a mist enshrouded the Giants outfielder. However, miraculously, Devore caught the ball in full stride, not in his glove but in his bare hand, and kept on running toward the Giants' clubhouse in center field with the ball clutched to his chest. The Boston fans, assuming Devore missed the ball and the Red Sox had won the game, went wild. However, umpire "Silk" O'Loughlin (who was known to say, "it's the Pope for religion, O'Loughlin for baseball; both infallible") made the correct call. The Giants win tied the series at one game each. It would not be the last unbelievable finish in a 1912 World Series game.

## Game Four (Friday, October 11)

Under threatening skies at the Polo Grounds, Smoky Joe Wood and Jeff Tesreau took the mound in a repeat of the first-game match-up before another record-breaking crowd of nearly 40,000. Another thousand gathered outside the stadium on Coogan's Bluff although they could not see the action in the new Polo Grounds. Rain had fallen all night, soaking the thousands of fans waiting to buy tickets at the box office, but just before the 2:15 P.M. start the sun broke through the clouds.

Despite Wood's dazzling performance in the opening game, the Giants claimed not to be impressed. Mathewson said Smoky Joe had gone to his fastball because he couldn't get his curve over. Meyers told a reporter Woods "depends too much on speed. That is bound to sap his reserve energy and his recuperative powers." In a tip of his hat to his friend Albert Bender, Meyers claimed Wood's speed was nothing like that of Bender in the first game of the 1911 series, and concluded, "he is not so hard a pitcher to beat."[45]

In the top of the first Meyers allowed Steve Yerkes to reach when he threw wildly on a bunt attempt, but two excellent fielding plays by Fletcher kept the Red Sox off the scoreboard. Boston took a 1–0 lead in the second. Larry Gardner tripled to right field and scored on a wild pitch when Meyers couldn't hold on to a Tesreau spitter. In a display of the "scientific game" even McGraw must have admired, Boston scored another run in the fourth when Jake Stahl reached on a force out, stole second, moved to third on a ground out, and scored on a weak single.

The Giants finally scored in the seventh. With one out and Buck Herzog on first, Meyers nearly tied the game with a long line drive to center, which stayed in the air just long enough for the limping Speaker to reach it. Fletcher then doubled, and Herzog crossed home.

The final Red Sox run came in the top of the ninth off Red Ames, who had relieved Tesreau, and the Giants went quietly in the bottom of the final frame. With a 3–1 victory the Red Sox, behind a pair of terrific performances by Smoky Joe Wood, had a two-games-to-one Series lead.

## Game Five (Saturday, October 12)

A "ghostlike fog" rolled in off the Atlantic, creating an eerie setting, as another sell-out crowd, recorded as 34,683, gathered in Fenway Park for the fifth game in the 1912 Series. Mathewson once again pitched well enough to win, giving up only two runs on five hits and setting down 17 batters in order. As McGraw said after the game, "I never saw him have more." Unfortunately for Matty two of the five hits he surrendered were triples in the two-run third inning.

Red Sox rookie Hugh Bedient allowed only one run on three hits. Along with Mathewson and Merkle, Meyers was the only Giant able to "fathom" Bedient's "benders."[46] The lone Giants run in the 2–1 loss came in the seventh when Merkle doubled and scored on an error.

For the game Meyers flied out in the second, singled in the fifth (after a dozen fouls), and hit a fly ball to Speaker in the seventh on which Merkle advanced from second to third.

On this day most of the action took place before the game. Boston players loudly complained that Art Fletcher had jumped on Red Sox catcher Hick Cady at the plate while trying to score in the seventh inning of Game 4. According to Smoky Joe Wood, Giants fans even threw overripe fruit, rocks and dirt on the Red Sox and their wives as they left the Polo Grounds.

At Copley Plaza where the Giants were housed, a cigar dropped from an open window caused a fire to erupt. One writer drew on a phrase popularly attributed to Indians at the time to describe how he assumed Meyers reacted to the fire: Chief Meyers, a cigar smoker himself, allegedly called the blaze "good medicine." According to the writer, Meyers was so caught up in helping the Boston firemen fight the fire, his teammates had to pull him away to make it to the game on time.[47]

During warm-ups Fred Snodgrass, smarting because of his .188 batting average in the Series and poor fielding, got into a scuffle with a Red Sox fan who leaped over the fence to grab a ball. Snow shouldered the man, picked up the ball, and threw it at another Boston spectator. Throughout the entire game Boston fans shouted catcalls at the Giants center fielder. Snodgrass made defiant gestures in response, until Larry Doyle, the Giants captain, told him to desist or get off the field.[48]

One effect of the growing rancor between the Red Sox and Giants was the blunting of an effort by some of the players on both teams to call a players' strike before the fifth game to protest the National Commission's refusal to give them a share of the proceeds from the extra game already played. To thwart the protest, the Commission announced before the game that from the first four games (including the tie) the players on the two teams would receive a total of nearly $150,000, an amount $20,000 more than the record the Giants and Athletics had split after the 1911 Series.[49]

## Game Six (Monday, October 14)

After taking Sunday off, as the law required in both Boston and New York, the 1912 World Series resumed at the Polo Grounds, with a smaller crowd of 30,622 in attendance. The Red Sox had the Giants on the ropes, leading the Series three games to one. Some Giants fans apparently gave up on their team. With Smoky Joe Wood ready to take the mound, it was easy to see why. However, in a move still debated nearly a century later by Red Sox supporters, Boston owner Jimmy McAleer overruled his manager and instructed Stahl to pitch the rookie Buck O'Brien, who had won 20 games during the season, instead of Wood.

With two out in the bottom of the first inning and Larry Doyle on third, O'Brien balked (the first in World Series history) allowing the run to score. Two more Giants soon crossed the plate, followed by a Meyers single to deep short that sent Buck Herzog to third. Meyers and Herzog next worked a double steal, which McGraw called, scoring another run. Then Fletcher bunted safely and Meyers scored from second, giving the Giants a 5–0 lead. After the inning an irate Wood confronted O'Brien on the bench and the two had to be separated by teammates. On the train ride back to Boston that evening, Wood's brother, Paul, who had lost $100 in a wager on the game, blackened O'Brien's eye.[50]

After the disastrous first inning Stahl replaced O'Brien with Ray Collins. The new Red Sox hurler held the Giants scoreless for seven innings, but the damage had been done. Marquard benefitted from the darkening conditions, making it difficult for the Red Sox to pick up his fastball. He allowed two runs in the second inning, but that was the end of Boston's scoring. The Giants took the sixth contest and closed to within a game in the Series.

Meyers again demonstrated his power hitting in the game. He tripled to left center in the fourth inning on a drive that would have been an inside-the-park home run for a faster man. Fletcher flied out to center and a strong throw by Speaker kept Meyers at third, where he was left stranded.

With the sixth game the 1912 World's Series set an attendance record, breaking the 1911 total of 179,351. Thus far 202,502 spectators had been in the stands for the six games. The total 1911 record receipts of $342,164.50 had been surpassed, with $403,137 already taken in. Each player on the winning team would receive about $4,000 (more than the average yearly salary for major leaguers at the time) and each player on the losing team would pocket close to $2,500.

Over the protests of McGraw and the Giants, the National Commission announced that a coin flip would decide the location of an eighth contest, if a Giants victory in the seventh game made one necessary. The coin toss took place with great ceremony on the field after the sixth game. Stahl won, ensuring that if there were an eighth game it would mean the Red Sox would have five home games in the 1912 Series to the Giants' three.

Despite the coin toss the Giants were upbeat about their prospects for the seventh game. "I hope they finally start Wood," Meyers told his teammates as they rode toward Boston. "I have no doubt that he can't come at us again the way he did the first two times. Nobody beats the Giants three times in a row if we have anything to say about it."[51] He would get his wish.

## Game Seven (Tuesday, October 15)

In the seventh game, with 32,694 in attendance at Fenway Park, Smoky Joe was called on to pitch. However, the Red Sox ace lasted only one inning as the Giants scored six runs on seven hits on only 13 pitches. From the third base coach's box McGraw directed the attack, ordering his batters to swing at Wood's first pitch and calling for double steals. These tactics and the strain of the first two games showed on the young Red Sox right-hander. His curve had little break and the Giants had no trouble with his fastball.

Wood's successor, Charley Hall, gave up nine more hits and five runs, and the Giants won going away, 11 to 4. With the Series tied there would be an eighth game. Half of the Red Sox fans left the stadium before the end of the first inning. Cynics in Boston accused the Red Sox of blowing the sixth and seventh games so the Series would go eight games and both teams' owners (though not the players) would profit.

Without explanation the Red Sox management had sold the 2,000 seats reserved for the Royal Rooters to VIP fans for the seventh game. Wood's first pitch was delayed for 30 minutes as the Rooters paraded around the field and tried to force their way into their grandstand seats. Thwarted by mounted policemen the raucous Rooters pushed down the bleachers fence and spread out into the crowd in what became known in Boston as "The Day of the Cossacks." From their seats the outraged Rooters chanted support for McGraw and the Giants. In addition, the dispute between O'Brien and Wood flared up again, and several other Red Sox players joined in the fracas before it ended.[52]

The New York press exulted that Smoky Joe Wood "is no longer the hero he was." Facing the greatest moment in his spectacular career he "cracked like the veriest minor league novice."[53]

For Meyers the seventh game of the 1912 Series was his personal best in the four World Series in which he appeared. He rocketed a single in the first inning and scored, then singled again in the third. In the Red Sox third he saved a run by blocking the plate, tagging out the sliding Charley Hall. Meyers notched his third hit in the fifth inning on a hot grounder. The official scorer awarded Meyers a single in the seventh, but reversed the call after the game and ruled the play a fielder's choice. If the original ruling had stood, Meyers would have been 4-for-4 in the game. McGraw sent Art Wilson in to replace the Cahuilla catcher behind the bat in the bottom of the seventh, denying Meyers the opportunity for yet another hit.

## Game Eight (Wednesday, October 16)

At the behest of offended Mayor Fitzgerald, the Royal Rooters boycotted the eighth game of the 1912 World Series and were joined by other enraged Boston fans. Shortly before the 2:00 P.M. start the stands were half full. The official count was only 17,034, and 1,500 of this number were Giants supporters who came from New York. Those who did show up would see one of the most memorable games in World Series history. In New York there was no boycott. A hundred thousand or more of the Giants faithful gathered around Manhattan to follow the game on large electric scoreboards, as they had for the previous seven contests.

The weather in Boston was again grim as a northwest wind blew across the field. Each manager tried to keep the other team guessing as to who would pitch, though the Red Sox assumed, correctly, the Giants hurler would be Christy Mathewson. Stahl sent his rookie Hugh Bedient to the mound, but was ready to call on Smoky Joe if Bedient faltered.

In the bottom of the first inning, with two out, Speaker singled. The Grey Eagle would later say that on that day, when you saw Mathewson from the bench, you wanted to grab your bat and get out there, because the veteran's stuff did not seem that good. Then you were at bat and "it was almost like he could read your mind. He knew *exactly* what he had to throw to make you look incredibly foolish."[54] However, the Red Sox center fielder was left stranded.

The Giants scored their first run in the third inning. Bedient seemed unsteady in walking Devore, who took second and then third on ground outs. Devore tore his pants sliding, and the game was held up briefly as McGraw patched the hole with a safety pin. The Giants outfielder then scored on Murray's double to left. Herzog hit a ball that stuck in the fence for a ground rule double in the fourth. Meyers then sacrificed him to third, but Herzog was still there when the inning ended.

In the fifth Red Sox right fielder Harry Hooper made a spectacular catch of a long drive by Doyle. He raced back, reached over the fence, and, half-supported by fans, speared the ball with his bare hand. Years later Doyle said he thought at the time and still did think it was a home run: "I never hit a ball better, and I still think Hooper was off the playing field when he caught the ball."[55] For his part Wood claimed Hooper's incredible catch was "almost impossible to believe even when you saw it" and "was the thing that really took the heart out of the Giants."[56]

In the sixth, Meyers walked but could not advance. In the bottom of the inning the Red Sox attempted a double steal, one of the Giants' favorite plays. Seeing Gardner square around to bunt tipped Matty off, and he unleashed a pitch that sailed at the batter, forcing him to dive out of the way. Yerkes, who had assumed Meyers would throw to second, broke for home. Meyers rose to catch the pitch and fired a strike to Mathewson who threw easily to Herzog, catching Yerkes before he could return to third. Reportedly, the Giants laughed as they walked off the field.

In the bottom of the seventh inning, pint-sized journeyman Olaf Hendriksen (known as "Swede" though he was actually from Denmark) pinch-hit for Bedient and drove in Boston's first run to tie the game. Matty had quickly put the diminutive Red Sox batter in the hole by tossing two fade-aways. With the count 0 and 2, Matty wasted two fastballs off the plate, bringing the count to 2 and 2. The next pitch was a curve. Swede stabbed at it, the ball hit the end of his bat, bounced off the third base bag, and then floated back toward the plate, eluding Herzog. Though a fluke, the hit would be scored as an RBI double.

In the eighth Stahl called on Smoky Joe Wood to relieve Bedient, a day after his ace had been bombed in the first inning of the seventh game. Fortunately for the Red Sox Wood recovered his form. Mathewson set the Red Sox down in order in the bottom of the inning to preserve the tie.

After a scoreless ninth, twilight descended on Fenway Park as the game went into extra innings. In the top of the tenth the Giants took the lead after Murray doubled and scored on a single by Merkle. Hundreds of Red Sox fans, convinced Mathewson would not allow another Boston run, left the stands. However, the Giants could not extend the lead. With two outs Meyers lined hard to Wood, who made a tremendous, barehanded stop, then threw the slow-running catcher out at first. The ball was hit with such velocity that it bloodied Wood's hand.

With the Giants now leading 2 to 1, Mathewson and the Giants needed only three more outs in the bottom of the tenth for a Giants win and the 1912 World Series crown. The lead-off batter for the Red Sox was light-hitting utility player Clyde Engle, pinch-hitting for the injured Wood. Engle floated a high fly to left center. Fred Snodgrass moved only a couple of steps toward the bleachers so he could camp under the ball and await its fall into his glove, but, almost unbelievably, he muffed the catch, allowing Engle to reach second on the error. In an uncharacteristic show of displeasure, Matty swung his glove. Seeing his battery mate's frustration, Meyers started toward the mound to calm Big Six down, but Mathewson waved the catcher back. Most who were present called Engle's fly an easy chance, though Tris Speaker, perhaps motivated by sympathy for a fellow center fielder, later said it would have been a difficult catch.[57] In a Los Angeles movie theater carrying the game by telegraph, Snow's mother fainted when her son's error was announced.

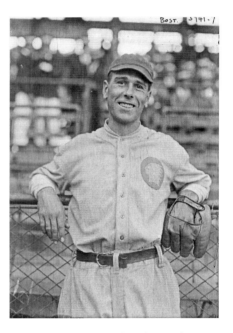

The next Red Sox batter, Harry Hooper, drove a pitch into deep center and Snodgrass made a great, running catch, one of the best in the history of World Series play. Speaker years later said, "I saw thousands of games, and I never, ever saw a catch like that before or after. It was like a magic trick."[58] This spectacular play would, as fate would have it, not be the play Snodgrass would be remembered for throughout the rest of his life. Instead it would be his infamous "muff."

Engle was able to advance to third base on the play. Then Matty's amazing control deserted him at the worst of times and he walked the next batter, light-hitting second baseman Steve Yerkes. After pitching 20 straight World Series innings without surrendering a pass, he would allow five walks in the eighth game of the 1912 Series.

Best remembered for his infamous "muff" of a fly ball in the 1912 World Series, center fielder Fred Snodgrass, shown here near the end of his career in a Boston Braves uniform (1916), was a teammate of Meyers when both played for the Giants (1908–1914, 1915). The two remained good friends when both retired to California. Meyers always defended Snodgrass when people asked about the "muff" (Library of Congress, Prints & Photographs Division, LC-DIG-ggbain-22463).

Next up was the Grey Eagle. Speaker popped up the first pitch, a fade-away, lofting a high foul toward the railing near first base. It was, in the opinion of most who witnessed it, the first baseman's ball. Some there that day said Fred Merkle immediately froze and caused what was to become one of the most famous missed foul balls in baseball history. Hugh Fullerton said he could have come down out of the press box to catch the ball, but Merkle "quit cold," not even starting for the ball, perhaps suffering from "financial paralysis" as he calculated the difference between the winner's and loser's share in the Series.[59]

Others present remembered Red Sox players were yelling loudly "Matty! Matty!" from their bench on the first base line, trying to confuse the Giants and freeze Merkle. Some say Merkle did move to catch the ball but was called off by Mathewson who was screaming "Chief! Chief!" Perhaps Mathewson subconsciously recalled Merkle's famous "bonehead" play in 1908 and was afraid history would repeat itself. Another possibility is that Mathewson was simply responding reflexively, instinctively calling for Meyers, with his large catcher's mitt, to take the fly.

Meyers recreates his famous lunge for a foul ball off the bat of Boston Red Sox star Tris Speaker in the bottom of the tenth inning of the eighth and deciding game of the 1912 World Series. However, in the game Meyers did not catch the ball (Library of Congress, Prints & Photographs Division, LC-DIG-ggbain-12046).

Still others argued that as catcher, it was Meyers's responsibility to call out the player who should field any ball in front of him, but he deferred to Matty. Merkle himself later said, "I could have made the catch any time, but Mathewson kept yelling for the Chief to take it. We were both big men; I wanted no collision. I kept way clear for Meyers, but he, too, stopped at the last moment, thinking I would take it, and the ball fell safe."[60]

According to most observers, at the last second Meyers lunged but couldn't make the catch. Almost unbelievably the Red Sox and Speaker now had another chance. Talking to *St. Louis Post-Dispatch* sportswriter Bob Broeg at the celebration of Stan Musial's 1,000th hit, Speaker said, "I was just about to holler 'Meyers,' aware it was closer to Merkle when, bless Mathewson's soul, Christy charged down hollering 'Meyers, Meyers.' The Chief couldn't get to the ball." Speaker's baritone boomed as it had during that game, Broeg recalled in describing the scene. In the game the normally cool Speaker let his emotion show, jumping up and down and shaking his fist at Mathewson. "'You just blew it, Matty,' I crowed," he told Broeg. "'You just blew the championship.'"[61]

Speaker singled on the next pitch, a curve, driving in the tying run. Yerkes went to third and Speaker to second on the throw to the plate and the stage was set. Matty walked Duffy Lewis intentionally, to load the bases, allowing a force at any base, but on a 3–1 count Larry Gardner drove a fly just deep enough to right for Yerkes to score. After catching the ball Devore made a desperate throw toward Meyers, who set up to block Yerkes off the plate. However, the throw was wide, and Mathewson, throwing up his hands, began walking off the field. Meyers turned away without even trying for the ball, and Yerkes raced across the plate with the winning run.

The Boston fans still in the stands erupted in joy and rushed onto the field to cheer the victorious Red Sox. Mathewson put on his linen duster and began the long walk to the clubhouse. Ring Lardner wrote that it was "one of the saddest sights in the history of a sport that is a strange and wonderful mixture of joy and gloom," to see Matty walking from the diamond "bowed head and drooping shoulders, with tears streaming from his eyes."[62] In the press box the tough *New York Globe* writer, Sid Mercer, broke down in tears.

John McGraw once again showed his class by elbowing his way through the crowd to the Boston clubhouse where he congratulated Jake Stahl and the Red Sox players. He said, "I can't say that I'm glad, Jake, but one of the teams had to win; it was to be the Red Sox, and congratulations are in order."[63]

Almost at once the tenth inning flub by Fred Snodgrass became known as the "$30,000 Muff," the approximate difference between the winners' and losers' shares of the receipts. However, McGraw came to Snow's defense as he had Merkle's four years earlier. "It could happen to anyone. If it hadn't been for a lot Snodgrass did," he said, "we wouldn't have been playing in that game at all." In *My Thirty Years in Baseball,* McGraw wrote, "Often I have been asked to tell what I did to Fred Snodgrass after he dropped that fly ball in the World Series of 1912.... Well, I will tell you exactly when I did: I raised his salary $1,000."[64]

For his part Mathewson never blamed Snodgrass for dropping the fly ball that started his downfall. He said to his teammates on the train taking the Giants back to New York after the game, "You can't blame a player for a physical error. The poor fellow feels miserable enough."[65]

The New York press was not so forgiving. In an article published on the front page of the *New York Times* the day after the game, Harry Cross wrote the indictment that would follow Snodgrass for the rest of his life[66]:

> Write in the pages of World's Series baseball history the name of Snodgrass. Write it large and black. Not a hero; truly not. Put him rather with Merkle, who was in such a hurry that he gave away a National League championship. It was because of Snodgrass' generous muff of an easy fly in the tenth inning that the decisive game of the world's series went to Boston this afternoon by a score of 3 to 2, instead of to the New York Giants by a score of 2 to 1.

Although Snow played four more years in the majors and had a successful business career in California after his playing days were over, when he died in 1974, the *New York Times* headlined its obituary: "FRED SNODGRASS, 86, DEAD; BALLPLAYER MUFFED 1912 FLY."[67]

Taking his lead from McGraw and Mathewson, John Tortes Meyers also refused to blame Snodgrass for losing the Series, calling the so-called muff "just a simple error" that "could happen to anybody."He also addressed the foul pop-up, saying, "I think the Red Sox dugout coached Merkle off it. The Boston bench called for Matty to take it, and called for me to take it, and I think that confused Fred.... Well, that's all right. It's all part of the game."[68] On another occasion Meyers was more direct, snapping, "It fell in the coaching box at first base. Who do you think should have caught it?"[69] Apparently he grew tired of discussing the incident. His grand-nephew, Colonel John V. Meyers, said in all the times his great-uncle talked about his baseball career, he never once mentioned missing Speaker's foul pop-up.[70]

For the 1912 World Series Meyers played in all eight games, with ten hits in 28 at-bats, for a .357 average, second only to Herzog's .400 (a World Series record for an eight-game series among players with at least ten at-bats). Meyers scored two runs and drove in three, struck out three times, and walked twice. When asked for his comment on the Series, Meyers said, "We lost to a good club and have every reason to hold up our heads and look our supporters squarely in the face. We gave Boston the very best we had and I think the victors will not begrudge us a share in the honors."[71]

## The 1912-13 Off-Season: Meyers as Sports Journalist

By the end of the 1912 season John Tortes Meyers was earning a reputation as something of a sports journalist. In addition to his *New York American* articles, he penned an essay after the 1912 season titled "When Ball Players Rest," with the byline "John ('Chief') Meyers." It received national circulation.[72]

In the article Meyers focused on the road trips Giants took in their two private Pullman cars. To pass the time the players mostly played cards or read. Meyers was among a group of four — with Crandall, Fletcher, and Becker — who regularly played pinochle, but he emphasized they never risked more than a nickel on their games. The time had passed, he wrote, when there was "tall gambling" among players with as much as $6,000 or $7,000 on the table. Some players sang and Leon Ames was known to recite Kipling's poem, "On the Road to Mandalay." The younger, smaller players sometimes kidded Jeff Tesreau until he chased them, sweeping them up with his big arms in a bear hug.

Reflecting the affection he always expressed for his teammates, Meyers claimed, "It's like one big family — a lively, noisy bunch of pals. I never saw a group of men in any business so genuinely attached to each other as the Giants."

When the Giants arrived at a town they would be transported in a fleet of taxis to a first class hotel. "We're an attraction, and we know it," Meyers wrote, "and that helps box office receipts. People always want to see this club that's got a Matty and a real Indian, and sometimes a Charley Faust or a 'Bugs' Raymond as an added attraction." Meyers had apparently grown accustomed to being singled out by fans. "The natives," he observed, with a touch of irony, "can always spot me, because of my Indian appearance, so I'm usually the one they make for. 'Hey, Chief, which is Matty?' they ask. 'Which one is Johnny McGraw? Who's going to pitch today, Chief?' The other boys give the laugh because I'm the goat for all the questioners. The fans can't recognize other players in their street make-ups."

According to Meyers each Giants player sported a diamond, which he noted was "the badge of big league class. As soon as a ball player gets out of the 'bushes' and into the big show the first thing he does is to buy a spark. Some of the boys have a half a dozen."

When it came to consuming alcohol, Meyers wanted to make clear to readers that most players did not drink at all and those who did only had an occasional beer. They always made it a practice, he said, apparently forgetting about Bugs Raymond, not to drink with fans.

After the morning practice on the road, players would pursue various pastimes. Some played billiards. Matty played chess or checkers with some local expert. "For my part," Meyers explained, "I'm an art bug; so I dig up some collection that is on exhibition or find a museum where there are good paintings and statuary, and spend all my time there. The Chicago Museum and Carnegie Institute in Pittsburgh are favorite morning haunts of mine." The college men on the team had clubs to go to. Meyers noted he spent "a good bit of time in the Dartmouth club in Chicago."

Meyers concluded the article by mentioning a letter he once received from a female admirer who told him where she would be sitting at the game the next day and what she would be wearing. "When you turn around and run back toward the stand for a foul as you often do," she wrote, "I wish that you would see me and give me some sign of recognition." Meyers claimed he turned over all his letters from female fans to "a little lady at home." He showed this particular letter to his wife Anna, and she sat near the place described in the letter. When the Giants catcher ran back for a foul ball, Anna reported seeing a woman in blue jump up and wait for a signal. Meyers noted in closing, "She didn't get it, but I got the foul."

Frustrated by the refusal of team owners and league officials to give them a larger share of the growing profits, Meyers joined with other players in both leagues to form the Fraternity of Professional Base Ball Players of America after the 1912 season. He became a leader in the group, serving on the Elections Committee.[73] The players argued that since they generated the income on the field, they should share more of the proceeds. They also wanted to end the hated reserve clause that kept them tied to one club until released or traded.[74] However, the owners mostly ignored the Fraternity and it dissolved in 1917. It would be more than 40 years before major leaguers succeeded in creating a successful union, the Major League Baseball Players Association, and more than a half-century before the first collective bargaining agreement. The reserve clause was not finally revoked until 1975, four years after Meyers died.[75]

Jack and Anna Meyers once again spent the off-season in southern California, where he played in the Winter League. One of the teams against which Meyers competed during an exhibition series that winter was Rube Foster's barnstorming Negro team, the Chicago American Giants.[76]

Without a doubt in 1912 John Tortes Meyers reached the pinnacle of success as a major league ballplayer. In a detailed analysis of the importance of the position of catcher, written in the 1912-1913 off-season, F. C. Lane concluded that two major league catchers stood out as the best — Jimmy Archer of the Cubs and Chief Meyers of the Giants. According to Lane, while Archer was the premier backstop defensively, "as a batter Meyers has few equals."[77]

In its list of the 40 leading players for the 1912 season, *Baseball Magazine* included Meyers, with the following note[78]:

> Chief Meyers is so phenomenal a batter that his slowness and his lack of finish are completely lost sight of. Last season was Meyers's best. The Indian batted as he had never batted before. All through the early days when McGraw's men were piling up that formidable lead, which was destined to last through the season, it was Meyers's formidable bat that counted the heaviest in the score. McGraw has said that Meyers is the greatest natural batter in the game.

# SEVEN

# Still a Star: The 1913
# Season and World Series

## 1913 Pre-Season: Thorpe Joins the Giants

The headline grabber during the Giants' 1913 spring training at Marlin, Texas, was 1912 Olympian and Carlisle Indian School standout Jim Thorpe. Writers gave Thorpe's power hitting the same attention they directed toward the batting prowess of John Tortes Meyers when the Giants catcher was a rookie four years earlier. McGraw called a home run Thorpe hit off Christy Mathewson with Meyers catching at a March 11 game "the longest hit in the world."[1] Aware of the publicity potential of having two Indians on his team, McGraw told reporters, "I can see no reason why he should not hit them on the nose as Chief Meyers does if he chokes his bat and drives the ball with his wrist and forearm."[2]

Although Thorpe was as yet unproven in the major leagues, the Giants were not the only team interested in him. As the New Yorkers prepared to leave Texas, McGraw kept Thorpe in Marlin when his regulars went south to play the minor league Beaumont team that was claiming the rights to Thorpe.[3] Before he had played a single game with the Giants, writers were placing Thorpe at "equal rank" with the two proven Native American stars in the majors, Meyers and Bender.[4]

Midway through the 1913 season McGraw added another college-educated player, Eddie Grant, an infielder with a Harvard degree. Meyers described an occasion when John McGraw ordered the brainy Grant to complain to an umpire about a bad decision. According to Meyers, Grant "marched right up to that umpire, bold as brass, and cried, 'On the strength of my personal belief, Mr. Umpire, that last decision seemed erroneous.'"[5] Another new Giant who shared Meyers's interest in philosophy was pitcher Al Demaree. Other additions to the team were Art Fromme, a pitcher, and Claude Cooper, an outfielder.[6]

Another widely covered story at the Giants' 1913 spring training concerned Meyers's battery mate Rube Marquard, who was late joining the team. Marquard had been on a vaudeville tour with the actress Blossom Seeley, and the two ended the run by getting married just as spring training began. The previous fall Seeley's estranged husband accused her of having an affair with Marquard and threatened to shoot her on stage. The irate husband filed a suit against the Giants pitcher but then withdrew it. Five months after her marriage to Marquard, Seeley gave birth to a baby boy.[7]

## "A Large Tribe"

In the third article in his series for the *New York American*, written early in the 1913 season, John Tortes Meyers celebrated the accomplishments of Indian major league ballplayers in general and four in particular[8]:

> If my race continues to devote the same attention to the diamond game that it has within the past few years, there will soon be a pretty large tribe in organized baseball. The national pastime has opened a profession to the Indian in which he can best employ those natural senses—I might almost say instincts that centuries of life in the open have endowed him with.
> It would be false modesty on my part to declare that I am not thoroughly delighted with the fact that my race has proven itself competent to master the white man's principal sport. In the two major leagues today are four young Indians who have attracted more or less attention: Albert Bender of the Athletics; George Johnson of the Cincinnati Reds; Jim Thorpe and myself of the Giants.

By 1913 Bender had already become, in Meyers's words, "one of the main dependencies of Connie Mack's wonderful Athletics. Fandom has endorsed him as one of the greatest pitchers of the age." Meyers believed George Johnson possessed the ability to become an effective major league pitcher, but also recognized, "It will take many years for Johnson to achieve such fame."

Knowing many readers would disagree with placing Jim Thorpe in his list of the top Indian ballplayers, when the Olympian had not yet proven himself as a major leaguer, Meyers was ready with a detailed argument defending his selection. His first point was that John McGraw, the best judge of talent in the major leagues, would not have signed Thorpe if he did not think he had real promise.

Meyers also wanted his readers to understand that Thorpe was showing he was willing to learn. In the few months since reporting to the Giants spring training camp, Thorpe had made remarkable progress, Meyers pointed out. He saw the rookie as "a real jewel in the rough," who would develop under McGraw's tutelage into a "real gem."

When he arrived at Marlin, Thorpe was dumbfounded by the curve ball but had learned to handle it just as well as the fastball, Meyers contended. Moreover, the rookie studied the top hitters on the club and drew on the best points of each. To the discerning observer, Thorpe displayed the qualities required to become a premier ballplayer. The Carlisle product had earnestness and good sense. He was willing to learn from his mistakes and he was quick-thinking. Meyers wanted readers to understand that despite Thorpe's renown, he was humble, even shy, and had a wonderful personality.

Only after mentioning the intangibles Meyers saw in Thorpe did the Giants catcher list the rookie's physical abilities. "No man in baseball is so beautifully equipped in a physical sense," Meyers wrote. However, he also knew Thorpe would have to refine his raw ability. For example, although the Olympian could run faster than any man on the club he was not yet the best base runner.

Meyers also saw a positive in the fact that Thorpe had not yet settled into one position. He looked good at first base, in the outfield, and showed he could pitch and catch as well. Not surprisingly, Meyers indicated he would prefer Thorpe pitch so that the two could become the only Indian battery in the major leagues.

In short, Thorpe should become an excellent ballplayer, Meyers contended, because he had natural ability and the willingness to develop his talent through practice into real skill.

Later in 1913, Ed Goewey cited three of those on Meyers's list of top Indian ballplayers, albeit in a patronizing fashion. Once again, clearly alluding to the well-known expression of General Philip Sheridan in 1869 that "the only good Indian is a dead Indian," Goewey wrote[9]:

> All arguments to the contrary notwithstanding, there are good Indians, and three of the greatest of these *are* "Chief" Bender of the World's Champion Athletics and "Chief" Meyers and "Jim" Thorpe of the Giants, leaders of the National League. This trio represents the highest type of red man, viewed from the standpoint of the athlete, in the public today, and some of their achievements have never been equaled by a white man.

In his article Meyers stated that Indians were well suited for success in baseball, because for centuries they had lived close to the land and developed the instincts that prepared them well for the national pastime. This assertion did not mean he was echoing the popular view that Indians had inherited a "warlike, savage" character that could be exploited on the baseball diamond. To the contrary, the skills honed by the Cahuilla and other indigenous peoples were hardly "primitive" or "uncivilized." Rather, they were well matched to a game requiring skills of physical strength, dexterity and a quick and agile mind.

The participation by Native Americans in professional baseball *was* on the rise in 1913. *Baseball Magazine* identified 17 Indians playing in the majors or the top minor leagues, and exuded, "Arise, ye braves, and get in the running for the wampum of the pale face!"[10] At the end of the 1913 season William Phelon calculated "in proportion to the total population, the North American Indian now furnishes more ballplayers to the professional game than any other race or nationality within our borders."[11]

However, Meyers's hope that a "large tribe" of Indians would take up baseball did not come to pass. Despite the "blip" in 1913, he and other Native American major league ballplayers would never constitute more than a small minority and would all feel the same sting of racism Meyers experienced. A half-century after Meyers began his major league career, the great New York Yankees pitcher Allie Reynolds, whose mother was Creek, was still being known by the racially charged nickname "Super Chief." Reynolds told a reporter in 1991, "I've gone through hard times being an Indian too. I've been called Copperhead and Chief and Superchief and Gut-eater, and what have you."[12]

As he reflected on the success he and Bender had already achieved, and the potential of players like Johnson and Thorpe, John Tortes Meyers could not restrain the pride he felt knowing Native Americans had demonstrated themselves "competent to master the white man's principal sport." In other words, Indians had proven they could compete with whites as professionals at the highest level in the sport white Americans created and most valued. What Meyers left unsaid in his article was that Native Americans excelled despite having to cope with an unceasing barrage of bigotry. That must have made their success all the more satisfying to him.

For three years (1913–1915) Meyers (left) roomed with the famed Olympian Jim Thorpe (right) while both played for the New York Giants.

## Meyers and Thorpe: Friends and Teammates on Different Paths

John McGraw signed Jim Thorpe to a three-year contract with the Giants on February 2, 1913, at a salary of $6,000 a year, with a $500 signing bonus. The timing was fortuitous. Thorpe had no plans for the future after having been forced to return the medals he won in the 1912 Olympics. Encouraged by his coach and mentor at Carlisle Indian Boarding School, Glenn "Pop" Warner, Thorpe jumped at the opportunity to play major league baseball. At least three teams besides the Giants (the Chicago White Sox, Cincinnati Reds, and St. Louis Browns) expressed interest in signing Thorpe, but McGraw and the Giants offered the best deal.

Warner made sure to present a clean, wholesome image of Thorpe, downplaying his Native American heritage. At Thorpe's signing with the Giants, one reporter noted, "There is little to suggest the redman of the forest. He looked more like a big college student who had stepped out of a Broadway toggery shop."[13] When asked by another reporter at his signing if he had ever met Chief Meyers, Thorpe said innocuously, "No, I never did. But I guess we'll get along together all right. I always have got along with everybody."[14]

When McGraw told the Giants he signed Thorpe because he was convinced of the Olympian's potential as a baseball player, as Meyers always maintained, the Giants manager was not entirely truthful. When a friend asked him how he knew Thorpe could play baseball at the major league level, McGraw responded more honestly, "I don't know. All I know is that he is the one all the sports fans in the country want to see. I've got the ball players I need to win — and Thorpe isn't going to hurt us at the gate."[15] With major league attendance continuing to slide from its high mark in 1909, the Giants manager realized the team needed all the help it could get in luring fans to the games.

The shrewd McGraw clearly recognized the publicity potential in fielding the first all–Indian battery in baseball history if Thorpe developed as a pitcher and could be teamed with Meyers. In this case, however, McGraw was wrong on two counts. Thorpe did not become a pitcher, and there is no evidence that his presence on the Giants boosted game attendance.[16]

As it turned out, Jim Thorpe did not reach the same level of success in major league baseball as Albert Bender or John Tortes Meyers. During his first three years with the Giants he played in a total of only 66 games and did not bat over .200 until 1915. He spent parts of all three seasons in the minor leagues, and, while playing for Jersey City, was sued for being involved in a barroom brawl and dismissed from the team.[17] Thorpe spent the entire 1916 season with the minor league Milwaukee team.

During part of the 1917 season McGraw "loaned" Thorpe to Cincinnati, where Christy Mathewson was then manager, believing Matty would be able to inspire Thorpe as he had Meyers. In 1918 Thorpe played in only 58 games for the Giants. Responding to his complaints at playing so little, McGraw traded Thorpe to the Boston Braves in 1919 where he played in 60 games and had his best year at the plate in the majors, batting .327. For his career, Thorpe appeared in only 289 major league games and had a .252 batting average, with seven home runs and 29 stolen bases. After leaving the majors in 1920, Thorpe continued playing baseball in the minor leagues for three more years and had more success at the plate, batting over .300 each year.

Jim Thorpe never developed the close relationship with John McGraw that John Tortes Meyers did. Thorpe and the Giants skipper often argued, sometimes bitterly. When McGraw used racially charged taunts to try to motivate Thorpe, the former Olympian responded defiantly. He did not simply accept the Giants manager's tirades as other players, including Meyers, learned to do.

Thorpe had excelled so easily at track and football, his coaches did not need to give him much instruction. By contrast, McGraw pushed him hard on the baseball diamond and hovered over him. "His way of telling me when to swing and when to take one — all that McGraw stuff," Thorpe said, "bothered" him, while, by contrast, Meyers thrived on the close attention.[18]

It may well have been that the constant clashes with McGraw "affected [Thorpe's] general disposition, his performance on the field, and his general enthusiasm for the game of baseball."[19] According to McGraw's wife Blanche, her husband felt he had to keep particularly close tabs on Thorpe, even enlisting Chief Meyers to read his roommate's mail. One day, according to Mrs. McGraw, Thorpe found an opened letter addressed to him from his wife Iva in Meyers's locker, and "exploded."[20] At least in this case, by spying on a teammate Meyers had allowed his close relationship with McGraw to cloud his judgment, causing him to violate his own Cahuilla value of integrity.

During most of his baseball years and after, Thorpe was also immersed in professional football. He even barnstormed for a time with an all–Indian basketball team.

Thorpe was willing to enact whites' stereotypes of Indians if he profited from them. Such was the case in the early 1920s when he managed and played for the Oorang Indians, an all–Indian National Football League franchise. Thorpe and the rest of the team would sometimes dress in feathers and "war paint" for a half-time show featuring "Indian" dances and war whoops.[21]

After his career in professional sports ended in 1929, Thorpe continued to cash in on the public's fascination with Indians, taking an all–Indian song and dance troupe on tour. He also took bit parts in movies that portrayed

Indians stereotypically. However, he did demonstrate his concern for Indian rights, insisting that other Indians be hired for Native American roles in the movies in which he appeared.

Unlike John Tortes Meyers, who most often found constructive ways to channel the tension of living in two worlds, Thorpe seemed, especially in his later years, to succumb to the pressure. Sometimes he externalized the stress. More frequently he turned the hostility he felt inward. He struggled with alcoholism and barely eked out a living when his sports career ended.[22]

Writing after Thorpe had died in 1953 at age 65, Grantland Rice summed up Thorpe's career succinctly, but in stereotypical language: "[Thorpe] rose to great fame in a hurry, and then sank. He was a gentleman but there were times when firewater got the better of their long feud." According to Rice, Thorpe was "the greatest athlete of his day, if not all time," but was "pilloried by the shabby treatment he received from most of the press and the public." His proposal for a remedy was to honor Thorpe not simply as the amazing athlete he was but rather as a stereotypical Indian, with "an effigy ... in the entry to the Indian wing of the Museum of Natural History in New York." A captive of his times, Rice missed the point. Thorpe was "pilloried" because he *was* an Indian who outshone white men at their own games, and, therefore, could not be given the full recognition he deserved as a premier athlete.[23]

For the three years the two were teammates on the New York Giants (1913–1915), Meyers and Thorpe were roommates. They remained friends until Thorpe died. The two former Giants did not have much contact in Thorpe's later years,[24] but on occasion their paths crossed.[25]

When Thorpe died, Meyers felt it important to honor his friend and teammate. On the day before Thorpe's body was shipped to Oklahoma for burial, John Tortes Meyers went to Los Angeles to pay his respects and attend a rosary said for Thorpe.[26]

A half-century after their years together on the Giants, Meyers described Jim Thorpe as "an Adonis! Built like a Greek god." He was, according to his friend, "[t]he greatest all-around athlete who ever lived." What Meyers most wanted understood was that "Jim was very proud of the great things he'd done. A very proud man. Not conceited, he never was that. But proud." Thorpe rarely talked about his feelings at having been stripped of his medals after the 1912 Olympics. However, he opened up to Meyers late one night during the period they roomed together. "Jim came in and woke me up. I remember it like it was only last night," Meyers said 50 years afterwards. "He was crying, and tears were rolling down his cheeks. 'You know, Chief,' he said, 'the King of Sweden gave me those trophies, he gave them to me. But they took them away from me, even though the guy who finished second refused to take them. They're mine, Chief, I won them fair and square.' It broke his heart, and he never really recovered."[27]

There is a tragic irony in the story of Jim Thorpe, and John Tortes Meyers recognized it better than anyone. As Philip Deloria has observed, "Jim Thorpe, the great icon of Indian athleticism ... stands alone as an anomaly, the only Indian that anyone not Indian can seem to remember when it comes to American sports."[28] Despite unparalleled recognition, making him the most famous American Indian athlete and the most honored athlete of the twentieth century, the path of assimilation for Jim Thorpe led not only to dominance in the white man's sporting world, but also to dressing up in "Indian" attire foreign to his own heritage and performing made-up "Indian dances" before white audiences in order to earn money.

Though he did not attain the same level of renown as his friend, John Tortes Meyers followed a different path than Jim Thorpe. In the final analysis, despite their success as athletes, both Thorpe and Meyers knew the pain of being "strangers in a strange land." The difference was in how each coped with living at the boundary between cultures, in an arena that exploited their talents but did not grant them full equality. As it did for Louis Sockalexis and Albert Bender, the tension for Jim Thorpe became at times unbearable,

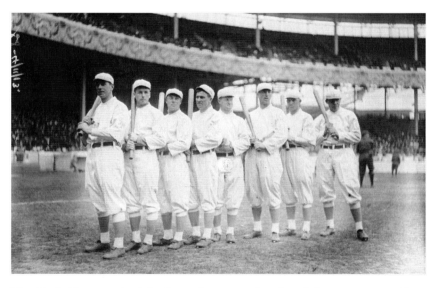

New York Giants at the Polo Grounds on opening day of the 1913 season. Identified by the Pictorial History Committee of the Society for American Baseball Research, left to right, are: Fred Snodgrass, Tillie Shafer, George Burns, Larry Doyle, Red Murray, Fred Merkle, Buck Herzog, and Meyers (Library of Congress, Prints & Photographs Division, LC-DIG-ggbain-11468).

relieved only through self-destructive outbursts of anger and bouts of drunkenness. Meyers found other, more positive, outlets for his frustration and ways to stand up for himself and for his people.

## The 1913 Season: Another Great Year

Playing in cream-colored, velvet-trimmed uniforms modeled after the New York University colors, the Giants got off to a slow start offensively during the 1913 season, but pitching kept them in the pennant race. Mathewson, Marquard, and Tesreau continued in their winning ways, with rookie Al Demaree also contributing victories.

Jim Thorpe made his Giants debut in the second game of the season, a loss to Brooklyn. The *New York Times* described his entry, making clear his ethnicity: "As a last straw with two down in the ninth, McGraw sent Jim Thorpe into bat. The Indian went the way of his white brothers and was tossed out at first base after hopping a grounder to Cutshaw."[29] For the 1913 season Thorpe would play in only 19 games, with only 36 plate appearances. His batting average was an anemic .143, and his on-base percentage only .167.[30]

A May 9 game exemplified the Giants' early play. Meyers was 1-for-3 in a losing effort to Cincinnati. Marquard took the loss. Alluding to Marquard's off-season vaudeville adventure, one writer commented, "During seven of the eight innings that he occupied the mound at the Polo Grounds yesterday Rube Marquard acted like a pitcher. In the other inning he pitched like an actor."[31]

The previous day Chief Johnson was on the mound for the Reds in a game marked by a controversy involving Meyers. In the seventh inning the Cahuilla catcher blocked the plate and apparently tagged out a Reds player trying to score. However, he dropped the ball, and "as there were no windows in Meyers's massive frame" Umpire Bill Egan "blew the call, not seeing the sphere roll away. Twenty Reds stormed out to protest. Manager Joe Tinker danced up and down waving his arms, but to no avail. Egan refused to reverse his ruling."[32]

W. A. Phelon created the following imaginary encounter between Meyers and Johnson at this game, replete with what the writer apparently thought to be authentic Indian dialogue: "Said Chief Johnson to Chief Meyers—'We Indians should stick together—be a true brave and strike out!' Said Chief Meyers to Chief Johnson: 'Tat sticking together goes with Sweeney [a horse racing expression for "fixing the race"]. I prefer the wampum of the pale face.' A bang went a hot single."[33]

In May the *New York American* published the fourth and final article in the series by "John ('Chief') Meyers, Star catcher of the champion Giants and one of the greatest hitters in the National League." Appropriately, the topic was hitting.[34]

According to Meyers, "Batting ability is the high art of baseball.... 'Can he hit?' is the universal question which greets the announcement of every new arrival to the game. The three magic words embody the chief concern of scout, manager and public." Certainly, this was true in Meyers's case. His lack of speed and sometimes shaky fielding were more than compensated for by his remarkable ability at the plate.

The Giants' power hitter took exception to the conventional wisdom that "batters are born, not made." In his opinion, good hitting could be taught, just like fielding and base running. Of course, not every player could become a Ty Cobb with his lightning speed or Honus Wagner with his raw power merely by studying. However, the Giants catcher believed careful attention to the basics of hitting and diligent practice could help turn an average hitter into a real threat.

Meyers asserted that the obstacles the batter faces are significant: hitting a round sphere, which has been thrown as hard as humanly possible, with a round bat, a half-second to decide whether and where to swing, nine agile fielders even if he hits the ball, and a pitcher able to make the ball vary on its way to the plate.

Nevertheless, Meyers proposed, there are various principles of "batting science" that can help meet these challenges. In his view, the most important were remaining still as the ball approached and waiting to meet the projectile as it passed in front of the body. He contended that learning these skills made a so-called "natural hitter," like "Heine" Zimmerman, Wagner, Napoleon "Nap" Lajoie, Larry Doyle and even Cobb. The Giants' power hitter credited John McGraw with drilling this idea into the Giants players and turning men with average ability into excellent hitters.

Not only did Meyers assert this principle, he explained why it worked. By providing the "steadiest possible attitude" it does not "handicap the eye." Since curves and spitters break late, keeping the body back allowed the batter to swing when it was easiest for him to meet the ball.

Another principle Meyers identified was to keep the swing in a horizontal arc rather than swinging upward or downward. A level swing will propel the ball harder and keep it on the ground, resulting in more hits, he asserted.

Beyond basic principles the keys to batting success Meyers had discovered were constant practice, focusing on overcoming batting weaknesses, and carefully studying the opposing pitcher's repertoire — his strengths and his weaknesses. Working on hitting the ball to all fields was also an essential. Finally, Meyers contended, since baseball is "nothing more than a battle of wits, the best batter is the one who masks his hand."

The article is clear evidence of what McGraw and other players often said about Meyers. He was a serious student of the game, one of the best in his generation, who took a scientific approach to all aspects of baseball.

A total of 60,000 "frenzied fans" were present at the Polo Grounds on May 30, 1913, for a doubleheader against the Phillies.[35] A month later, with the Phillies and their ace pitcher Grover Cleveland Alexander leading the league, McGraw fired up the Giants by telling his players, "If a team like the Phillies can win a pennant in the National League, then the League is a joke." A June 30 victory, 11–10, over the Phillies put the Giants ahead for good as they won 30 out of 34 games.[36]

Meyers's fluency in Spanish was the basis of a humorous incident in June 1913. Victor Munoz, a Cuban reporter, interviewed Meyers and was astonished when the Giants catcher answered his questions in excellent Spanish. Munoz immediately cabled home a report saying Meyers was a Mexican, not an Indian, as had been assumed. Meyers apparently did not correct him.[37]

In mid–July Meyers and the Giants once again witnessed for themselves the pitching potential of Chief Johnson. Calling him the "Winnebago tribesman" and "the Injun," the *New York Times* reported that Johnson relieved for the Reds in the fifth inning of a July 14 contest, with the Giants leading 5 to 3, and shut the Giants down. However, the Giants' lead held up. The Giants had scored on one of Meyers's crashing blows in the second, a double driving in Fred Merkle. He recorded another RBI with a sacrifice fly in the fourth to provide the winning margin.[38]

Though not duplicating his sizzling season of the previous year, Meyers was still hitting very well. He was the hero in a July 7 Giants victory, 6 to 1 over Brooklyn. In the fourth inning Meyers stole second. The theft stood out, according to one writer, like "a snoring deacon in church." After getting to first on a pass, Meyers "started for second like Truck No. 6 going to a fire. Nearing the base, he thundered along until the infield shook. The big Indian hit the earth and slid into the cushion with a thump which could be heard all over Long Island." Even more impressive was his speed the next inning. When "Tillie" Shafer's throw sailed wide of Merkle at first on a grounder, Meyers raced down the line to back up the play, retrieved the ball, and nailed a Brooklyn runner at third. He also singled and drove in a run in the sixth.[39]

For most of the month of August, Meyers was out of action after tearing a finger in an August 4 game. Replacing Meyers behind the bat were Arthur Wilson and the lanky Larry ("Long Larry") McLean, whom McGraw acquired in mid-season from the Cincinnati Reds.

Meyers returned to action at the end of August in time for one of the more memorable contests of the 1913 season. An August 30 game, played in Philadelphia, paired pitching greats Christy Mathewson and Grover Cleveland

Alexander. Alexander was hit hard by the Giants and exited in the third inning, with the New Yorkers ahead. However, Philadelphia rallied to take the lead. With the Phillies about to finish off the Giants for the third time in a row, leading 8 to 6 in the ninth, McGraw sprang into action. The Giants skipper complained to home plate umpire Bill Brennan that spectators in the center field bleachers were blinding the Giants' batsmen. He said they were waving their straw hats, causing the sun to be reflected into the batters' eyes. When the Philadelphia manager said he could do nothing about it, Brennan called in the police who asked those directly in line with the pitcher and batter to move. The park was full, and the fans refused to budge. After a long discussion the game was forfeited to the Giants, who had to push their way through enraged fans to reach their clubhouse.

The Phillies' appeal of the ruling was upheld and the game was finished on the 2nd of October, with the Phillies winning. Meyers singled with two outs in the ninth, keeping the Giants' hopes alive. He was replaced with a pinch-runner, but the Giants failed to score. However, at the August 30 contest McGraw had accomplished his objective, arousing his players for the crucial stretch run. The Giants returned home after the August contest to win eight of their next 12 games. By early October the Giants clinched the pennant.[40]

The Giants' 1913 season record of 101 wins and 51 losses put New York 12½ games ahead of Philadelphia. Only in 1904, when they finished 13 games ahead of Chicago, did the Giants win the pennant by a wider margin during the Deadball Era. For the 1913 season Meyers was the only Giant to bat above .300 (.312), but pitching, speed (296 stolen bases), and McGraw's unique motivational style seemed to many to make what was otherwise a very ordinary ball club into the pennant winner for the third year in a row. As the Cubs' Johnny Evers famously said, "The Giants were a second-rate club with a first-rate manager."

Meyers had appeared in 120 games, had 378 at-bats, scored 37 runs, drove in 47 runs, knocked out 118 hits for 155 total bases (including 18 doubles, five triples and three home runs).[41] For the third consecutive season, the modern company STATS, Inc. has chosen Meyers as catcher on its 1913 National League All-Star team.[42] He finished fifth in the Most Valuable Player balloting, behind Jake Daubert of the Superbas, Gavvy Cravath of the Phillies, Rabbit Maranville of the Braves, and Christy Mathewson.

## The 1913 World Series: A Contrast in Managerial Styles

In 1913, for the third time in nine years, John McGraw's New York Giants met Connie Mack's Philadelphia Athletics in the World Series. The Giants won in 1905, four games to one, the Athletics in 1911, four games to two. This would be the "rubber match" between the two recognized managerial geniuses of the era, so different in temperament and style.

Having already played in the two previous series, Christy Mathewson sensed Mack's approach to managing gave the A's an edge. Writing just before the 1913 World Series began, Matty compared the A's to a college team, saying, "There is never any dissension.... They are all whooping it up for one another. No politics mars the workings of the club and you never hear one member of the team knocking some fellow player." According to Mathewson, "This is all Connie Mack. He is a marvel at handling men." Not even the fact that Mack was notoriously tight, paying players less than they would have made on other clubs, caused the players to complain. By contrast, under the hard-driving McGraw, the Giants were, Matty claimed, wound up tight going into this as well as other World Series.[43]

Shown here in a 1913 photograph, Connie Mack (in bowler hat), manager of the Philadelphia Athletics for a half-century (1901–1950), led his team to victory in two World Series (1911 and 1913) against New York Giants teams on which Meyers played. Respected both by his own players and opponents alike, Mack holds the record for most career wins by a manager (3,731) (Library of Congress, Prints & Photographs Division, LC-DIG-hec-03263).

In a prelude to the 1913 Series Hugh Fullerton rated the Giants and A's and found that given the likelihood the match-up would be a free-hitting affair with many base runners, catchers would be second in importance only to pitchers.[44] According to Fullerton, of the two starting catchers Meyers ranked higher in hitting, but below newcomer Wally Schang of the A's in speed, throwing, and fielding.

Fullerton's was probably the most objective overall assessment of the Cahuilla catcher's strengths and weaknesses of any sportswriter who saw him play. He called Meyers "an old-fashioned type of hitter — a stolid, heavy-driving fellow, hitting the ball with immense power and with all his weight behind it. Pitchers who get the ball in too close to him should signal the third baseman to dodge before they pitch." He credited the Giants backstop with hitting all kinds of pitching. If it were not for his "excessive slowness," Meyers would be, in Fullerton's estimation, the best right-handed batsman in the major leagues, the equal of Hans Wagner and Nap Lajoie.

Defensively, Fullerton claimed Meyers was particularly adept at figuring out what hitters and runners were planning to do and steadying and slowing down pitchers when the situation required. Although perhaps not as sound mechanically as other catchers, allowing too many balls to get by him, Fullerton noted the Giants catcher was not "afraid of spikes" as some claimed. To the contrary, Meyers stood his ground and blocked the plate well.

In a more succinct evaluation of the catchers in the 1913 Series, Irwin Howe contended, "Meyers comes close to being the best all-around backstop in the game to-day." Howe's final comment turned out to be prophetic: Meyers "will do all the receiving for the Giants unless injured."[45]

After the Giants clinched the pennant, Meyers was miffed when McGraw assigned him to catch both games in a doubleheader. Years later he remembered telling teammates, "I'm sore and I hope I get a split finger in the first game. I've been working like a dog to bring us through and now that it is settled I've got to work in a doubleheader that doesn't mean anything."[46]

Expectations for the economic success of the 1913 Series were high. The Commercial Moving Picture Company bought the rights from the National Commission to film the Series and was showing highlights in theaters in New York and Philadelphia hours after games finished. Having been rebuffed in their earlier appeals, the Giants and A's players did not bother to petition for a portion of the fee.[47]

It did not escape the notice of the press that with Chief Bender and Chief Meyers once again squaring off in the Fall Classic, Indians across the country were enthused. Fifty "blanketed Indians from the reservations of Oregon and Washington" who were "intent upon seeing how their fellow redmen distinguished themselves" traveled as far as 150 miles to watch real-time displays of the game results on an outdoor scoreboard in Portland, Oregon.[48]

Two days before the first game of the 1913 Series, Meyers joined Christy Mathewson, Fred Snodgrass, Hooks Wiltse, Jim Thorpe and other Giants for the Sunday morning service at Grace Methodist Episcopal Church on 104th Street in New York City. When the Reverend C. F. Reisner named Christy Mathewson as "a fine example of Christian manhood," the packed congregation erupted in cheers. Also speaking from the pulpit was David Fultz, a former A's player, who a year before had led the effort to unionize major league players by creating the Baseball Players' Fraternity. A month after the 1913 Series ended Fultz presented a petition signed by nearly 500 players, with a list of 17 demands. Although the Fraternity did not survive, Fultz did succeed in getting the baseball owners to agree to address most of the players' stated concerns.[49]

## Game One (Tuesday, October 7)

On an overcast day McGraw chose Rube Marquard to start the first game of the 1913 World Series at the Polo Grounds before an enthusiastic crowd of 36,291. The Giants pitcher looked strong in warm-ups, but later admitted he was very nervous when he took the field. On this day Meyers could not calm his battery mate. Marquard gave up five runs on eight hits in five innings before being relieved. Frank "Home Run" Baker and Eddie Collins had three hits each in the game for the A's.

Baker drove in a run with a single in the fourth, one of three runs scored by the A's in the inning. When the A's third baseman came up in the fifth with Collins on second and two out, Marquard said he intended to pitch Baker low and away but instead delivered a knee-high fastball on the inside corner. Baker deposited the ball into the stands for a two-run home run. The A's third baseman would be the hitting star for the Series and MVP if one had been selected. He hit .450, with nine hits in 20 at-bats, and collected seven RBI.

Albert Bender started for the A's, but was not sharp, giving up 11 hits. Nevertheless, the ace of the Athletics staff pitched well enough to earn the win, holding the Giants to four runs, while Philadelphia tallied a total of six.

At a crucial point in the game McGraw hurled insults at the A's pitcher from the bench. Bender walked toward McGraw, smiled, held his hand to his ear, mockingly urging the Giants manager to yell louder so he could hear him. The next inning Bender set down the Giants in order. That evening Bender told a reporter how an article sent to him by a friend had motivated him. An underlined sentence said, "McGraw knows that he can beat Bender and hopes that Mack will start with the Indian." The A's pitcher said, "when I got in the box I thought of the clipping, and that was enough."[50]

Meyers did not live up to Fullerton's expectations, going hitless in the game, 0-for-4. When he tried to surprise Bender with a bunt in front of the plate, the A's hurler was off the mound in a flash, easily throwing Meyers out. Defensively the Giants catcher was sharper; he nailed an Athletics runner trying to steal second in the top of the ninth.[51]

## Game Two (Wednesday, October 8)

A sold-out crowed of 20,563 watched the second game of the Series at Shibe Park in Philadelphia on a rainy day. Two collegians were on the mound, with Mathewson of Bucknell University pitching for the Giants and Eddie Plank of Gettysburg College for the A's. Both rose to the occasion and hurled nearly perfect games through nine scoreless innings.

With the word out that Mathewson would be relying almost solely on his fadeaway and curve, he threw nothing but fastballs, crossing up the A's batters. When the A's put men at second and third with no one out in the bottom of the ninth, Matty went to work and sent the game into extra innings.

Big Six was also a star at the plate for the Giants, singling in the top of the tenth to knock in what turned out to be the winning run. That tally was followed by two insurance runs, and Matty proceeded to set down the A's three up, three down in the bottom of the tenth for a 3–0 Giants victory.

Meyers watched Mathewson's outstanding performance from the bench. His wish for a sore finger before the doubleheader at the end of the season had not been fulfilled then, but an injury before the second game kept him from playing for the rest of the 1913 World Series. While warming up, Meyers split the thumb on his throwing hand and badly bruised or broke his index finger catching a hard throw from Buck Herzog at third. As Meyers walked off the field, McGraw "threw out his hands in a gesture that clearly indicated despair."[52]

Larry McLean took over behind the bat, with support from Art Wilson. McLean would take full advantage of the opportunity offensively, batting .500 with six hits in 12 at-bats and two RBIs during the series. However, Meyers was missed. As Richard Alder concluded in a careful analysis of the 1913 Series, "[Meyers's] presence ... at the least might have resulted in a much closer series."[53] Although Matty did not seem to be affected in the second game, it was a fact that Mathewson and Meyers had an "excellent rhythm."[54]

## Game Three (Thursday, October 9)

Responding to complaints from members of the Baseball Writers Association that their livelihood was being threatened, Ban Johnson of the National Commission attempted to forbid articles ghostwritten for players during the 1913 Series. Meyers was among the players who had signed with ghostwriters to let their names be used in articles. Johnson first attempted to impose a rule saying any player whose name appeared in a byline could not appear in the Series. When Connie Mack said that if the ruling were enforced he would find substitutes for two of his stars, Baker and Collins, because he would not interfere with their writing deals, Johnson relented, saying that if players

wrote their own articles they would be allowed to play. That was a greater
challenge for some than others. Mathewson and Meyers were certainly capable
of writing their own pieces, but Jeff Tesreau, whose ghostwritten articles
appeared during the 1912 Series, and who signed a contract for the 1913 Series,
had a reputation as a man of few words. After the exciting second game the
ghostwriter assigned to pen the articles attributed to Tesreau went to him for
a comment. According to the writer, playing to the stereotype of Tesreau as
the Ozarks hillbilly, the pitcher said only four words: "I hurt muh thumb."[55]

With the series knotted at a game each, Connie Mack tapped a rookie,
"Bullet" Joe Bush, who had 14 victories during the regular season, to start the
third game. McGraw countered with spitballer Jeff Tesreau, who had pitched
well in the 1912 Series. Scouting reports indicated the A's were weak against
spitters. Tesreau assured his manager he was ready to take the mound despite
his sore thumb.

The game was played at the Polo Grounds before a sell-out crowd of
36,896 on another overcast day. Rain overnight left the field soggy.

The cagey A's noticed Tesreau was tipping his spitball by moving his
fingers from side to side on the ball when he was about to throw the pitch,
so they sat on his spitter and scored three runs in the top of the first. Mack
turned the tables on McGraw by pulling a double steal. That would be all the
A's needed as Bush held the Giants bats in check, and Philadelphia ran away
with an 8 to 2 rout.

## Game Four (Friday, October 10)

Christy Mathewson was tired after pitching 306 innings during the regular season and into extra innings in the second game of the 1913 World
Series. Consequently, he was not available for the fourth contest, played in
Shibe Park before another capacity crowd of 20,568. Scalpers sold tickets for
as much as $15, while thousands gathered in New York to follow the game on
the popular electronic scoreboards.

McGraw passed over Marquard because of his performance in the first
game and started his rookie sensation Al Demaree, who had a 13–4 regular
season record. Mack did not have to think twice about who would be his
pitcher in the game. It would be Albert Bender, and Bender was ready.

Demaree was able to handle the A's hitting stars, Baker and Collins, but
not shortstop Jack Barry and catcher Wally Schang, who were ordinarily not
offensive threats. Barry was 3-for-4, scored two runs and drove in another.
Schang went 2-for-2, scored a run, and drove in four of the six A's tallies.
Demaree lasted only four innings before being relieved by Marquard.

Bender was sharp, holding the Giants scoreless through six innings.

However, he was shaky in the seventh, giving up a three-run homer to Fred Merkle. The Giants plated two more runs in the eighth to close within one tally. A throwing error by Bender contributed to the Giants' scoring. When Mack sent a player to the mound to ask Bender if he had anything left, Bender said he was fine. With his deep sense of pride, Bender always considered it shameful to be taken out of a game. He bore down and held off the Giants to win his fourth straight World Series game, by a score of 6 to 5.

After the game Grantland Rice observed that Bender's "sharp reflexes" and his ability to "take the game as it comes to him, rarely getting excited or off-balance," were tremendous assets. Rice considered Bender, with whom he frequently played golf, a "pal of mine" but still viewed the A's pitcher through the prism of racial stereotyping. The Indian, Rice wrote in his memoir *The Tumult and the Shouting,* "is a great natural athlete. Given the same chance, he has the white man lashed to the post. His heritage is all outdoors."[56] Bender biographer William Kashatus has offered this interpretation of Rice's vivid image: "No matter how successful he became, Bender would remain at best a fascinating specimen, at worst a threat to popular notions of white superiority."[57]

## Game Five (Saturday, October 11)

The weather was again rainy and overcast in New York, but that did not keep 36,632 fans from buying tickets for the fifth game of the 1913 World Series. In an effort to keep the Series alive, McGraw put his last, best hope on the mound — Christy Mathewson. The Giants supporters cheered madly when Mathewson took the long walk from the center field Polo Grounds clubhouse to the bench. It would be Matty's final World Series appearance.

Mack countered with Eddie Plank and challenged the A's players to finish off the Giants by telling them the club would give its share of the game receipts — over $30,000 — to the players if they won. The pledge amounted to an extra $1,000 on top of the official $3,000 share for players on the winning team. Mack made the promise even though to fulfill it would violate the National Commission's policy that players in World Series be compensated only from the receipts for the initial four games, lest they be tempted to throw games to extend the series.

Plank held the Giants to only two hits and would have kept them from scoring except for an error he committed. Mathewson was nearly as effective. He later said he knew this might be his last World Series appearance and he desperately wanted to win.

Fred Merkle was once again at the center of controversy when he froze on a play in the third inning, allowing a run to score. With that tally the A's had a two-run lead, and the Giants' fate was sealed. The Giants could muster only one run, when Meyers's substitute Larry McLean drove Big Six in after Plank's fielding error in the fifth. The game and the 1913 World Series were over, with the A's taking four of five games.

After the game McGraw was effusive in his praise of Mathewson, telling writers, "[Matty] has the greatest heart of any ballplayer I ever knew, and by heart I mean courage.... I don't believe that there will ever be another like him for ability, brains, and courage."[58]

Despite losing the fifth game, for the series Mathewson's ERA was 0.95 and he led the Giants with a .600 batting average. His career World Series record would be five wins and five losses, but he completed ten of the eleven games he started and had an ERA of 0.97, giving up only ten walks in 101 innings. Four of his five victories were shutouts.

As in 1911 McGraw was the first to congratulate Mack and the A's. However, the loss left the Giants manager seething. At a team dinner several days after the 1913 Series a drunk McGraw berated his old friend, coach Wilbert Robinson, for misreading a sign from McGraw and sending Snodgrass on an unsuccessful steal. McGraw angrily alleged that Robinson, who had been his right-hand man on the Giants for five years, had made more mistakes than anyone else on the team. McGraw grew hotter and hotter until he fired "Uncle Robby" on the spot and threw him out of the party. According to umpire Bill Klem, who was present at the dinner, Robinson responded by dousing McGraw with beer before he left. The two former teammates did not speak again for 17 years.[59]

Meyers never complained about his bad luck in missing all but the first game of the 1913 World Series due to the injury he incurred during warm-ups for the second game. His quiet acceptance of this and other misfortunes in his life is a reflection of the Cahuilla teaching that life is unpredictable, and one must learn to take the bad with the good.

The winning players in the 1913 Series pocketed $3,244 each while the losers' share was $2,162 per player. Among the Giants on the roster for the 1913 Series who did not play was Jim Thorpe.

## The 1913-14 Off-Season: The Round-the-World Tour

During the 1913-14 off-season John Tortes Meyers and other Giants players were invited to join a 139-day round-the-world baseball tour organized by John McGraw and Charles Comiskey, owner of the Chicago White Sox. It was to be, its promoters claimed, a trip of "epic proportions—a tour to end all tours."[60] The extravaganza began with a 31-game barnstorming trip across the United States, after which the teams sailed to Japan, China, the Philippines, Hong Kong, Australia, India, Ceylon, Egypt, Italy (where McGraw had a private audience with Pope Pius X), Monte Carlo, France (where McGraw visited Napoleon's tomb), and London (where they played before 35,000 baffled Englishmen, including King George V). The teams returned on the Cunard Line's luxury ocean liner *Lusitania,* arriving in New York on March 4, 1914, a year before a German U-boat torpedoed the *Lusitania* off the Irish coast.[61]

The original plan, hatched in December 1912, when McGraw was in Chicago on a vaudeville tour, was for only Giants and White Sox players to be on the round-the-world jaunt. McGraw was able to convince Meyers along with Christy Mathewson and other New York Giants (including Jim Thorpe, Larry Doyle, Fred Merkle, Fred Snodgrass, George Wiltse, Art Fromme, Al Demaree, and Jeff Tesreau) to join the trip. However, not enough signed up from the two teams, so other star players were recruited. A half-dozen future Hall of Famers were scheduled for the tour, including Walter Johnson and Tris Speaker. Bill Klem and Jack Sheridan agreed to go along as umpires. One of the attractions for the married players was that wives would be allowed to accompany their husbands. Meyers's wife Anna was to be among them, as was Mathewson's wife, Jane, and Thorpe's first wife, Iva, whom he had just married.

The first game of the barnstorming phase was in Cincinnati on October 18, 1913. The weather was so raw and cold only about 2,000 fans showed up. A meager crowd of 7,000 paid to see the teams play the next day in Chicago. McGraw was concerned that the Giants' poor showing in the 1913 World Series was affecting attendance, but the harsh weather was the factor the trip organizers had not adequately considered.[62]

For the fifth game in the tour, played in Sioux City, Iowa, Winnebago and Omaha Indians came from their reservations across the Missouri River in Nebraska to cheer Thorpe and Meyers. In an article titled "Indian War Whoops For Giants' Red Men," which appeared in a series on the tour he had contracted to write for the *New York Times,* John McGraw focused on the reaction at the Sioux City game to Meyers and Thorpe. "Polo Grounds fans who have delighted since Chief Meyers joined my club in giving those imitation war whoops when the Indian came to bat, should have been with us today," the Giants manager explained. "[In Sioux City] they would have heard some whooping of the real variety. There are a number of reservations not far from Sioux City and the Indians were out in large numbers today to see Meyers and Thorpe. In their own way the redskins furnished enough noise to prove to Chief and Jim that they were among friends."[63]

Four thousand were in attendance for the October 23 game. It was the largest crowd to see a baseball game in the history of Sioux City. However, to the disappointment of the Winnebago and Omaha Indians present, McGraw inexplicably did not play Meyers, and Thorpe failed to record a hit in three appearances.

While the teams were in town, the *Sioux City Tribune* reported that hundreds gathered at the their hotel "to take a peek at the most advertised athletes in the world." According to the article, the two main objects of curiosity, Mathewson and Meyers, reacted differently to the attention. Matty was gracious and all smiles during brief conversations as he pushed through the crowd. By contrast, "The 'Big Chief' did not enjoy the homage, as could be seen by his facial expression. He shifted his gaze rapidly around the lobby until he saw a side door leading to Pierce Street. He bolted for the exit, leaving his admirers in the hotel except for two or three of the more persistent hero worshippers who followed in the immediate vicinity of his greatness."[64]

Before the game in Tulsa, Oklahoma, six days later, the overloaded right-field bleachers collapsed, spilling several hundred fans onto a contingent of soldiers passing underneath them. One soldier died and 50 people were hurt, some seriously. A trio of Giants wives (Anna Meyers, Rea Lobert, and Edith Doyle) narrowly missed being struck by the falling debris. As in Sioux City hundreds of Indians came to the Tulsa game to cheer Meyers and Thorpe. Their turnout was one of the reasons for the packed stadium. Oklahoma Governor Lee Cruce was feet away from the collapse and insisted the game go on as scheduled, and Walter Johnson pitched a complete game shutout against Mathewson.[65]

The most enthusiastic fan response during the barnstorming phase was at a November 5 game played in Blue Rapids, Kansas, before an ecstatic crowd of nearly 4,000 fans, more than twice the town's population of 1,500.[66]

After a November 9 game in Los Angeles, the teams left for a contest the next day in San Diego, billed by the organizers as "Chief Meyers's hometown." Some 4,400 fans squeezed into San Diego's Athletic Park, which had 2,600 seats. Not surprisingly, the crowd was swelled by large numbers of Cahuilla and other Indians from the area who came to see Meyers play. They would not be disappointed.

The title for McGraw's article on the game told it all: "Native Son Meyers Wins for Giants." According to McGraw, "Chief Meyers was a hero in his native state to-day when he thrilled a big crowd here by smashing a home run over the right-field fence in the ninth inning with the score tied and won the game for us from the White Sox by a score of 4 to 3."[67]

Meyers's heroics were due largely to an error made by umpire Bill Klem. With the score tied 3–3 Klem announced the bottom of the ninth, when in reality the game was in the top of the ninth. Thinking nine full innings had been played, Klem declared the game a tie. According to one sportswriter in attendance, "Meyers and his wife were already out of the stadium sitting next to [San Diego team owner] Will Palmer in his automobile, preparing to drive off for the U.S. Grand Hotel, when Klem realized his mistake and called everyone back to their places. The Giants would get one more chance to bat."[68]

McGraw rushed to the parking lot to retrieve Meyers, who was scheduled to be the leadoff hitter. According to one account, "Meyers came back grudgingly and told Klem what he thought of umpires in general and Bill Klem in particular." Perhaps eager for the game to end, the pitcher grooved the ball and Meyers drove it well out of the park. As Meyers rounded the bases, a local reporter claimed the Indians in attendance responded with a war whoop that could be heard at the San Diego city hall.[69]

After the game Meyers asked reporters whether a local haberdasher was still giving hats to players who hit home runs. Meyers owned several of them, given to him while he was playing in San Diego during previous winters. He did not receive a hat on this occasion, but he did earn a blister abalone tiepin given to him by another San Diego businessman for hitting his game-winning home run. It was a happy trip up the California coast that night on the Honeymoon Special, as the team's train had been dubbed.[70]

Both John Tortes Meyers and Jim Thorpe would have been closely following reports being wired across the nation about a football game being played at the Polo Grounds on November 15, 1913, between the Carlisle Indians and the Dartmouth Indians. At halftime, Carlisle was trailing 10–7, and it appeared Meyers would have bragging rights over Thorpe in the battle of their *alma maters*. However, in his halftime pep talk, "Pop" Warner (who had a $300 wager on the game) promised to give the Carlisle players $5 each to spend "having fun" in New York City if they came back to win. The inspired Carlisle players scored four touchdowns in the second half and held the Dartmouth squad scoreless to win the game, 35–10.[71]

At the end of the barnstorming phase of the round-the-world tour, various factors contributed to the decision by Jack and Anna Meyers not to continue abroad. Unspecified business concerns, the need to spend time in California with his extended family, as well as the decision of Matty and his wife Jane not to go overseas, all influenced the Meyers.[72] Whatever their reasons Meyers and Mathewson both left the tour together in San Francisco.[73]

Meyers's decision not to sail with the tour may also have been affected by the constant attention heaped upon the players during the barnstorming phase. According to historian James Elfers, "Studious John 'Chief' Meyers was as quiet as ['Laughing Larry'] Doyle was loud."[74] Meyers certainly knew what it was like to be at the center of fan curiosity. However, unlike other players, who relished fans making a fuss over them, Meyers did not. Invariably, the attention included insensitive comments on and questions about his Indian heritage.

The newlywed Jim Thorpe and his wife Iva made the whole trip, but apparently it did not go well for them. On more than one occasion, McGraw lectured Thorpe for doing so much drinking and card playing he was neglecting his wife.[75]

After leaving the tour the Meyers went directly to Riverside to visit Jack's aging mother, Felicité, and other members of his family and apparently planned to spend the winter on their farm near Riverside. However, Will Palmer convinced Meyers and Jeff Tesreau to join his San Diego Bears in the eight-team Southern California Winter Association. The Bears owner advertized Meyers and Tesreau as "the greatest winter league battery that ever exhibited on any team." According to an account in the San Diego press, Meyers "used his 'war club' to beat the Mathies of Los Angeles into submission" in the opening game.[76]

Meyers and his Giants teammates undoubtedly followed closely the emergence of the Federal League during the 1913-1914 off season.[77] The new rival professional baseball circuit worked hard to attract National and American League players to teams in established major league cities (Chicago, St. Louis, Pittsburgh, Brooklyn) and cities without teams (Indianapolis, Kansas City, Baltimore, and Buffalo). Mostly younger players and a few aging stars like Albert Bender and Mordecai "Three Finger" Brown signed in response to huge offers. Walter Johnson agreed to play for the Federal League team in Chicago, but withdrew from the contract when the Washington Senators made a large counter offer.

Aware of plans for the new league, the Giants moved to head off desertions by signing players to new two- or three-year contracts at substantial pay raises. Meyers may have been considering Federal League offers into the 1914 season, because he did not sign a new three-year deal with the Giants until April 30.[78] Relief pitcher Doc Crandall, back-up catcher Art Wilson, and promising young outfielder Claude Cooper were the only Giants to bolt to the new league. Christy Mathewson was nearing the end of his career, but the Federal League owners clearly wanted to sign him because of the credibility and integrity he would bring. They made a huge offer, but Matty instead inked a new contract with the Giants paying him $12,000 a year. McGraw was offered $100,000 to jump to the Federals, but fearing the new league might destroy professional baseball he rejected the lucrative deal.

If Meyers was reading the papers during the Christmas holidays in 1913 he saw obituaries for Louis Sockalexis, the first Native American major league baseball player who had acknowledged his heritage. Sockalexis died on Christmas Eve, 1913. Like Meyers and other Native American major leaguers,

Sockalexis, who played for only three years with Cleveland, knew the sting of racist taunts and demeaning stereotypes. Like Jim Thorpe and Albert Bender, but in contrast to Meyers, Sockalexis turned to drinking to excess to deaden the pain. As biographer Brian McDonald put it, Sockalexis "flushed away his talent in a river of alcohol."[79] Within a year of being let go by Cleveland, he was living on the streets, begging for money to buy liquor. In his final years Socaklexis returned to the Penobscot reservation in Maine and found some peace in teaching children to play baseball, but, weakened by years of alcoholism, he died of heart failure at the age of 42.

# EIGHT

# Final Years in Baseball (1914–1920)

## The 1914 Pre-Season: Befriending a Stranger

By 1914 John Tortes Meyers had become one of the best hitters in the major leagues. Impressively, he was among only 26 players who had hit .350 or better at least once between 1901 and 1913.

Though his past success made him eager for the 1914 season to begin, Meyers was deeply concerned about the welfare of the Cahuilla people living on the Santa Rosa and other reservations in southern California. During the winter a famine struck the reservations. Cahuilla women, perhaps including Meyers's mother Felicité, who was known to be a skilled basket maker, were making and selling their wares to tourists in order to earn much-needed cash to support those on the reservations without resources. Some of their baskets were sent to New York to be sold by the American Indian League, a charitable organization. They were advertised as "specimens of the basket work foreign observers have said is the only genuine American art." Without naming the Cahuilla, the *New York Times* reported, "[T]he present sale is for the benefit of three tribes—to one of which Chief Meyers, the Giant catcher, belongs."[1]

After spending the winter in California, Meyers, accompanied by his wife Anna, arrived at the 1914 Giants spring training camp in Marlin, Texas, on the 22nd of February, complaining about the cold weather. Meyers delivered the news that Giants catcher Art Wilson was going to report to a Federal League team. Meyers added, perhaps not entirely truthfully, he never considered leaving the Giants himself for the new league.[2]

Not having seen the Giants third baseman Art "Tillie" Shafer all winter, Meyers was unsure whether Shafer would report to Marlin, though he knew Matty had been "working on him." The Giants would later learn Shafer had left the team for good. He may be the only player ever to have been driven from major league baseball by fan mail. Twenty-four and single in 1913, Shafer often received scented letters from female fans, which he refused to open and let pile up in the clubhouse. Throughout the 1913 season other Giants players were unrelenting in their teasing of Shafer, a Notre Dame graduate who had first played for the Giants in 1909. Despite playing regularly and batting .287 in 1913, Shafer never returned to the Giants or to major league baseball after going home to Los Angeles at the end of the 1913 season.[3]

It was still too cold for baseball the day after Meyers reported, so the Giants played medicine ball, handball, and football. Half a dozen Giants had played football in college so some elaborate plays were run. Having been soured by his brief foray into football at Dartmouth a decade earlier, Meyers joined in the handball contest instead and displayed, according to a witness, "considerable agility."[4] With John McGraw still on the round-the-world tour, former major leaguer Ed Kinsella was serving as the acting Giants skipper.

At 4:00 A.M. the next morning Emilio Palmero, a left-handed pitcher, arrived in Marlin after traveling from his native Cuba. Knowing what it was like to be a newcomer from a different culture, Meyers befriended the Cuban. Since the Giants catcher had grown up speaking Spanish as well as English and Palmero spoke very little English, Meyers served as his interpreter, introducing Palmero to the 16 other players in camp. The Cahuilla catcher even furnished a uniform for the young pitcher, although the diminutive Palmero was swallowed up in the catcher's much larger outfit.[5]

In an early March exhibition game against Dallas, Meyers batted against an Indian pitcher named Scott who had just broken into professional baseball. Aware they were watching a contest between two Indians, the fans gave louder than normal ear-splitting war whoops when each player stepped to the plate. A reporter present noted that Scott seemed flustered by the deafening shouts, but "Chief Meyers [was] familiar with war whoop greetings on the big league circuit [and] was quite at home when said noises greeted him."[6]

When McGraw finally joined the team late in the 1914 pre-season, the Giants manager once again demonstrated his ability to judge baseball talent. After seeing a 19-year-old lefthander named George Herman Ruth pitch in an exhibition game, McGraw extracted a promise from an old friend, manager-owner Jack Dunn of the International League's Baltimore Orioles, to give the Giants the first chance to buy the talented young hurler. Writers had already nicknamed Ruth "Dunn's baby" or simply "Babe." Three months later, without contacting McGraw, Dunn offered Connie Mack and the Philadelphia Athletics the opportunity to purchase Babe Ruth's contract. The parsimonious Mack demurred and referred Dunn to the Red Sox, who eagerly bought the rights to the pitching prospect.[7]

# The 1914 Season: On Display — Indians in Wild West Shows and the Major Leagues

Oddsmakers made the Giants heavy favorites to win a fourth straight pennant in 1914, but the New Yorkers stumbled out of the gate. McGraw's team lost the first two games at Philadelphia and a third game to Brooklyn, which had signed Wilbert Robinson as manager after McGraw fired him. The Brooklyn team had been known since 1899 as the Superbas, after a Brooklyn vaudeville troupe. In 1911 they added the moniker Dodgers, probably because it was a name associated with Brooklynites, who had to "dodge" trolley cars as they crossed the maze of lines in the borough. Soon after Robinson became manager in 1914 the Brooklyn team was also dubbed the "Robins." Sparked by their sensational outfielder Zack Wheat, the Brooklyn club, long the doormat of the National League, improved dramatically under Robinson's steady leadership.

According to the *New York Times*, the Giants April 23 home opener attracted "25,000 persons and several Indians, all of a whom had a nice time and crowed themselves hoarse just because the Giants buried the Quakers [a popular nickname at the time for the Philadelphia Phillies] under a 12-to-4 defeat."

The Indians, whom the *Times* apparently did not consider persons, were identified as "Chief Man-Afraid-of-His-Mother-in-Law and Chief Punish-the-Firewater, from the Wild West Show [and] several of their braves." The author of the article drew the two Indian ballplayers on the Giants into his stereotypical circle, noting, "Chief Meyers and Jim Thorpe tried to talk to the aborigines, but they learned that they didn't belong to the same lodge."[8]

Wild West shows peaked in popularity while John Tortes Meyers was playing major league baseball. The portrayal of Indians in these shows caused controversy at the time and continues to spark debate today. Dozens of shows flourished. Most popular were the Buffalo Bill Cody and Pawnee Bill shows. Both featured re-creations of famous scenes such as Indians attacking the cavalry in General George Custer's Battle of the Little Big Bighorn of 1876.

Cody, Pawnee Bill, and other Wild West show entrepreneurs contended their displays portrayed Indians as worthy adversaries and promoted respect and understanding for the noble warriors who once roamed the west. They also maintained that employment of Indians in their shows was helping ease the transition of a once proud and capable people to life in a market economy.

However, early twentieth-century advocates of assimilation were critical of Wild West shows for their stereotypical portrayal of Indians as savages incapable of being civilized. In 1913 Chauncey Yellow Robe, a Lakota reformer

Throughout Meyers's baseball career, "wild west shows" were popular. Virtually every show, as in this scene in a 1905 Pawnee Bill show, featured the "heroic death" of General George Armstrong Custer in 1876 at the hands of "savage" Indian warriors. Meyers liked paintings of Custer's death because he felt they depicted one of the only fair breaks Indians ever received (Library of Congress, Prints & Photographs Division, LC-USZ62-112856).

and member of the Society of American Indians, was asked what benefit Indians were deriving from Wild West shows. "None but what are degrading, demoralizing, and degenerating," he answered. It was inconsistent, most reformers argued, for the government to support programs seeking to civilize Indians while allowing Indians to join Wild West shows that were glorifications of the savage lifestyle they needed to leave behind.[9] Not all agreed. Meyers's predecessor at Dartmouth, Charles Eastman, for example, spoke approvingly of Wild West shows, noting "the circus tent and sawdust arena were often the only venues available to Indians for presenting themselves to general audiences."[10]

   This same disagreement is evident in modern discussions of "show Indians." Most modern historians contend that Wild West shows contributed to the perpetuation of negative stereotypes of Native Americans. However, on the basis of his own thorough study of the Wild West shows, L. G. Moses has offered a more affirming perspective, concluding that "show Indians" were not so much "representatives of an extinct civilization" as "one in transition." Moses argues the Indians in Wild West shows were, in their performances, taking a stand for the right of Indians to represent themselves in ways they and their children could celebrate.[11]

Historian Philip Deloria has taken a more nuanced view, suggesting "show Indians" and Native American athletes like Meyers, Bender, and Thorpe inspired both "racial repulsion" and "racial desire" in the white audiences before whom they performed. As representatives of a "savage race" overcome by the superior European civilization, Indians performing in the Wild West arena or on the athletic field were viewed with disgust expressed in negative images of primitivism. According to Deloria, as objects of "racial desire," the two groups called forth more admiring, but different, stereotypical reactions. Indians in Wild West Shows (re)enacted a recent but now bygone and already idealized historical time when great and noble Indian warriors roamed the west. By contrast, athletes like Bender and Meyers called to mind for white audiences an also lost but even more romanticized, mythic time of physical prowess "when natural men walked the earth."[12]

By the 1960s the Wild West shows were gone, but the stereotypical portrayal of Indians in motion pictures persisted. John Tortes Meyers indicated to Lawrence Ritter in his 1964 interview that he did not think the situation had changed as he watched western movies on television[13]:

> In those days, you know, the Indian was in the position of a minority group. Still is, for that matter. Nowadays, you can't ridicule an Irishman on the television, you can't ridicule a Jew, and you can't ridicule a Negro. But they can kill us all the time — make everything out of us they want. Every night you see them on the television — killing us Indians. That's all they do.

Meyers knew what it was like to be stereotypically labeled and objectified, though he was in greater control over the performances in which he was taking part as a major league ballplayer than the Indians on display in the scripted mock battles of Wild West shows or in the movies.

For the most part, as the 1914 season got under way, Meyers let his bat do his talking. The *New York Times* headlined its report on the Giants' May 9 victory over the Boston Braves, "Chief Meyers's Bat Wins for New York." In the game Meyers laced a scorching drive to the right field wall, driving in the only two runs of the game.[14]

By Independence Day the Giants had a record of 40 wins and 24 losses and were two games ahead of Chicago. However, weaknesses were apparent in the New York lineup. Meyers was one of the few consistent hitters. One report called him a "Dead Shot Dick" who used his bat as a rifle.[15]

As one of the elders on the 1914 Giants Meyers did his best to take that role seriously. He tried to motivate Marquard, whose pitching was erratic, telling a reporter in early August Rube was once again pitching the kind of ball that helped him to win a record 19 straight decisions two years earlier. "He has that hop on his fast once again and that is all he needs," Meyers was quoted as saying.[16] However, it was to no avail. Marquard suffered 12 straight losses and finished the season with a disappointing record of 12–22.

Indeed, Meyers tried to fire up all his teammates, commenting to another reporter, "[B]aseball is a game of equalization and ... in the long run all things about even themselves up." The Cahuilla belief in the harmony of opposing forces in life likely informed his sense of the balancing out of ups and downs through a long baseball season. Meyers predicted that since the Giants had not won a number of games in a row, they would soon have a run of wins to surge ahead in the pennant race.[17]

Meyers was continuing to do his part on the field. In a July 23 game he was 3-for-4 in a Giants rout of Cincinnati, 13 to 4. However, the lead story of the 1914 National League pennant race was the miraculous finish of the Boston Braves. They were in last place on the Fourth of July and then began one of the most sensational turnarounds in major league history. Known to major league historians as the "Miracle Team," the Braves rose as the Giants faded.

When the Giants took on the Braves in a September 7 doubleheader in Boston, the two teams were tied for the lead. A total of 70,000 fans were present for the games. After taking the first game, 5 to 4, the Braves were briefly in first place by themselves. The Giants won the second game, moving the two teams back into a tie.

However, the Giants could not keep pace with the Braves, and even Meyers's bat cooled off. On October 1 the Braves clinched the pennant, beating the Giants 7 to 6 at the Polo Grounds. Despite a record of 84 wins and 70 losses (the 12th straight year they had finished above .500) the Giants ended the 1914 campaign 10½ games behind the first-place Braves. Mathewson completed his 12th straight season of winning 20 or more games for the Giants, with a record of 24–13. It would be his last.

Meyers finished the 1914 season with a respectable .286 batting average. He appeared in 134 games, the most of any season of his career, with 381 at-bats (second only to his 391 in 1911). He scored 33 runs and had 135 total bases. His 109 hits included 13 doubles, five triples, and one home run. He drove in 55 runs and stole four bases.[18]

For the fourth consecutive season Meyers appears on the STATS, Inc. National League All-Star Team. The only other Giant on the 1914 STATS team is Jeff Tesreau, who had a record of 26 wins and 10 losses and a 2.37 ERA.[19]

During the 1914 season baseball writer William Connelly compiled what he considered to be "the greatest baseball team of all history." Based on an analysis of a combination of hitting and fielding, Connelly chose John J. Clements, long-time Phillies catcher, and John Tortes Meyers for the catcher's position. Others on his all-time best team included A. G. Spalding and C. Mathewson (pitchers), D. Brouthers (first base), N. Lajoie (second base), J. F. Baker (third base), J. Wagner (shortstop), E. Delahanty (left field), T. Cobb (center field), J. Jackson (right field).[20]

In 1914, for the first time since 1910, the Giants and Meyers did not appear in the World Series. After the season the Giants and Yankees played their second (and last) series of city exhibition games. The Giants won all four, attended by a total of only 40,000 fans, who jeered the Giants mercilessly. McGraw did not even show up for the games, choosing instead to watch the Braves–Athletics World Series.

With his mother Felicité in failing health, Meyers returned to his Cahuilla homeland and spent the rest of the off-season on his farm near Riverside. There is no record of his participation in any California exhibition or winter league games.

## The 1915 Pre-Season: Threat from the Federal League

With players jumping to the Federal League and attendance in the National and American Leagues falling in 1914, the owners agreed to trim regular rosters from 25 to 21 players for the 1915 season. The new league was still courting McGraw. However, out of a sense of loyalty to the Giants, the National League, and baseball, McGraw again rejected all offers. He also fought successfully to keep Rube Marquard, who had agreed to walk away from his Giants contract to sign with the Brooklyn Tip Tops of the Federal League.

After their swoon at the end of the 1914 season the Giants abandoned their violet trim and chose to emulate the Philadelphia A's' conical white caps with dark blue horizontal stripes, and dark blue stockings. The pinstripes on the uniforms were also switched from vertical to horizontal, creating the impression to some observers of a group of convicts rather than ballplayers.[21]

Meyers arrived at the Giants training camp in Marlin on February 27, 1915. Reflecting the growing threat that the United States might soon become embroiled in the Great War underway in Europe, the two Giants practice teams were called the Leather Necks and Flat Feet after enlisted men in the Marines and the Navy.[22]

The Giants tried to strengthen their line up by acquiring pitcher "Polly" Perritt from St. Louis and veteran third baseman Hans Lobert from Philadelphia. McGraw told reporters he expected Larry Doyle and Chief Meyers to return to their former hitting excellence after falling off in 1914.[23]

## The 1915 Season: Last Year with the Giants

Doyle and Meyers did not disappoint their manager in the April 14 opening game of the 1915 season at the Polo Grounds. Larry Doyle went 5-for-5 as the Giants manhandled the Robins, 16 to 3. Meyers got the game off to a good start in the top of the first when he tagged out a Brooklyn runner at the plate on a throw from left field. He then drove in two runs with a single in the bottom of the inning. Meyers also doubled to right in the sixth and scored. McGraw gave Jim Thorpe a rare start and he was 1-for-5 with a double.

The next day Rube Marquard totally silenced the Brooklyn bats as he threw a no-hitter, and the season was off to a promising start. However, the Giants' hopes were soon dashed. Mathewson lost the next game, and the Giants were defeated in ten of their next 11 contests.

The Giants slid into last place, and a frustrated McGraw forbade players to take their wives on a trip west in May. He also ordered players not to have as much as one glass of beer. Particularly hard hit by that ruling was "Long Larry" McLean. Though the catcher had a reputation as a problem player who could not stay sober, McGraw liked McLean's work in the 1913 World Series, when, after the injury to Meyers, he caught four games and batted .500. Through the 1914 season McLean had not caused problems, but that changed when he got drunk one evening in St. Louis early in the 1915 campaign and angrily accused McGraw of breaking a promise to pay him a $1,000 bonus for good behavior. When McGraw told him to be quiet and go to bed, McLean lunged at his manager and had to be restrained. McGraw immediately suspended the lanky catcher and ignored McLean's tearful entreaties for reinstatement. His dismissal meant Meyers would bear more of the catching responsibilities for the Giants until a replacement could be found. McLean never played in the majors again and was shot dead by a Boston saloonkeeper in a brawl six years later.[24]

Meyers did his best to fill the void and arouse his dispirited teammates with aggressive play. The Giants were struggling with an 18–24 record, when, at a June 14 game in Cincinnati, Meyers stood his ground as Reds third baseman Tommy Leach tried to run over him in a play at the plate. Leach got the worst of the collision and was out cold for several minutes.

However, the Giants were unable to mount sustained rallies and remained stuck below .500. A June 30 game against Brooklyn at Ebbets Field, which had become the Dodgers' home in 1913, was typical. Described by one sportswriter as being "like a visit to the dentist, painful but over quickly," the 7 to 0 pounding lasted only one hour and 18 minutes. Meyers was off his game, throwing a ball into center field on a double steal, allowing a run to score.[25]

The 1915 Giants rarely gave their fans much to cheer about except for the odd game, such as their 4 to 3 comeback win over the hated Cubs at the Polo Grounds in mid–July. The Chicago team was cruising toward a win, but, as one writer described the game, "summ[ed] up the poultry before they were out of the incubator." With the Cubs leading 3–0 in the eighth, Meyers led off and reached first after being hit by a pitch. As was his well-established custom late in games, McGraw lifted his slow-footed catcher for a pinch-runner. The Giants scored twice in the inning and won the game in the ninth.[26]

In a game a week later against the Cardinals at the Polo Grounds, Meyers showed his grit, and the fans responded as they did throughout his career by

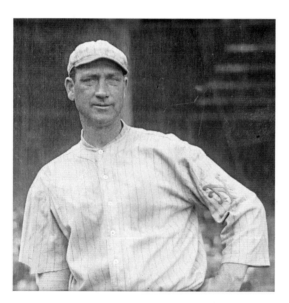

linking his determined play to the "Indian warrior" stereotype. With the bases loaded and two out, and the Giants trailing 3 to 1, the injured catcher "limped into the game as a pinch-hitter and the big stands resounded with all the war-whoops of every Indian tribe in the books." However, Meyers rolled to third, ending the contest.[27]

Veteran Larry McLean, shown here in a 1913 photograph, joined the Giants that year to back up Meyers at catcher, and starred in the 1913 Series after replacing Meyers, who had sustained an injury before the second game. After a violent encounter with John McGraw, McLean was released by the Giants in 1915 and died five years later in a barroom brawl (Library of Congress, Prints & Photographs Division, LC-DIG-ggbain-14752).

Hustling and playing hurt were not enough for McGraw to keep Meyers or any player on the Giants roster. McGraw had always been willing to trade his best players, even if they were still productive, if he thought they were beginning to fade in their abilities. The first indication the 1915 season would be

Meyers's last with the Giants came in August with the report that McGraw was planning "to do a Connie Mack" and clean house with the Giants lineup.[28] On the chopping block in addition to Meyers were Fred Snodgrass and Rube Marquard.

Meyers's fate was secured when McGraw acquired fleetfooted catcher Charley Dooin from the Reds on July 5. Though justified in order to provide support for Meyers after the dismissal of Larry McLean, the acquisition of Dooin was a bitter pill for Meyers to swallow. According to one account, the Reds catcher had been able to taunt Meyers and "get his goat" with racial slurs when Dooin was still with the Reds. The journalist describing the incidents chided Meyers for not being able to take the good-natured "kidding."[29]

Perhaps aroused by the impending shake-up, the Giants showed they were not quite ready to give up on the season. They won a September 6 doubleheader with the Boston Braves. Meyers's hitting surge continued as he blasted a four-bagger into the left field bleachers in the fifth inning of the second game, his only home run during the 1915 season.

However, the Giants could not sustain the effort. They lost nine of the next ten games and by the end of September were in the National League cellar. Only 200 spectators were present at the Polo Grounds for a September 30 match-up with the Giants losing to the Robins 2 to 0. The mood on the team turned ugly. Nineteen Giants and McGraw were ejected from the nightcap of a doubleheader defeat at Pittsburgh. After another doubleheader loss in Boston, McGraw pulled a knife on a rowdy fan.

The Giants ended the 1915 season in last place in the National League for only the second time during the Deadball Era. Their record of 69 wins and 83 losses left them 21 games behind the pennant-winning Phillies.

The rumors that Meyers was about to be traded to the Brooklyn Robins heated up in December 1915. One writer claimed, "[A] deal practically is complete for the transfer of Catcher Jack Meyers by the Giants to the Dodgers. While John McGraw and the Indian have not agreed, [Brooklyn Manager Wilbert] Robinson believes Jack would be a great help in developing his pitchers."[30]

It was true Meyers's production had fallen off, but virtually all the Giants were playing poorly. Only Larry Doyle, who finished the season with a .320 average, was performing up to expectation. Meyers appeared in 110 games in 1915, the fewest since 1909, and batted only .232, more than 50 points lower than in 1914 and more than 130 points off his 1912 high of .358. His 289 atbats were also his lowest since 1909. He scored only 24 runs on 67 hits, with 90 total bases. His hits included ten doubles, five triples, and a single home run. He drove in only 26 runs.[31]

An article published after the 1915 season, entitled "The Sunset Race," lamented the fading away of the Indian ballplayer and reflected the "vanishing American" stereotype commonly applied to Indians at the time. It noted that as recently as 1913 Indians were playing a vital role in the national game. Chief Bender and Chief Meyers were leading lights, and others like Jim Thorpe, Jim Bluejacket, and Chief Johnson showed promise. Just two years later Bender and Meyers were fading, Thorpe was in the minors, and the other two were largely forgotten. The article suggested the following image for the fate of Indians in major league baseball: "the last Red star has set in the midnight sky."[32]

By 1915 the situation for Indians in general in the United States was increasingly dire. For a quarter-century allotment programs had decimated tribal lands across the country by breaking up communally held land, distributing parts of it to individual Indians, and selling the rest as "surplus land." Many Native Americans were being forced to try to survive on small, often unproductive, acreages. Schools both on and off reservations and missionaries had relentlessly worked to force Indians into the mold of the white man's image of the "good Indian."

The pressure for Indians to assimilate to the dominant culture was at its peak, as reflected in "competency commissions" instituted in 1915 by Commissioner of Indian Affairs Cato Sells. Their purpose was to declare Indians, on a case-by-case basis, competent or incompetent to run their own business affairs. If the judgment was "incompetent," a legal guardian was appointed to help the person. "Competent" Indians were encouraged to go through a citizenship ceremony in which the Secretary of the Interior called each applicant forward by his white name, handed him a bow and told him to shoot an arrow. Then the Secretary would say, "You have shot your last arrow. That means you are no longer to live the life of an Indian. You are from this day forward to live the life of the white man. But you may keep the arrow; it will be to you a symbol of your noble race and the pride you feel that you come from the first of all Americans." The applicant was told to put his hand on a plow as a symbol of the choice to live as a white man, by the sweat of his brow. Finally, the "competent" Indian was given a U.S. flag, a badge with the inscription "A Citizen of the United States," and a purse to remind him the money he earned by his labor was his alone and must be wisely spent."[33]

In response to the reports that Meyers was about to be released and picked up by the Brooklyn Robins, tributes to his impact on the Giants and laments about his departure appeared. One writer claimed, "Next to Mathewson and McGraw himself there has been no more notable figure with the modern day Giants than Jack Meyers, the Indian catcher, and there is nothing more significant of the gradual breaking up of the National League's most famous team than his release to Brooklyn."[34]

**John McGraw traded Meyers (here shown in a Dodgers uniform) to Brooklyn in 1916, where he joined what he called a "crippled up" club (Library of Congress, Prints & Photographs Division, LC-DIG-ggbain-22979).**

By February 1916, it was official. John Tortes Meyers had played his last game with the Giants. "The Indian was purchased," according to one report, "at the waiver price by the Brooklyns ... much to the delight of Wilbert Robinson." Dodgers owner Charles Ebbets picked up Meyers's $6,000 contract from the Giants. Apparently, Meyers had paid a visit to Ebbets Field and told the owner "he would show McGraw and the Giants that he still could catch and hit."[35] However, writing in *Baseball Magazine* W. A. Phelon questioned Ebbets's decision, claiming, "The Chief is fading, and he draws a "gigantic salary."[36]

## The 1916 Season: Joining "An Old Crippled-Up Club"

Meyers reported to Brooklyn's Florida spring training camp in March 1916, joining ex–Giants Rube Marquard and Fred Merkle and reuniting with Brooklyn skipper Wilbert Robinson. As Meyers recalled, "[Robinson] didn't have to do much managing ... because it was a team of veterans. Nap Rucker, Jake Daubert, Jack Coombs, Rube, Zack Wheat, Hi Myers—we'd all been around a long time. And, of course, Casey Stengel. He was one of the few younger ones on that team." Meyers jokingly called the 1916 Robins "an old crippled-up club."[37]

By 1916 Zack Wheat was regarded as one of the best outfielders in base-ball. He was also a Native American. Wheat's mother was a full-blooded Cherokee and his father was of Euroamerican descent. Unlike Meyers, however, Wheat chose to hide his Indian heritage, and thus largely avoided the nickname "Chief" and the constant "war whoops" and slurs Meyers, Bender, and other Native American major leaguers endured.

However, Wheat could not completely avoid being stereotyped in the same way as other Indians. A 1917 article heralding Wheat as the "most grace-ful of outfielders," attributed his talents to the "instincts of the warrior and huntsman" he inherited as an Indian. "With his crude ideas of civilization, the early chiefs of the New World forest left ordinary tasks to the women of the tribe," the article claimed. "The men concerned themselves solely with the excitements of the chase and grimmer excitements of war." Hence, Indian athletes like Wheat (who has "a liberal portion of Indian blood in his veins") naturally possessed "keenness of eye, speed of foot and strength of arm.... He is the most easy and graceful of fielders because it is natural for him to be so. The lithe muscles, the panther-like motions of the Indian are his by divine right."[38]

Eight years younger than Meyers, Wheat was able to have a much longer career, remaining with the Dodgers for 18 seasons (1909–26). Though he threw right-handed, he was a natural left-handed batter. In 14 seasons his average was over .300. In 1916, the first year Meyers played with him, Wheat hit in 29 consecutive games and batted .312. In 1918 Wheat won the National League batting title with a .335 average. Wheat was so good at hitting curve balls that John McGraw instructed his pitchers not to throw hooks to the Dodgers slugger any more.

Wheat still holds the Dodgers all-time club records for most games (2,322), at-bats (8,859), hits (2,804) doubles, triples, and total bases. With the advent of a lively ball, Wheat's batting average soared to .375 in 1923 and 1924. When he finished his major league career with the Philadelphia Athletics in 1927, he had a lifetime batting average of .317. In addition to his reputation as a hitter he was also heralded as an outstanding outfielder. Known as "165 pounds of scrap iron, rawhide, and guts," in 1959 Zack Wheat was elected by the Veterans Committee to the Baseball Hall of Fame. He died in 1972, a year after Meyers.[39]

It was Wheat who recommended the Robins sign one of his old friends from Kansas City, another legendary player who would become a good friend of Meyers. As a youth Wheat had played basketball with the prospect, a profi-cient minor league outfielder named Charles Dillon Stengel, better known then as "Dutch," and later as "Casey" (after K.C., for Kansas City). Stengel joined the Dodgers in 1912 and remained with the Brooklynites for six years.

On the 1916 National League champion Brooklyn Dodgers Meyers teamed with a young Casey Stengel (far left) and another Native American star, Hall of Famer Zack Wheat (far right). Next to Stengel is Jimmy Johnston; Hy Myers is next to Wheat (Library of Congress, Prints & Photographs Division, LC-DIG-ggbain-22985).

An excellent defensive outfielder, Stengel was also a solid hitter and had one of his best years at the plate in 1916, batting .279. Meyers credited Stengel with Brooklyn's success in 1916, saying, "It was Casey who kept us on our toes. He was the life of the party and kept us old-timers pepped up all season."[40]

The Dodgers finished third in 1915, and because of the age of the players were not given much chance to compete for the National League title in 1916. However, Robinson, a one-time major league catcher himself, thought the addition of Meyers would be a critical factor in making the Dodgers dangerous as pennant contenders. While serving as a coach with the Giants, the Dodgers manager had seen for himself Meyers's ability to work effectively with pitchers. Robinson also believed a largely veteran pitching staff would work well with Meyers.[41]

Robinson was renowned for his ability to keep his team loose. During spring training in 1916 he agreed to catch a baseball dropped from a biplane circling the practice field. However, the pilot, aviatrix Ruth Law, forgot to bring a baseball (or, some say, intentionally neglected to pick up a ball) and dropped a grapefruit from 500 feet instead. Wearing a chest protector, Robbie circled under the falling object, which hit his catcher's mitt and bounded onto his chest, knocking him down. The grapefruit exploded, showering the Dodgers manager with warm juice, and he cried out, "Jesus, I'm hit! Help me, lads. I'm covered with my own blood." Meyers and his new teammates roared with laughter.[42]

As fate would have it, the Robins' first game of the season, on April 19, 1916, was against the Giants, and Brooklyn won 7 to 3. Meyers was the star, as the *New York Times* reported[43]:

> Chief Meyers was told by the Giants that as a major league ball player he was through. Yesterday was the first opportunity to show McGraw he was wrong in selling him. The Chief did some nice work behind the plate, but what pleased him most was the fact that he got a crashing double in the seventh inning that paved the way for the run which tied the game.

Brooklyn took the league lead after beating the Phillies 2 to 0 in a May 4 game. Meyers was 1-for-3 and drove in the second run in the two-run fifth.

As Uncle Robbie predicted, Meyers was a key factor in the Robins' success, both offensively and defensively. Three games in June demonstrate his impact. In a June 5 victory, 3 to 2, against the Pirates, Meyers made a key defensive play, tagging out a runner at the plate in the sixth inning. He also drove in a crucial run on a long double in the second inning. In a 14-inning game against the Cardinals five days later Meyers kept the Giants in the game, driving in a run. The legendary Rogers Hornsby, who began his career with St. Louis in 1915, was in the lineup. An intentional walk to Meyers in the 11th inning in a June 17 win over the Cubs turned out to be the decisive play. With a man on second Cubs manager Joe Tinker called for the pass after Meyers had scorched a ball just foul along the third base line. However, Robins pitcher Jack Coombs singled in the run to win the game.

Despite his devastating hitting one writer could not resist penning a piece of doggerel about Meyers's lack of speed on the base paths[44]:

> What is so rare a day in June,
> When, in the thick of the pennant chase,
> We lamp the sport sheet and nearly swoon
> To read, "Chief Meyers has swiped a base."

While Meyers was helping the Dodgers in their pennant drive, he also testified as a witness in a highly publicized New York court case pitting members of two controversial new religious movements against one another.[45] The plaintiff in the $250,000 civil suit was Mrs. Brownie Rathbone Weaverson. Mrs. Weaverson (age 64), a believer in the Mazdaznan religion, accused Mrs. Caroline Frame (age 72), a Christian Scientist, of "alienation of affection" for allegedly convincing Weaverson's husband (age 52) to move into Mrs. Frame's apartment in the guise of working with him to promote Christian Science.

In her defense, Mrs. Frame's attorney claimed Mrs. Weaverson lost the affections of her husband when she took up with the founder and leader of the Mazdaznan "cult," the Rev. Dr. Otoman Zar-Adhusht Hanish.

In his testimony during the trial Meyers acknowledged that he and his wife Anna were close friends with Mrs. Weaverson, who was known as "Mother" among her fellow Mazdaznans and for a time played a key role in the religion. That he was called to testify in her behalf during the trial raises the question of whether one or both of the Meyers were followers of Mazdaznanism, an eclectic religion with roots in the Zoroastrian religion of ancient Persia, but also having Hindu and Christian elements. Its practices focus on awareness of God's mysterious power present in all of life through "a discipline of breath control, rhythmic praying and chanting ... supplemented by a recommended vegetarian diet."[46]

Though formally Roman Catholic throughout his life, and, according to his grandnephew, agnostic in his personal beliefs,[47] Meyers may have found the Mazdaznan emphasis on personal discipline and responsibility compatible

Meyers met his wife Anna, identified (left) in this 1916 photograph as "Mrs. Chief Meyers," in St. Paul in 1908. The two were married in 1909 or 1910 and remained together until the 1930s. Seated at right is the wife of Meyers's Dodgers teammate, Larry Cheney (Library of Congress, Prints & Photographs Division, LC-DIG-ggbain-22472).

with similar principles in his own Cahuilla heritage. In addition, the Mazdaznan emphasis on a mysterious power that can be drawn on in addressing
life's challenges may have reminded him of the Cahuilla teaching of ʔivaʔa.

By July 1916, Meyers's excellent performance on the diamond was creating a national stir. Calling him "the college bred aborigine," a story on the
wires chided McGraw for "discarding" the catcher and claimed "the Chief has
accomplished a wonderful come back and is an idol in Brooklyn today."[48]

In late July Christy Mathewson, who in 1916 had become player/manager
of the Cincinnati Reds, made his first appearance at Ebbets Field before 20,000
enthusiastic fans. The Dodgers lost the first game of the doubleheader, 6–1,
but won the second game, 3–2. In the first game Rube Marquard was on the
mound with Meyers catching. In the second inning Meyers ended a Reds rally
by catching a runner napping off first. He tied the score in the bottom of the
inning, driving in the Robins' only run with a single to center, scoring Casey
Stengel.

Down the stretch both Meyers and Wheat were critical to Brooklyn's
success. In an August 15 win, 5 to 1, the Robins played like "coming champions," taking advantage of every opportunity allowed by the Pittsburgh nine.
Wheat collected two doubles and a triple and "Chief Meyers regained his batting eye," recording a single and a double.[49]

However, plagued by injuries and weak hitting the Robins faded. The
Phillies took first place after five victories over the Brooklyn team in September, including two by their ace, Grover Cleveland Alexander. After sliding
into third place, the Robins rallied due to timely hitting by Stengel and Wheat,
and Robinson's skilled use of the "scientific game" he learned from John
McGraw to scratch out runs. They regained the lead, winning a crucial September 30 game against the Phillies and Alexander.

As though planned by the baseball gods, the 1916 National League pennant race came down to the last series of the season, a four-game set at Ebbets
Field, matching the old friends, now bitter rivals, McGraw and Robinson.
The Giants had come from nowhere to challenge for the pennant, winning a
major league record 26 consecutive games in September. However, the Giants
were unable to catch Brooklyn and Philadelphia.

The Robins won the two first games of their season-ending series with
New York, and, with the Braves sweeping the Phillies in a doubleheader,
Brooklyn had secured first place with two games left to play. The pennant-
clinching game raised some serious questions. New York took a 3–0 lead but
then played with little enthusiasm. One writer in attendance called the game
a "farce," claiming the Giants had "little snap in their play." With the Robins
leading 6–5 in the sixth, McGraw suddenly stormed off the field and refused
to manage the remaining two games. The Dodgers scored three more runs

and won the game, 9–6. When he caught a fly for the final out, the normally restrained Zack Wheat tossed the ball into the stands and joined Meyers and his other teammates as they snake-danced into the clubhouse.

Some who saw the game speculated that the Giants were taking it easy in deference to former teammates Chief Meyers, Rube Marquard, and Fred Merkle, all now playing for the Robins. Others said it was as a result of the Giants' hard feelings against Philadelphia because the Phillies spoiled the Giants' pennant chances with late-season victories. Still others claimed McGraw was angry because he placed a large bet that the Giants would finish at least third in the pennant race, and with their final-week collapse, they slipped into fourth behind the Dodgers, Phillies, and Braves.

After reporters told Robinson that McGraw had called the Giants "quitters," the Dodgers manager laughed and said, "That's a lot of shit. That's a joke. The fact is, we're a better ball club, and McGraw knows it. We outclassed them. We beat the Giants fifteen times in twenty-two games. Tell McGraw to stop pissing on my pennant."[50]

Brooklyn finished the 1916 season with a record of 94 wins, 60 losses, and two ties, 2½ games ahead of the Phillies, four games ahead of the Braves, and seven games in front of the fourth-place Giants. The hitting star for the Robins was Zack Wheat, who finished with a .312 batting average, an on-base percentage of .366, and a slugging percentage of .461.

Meyers played in 80 games during the 1916 season, with 239 at-bats, 24 runs, 67 hits (including ten doubles, three triples and no home runs), and 90 total bases. He drove in only 21 runs, the lowest total in his major league career. However, he did raise his batting average of the previous year (.232) to .247.[51]

## The 1916 World Series: Casey and the Babe

By 1916 John Tortes Meyers had already appeared in three World Series with the Giants (1911, 1912, 1913), but the New Yorkers had been losers in all of them. He would have one last opportunity to be on a World Series winner in 1916, this time with the Robins. Most observers favored the American League pennant-winning Boston Red Sox, who had never lost a World Series—winning in 1903, 1912 and 1915, but to a few Brooklyn seemed to have the edge.

### Game One (Saturday, October 7)

The first game of the 1916 World Series was played in Boston on a crisp, autumn day under a clear blue sky before a crowd of 36,117. The Red Sox management decided to play the game in the National League Boston Braves Field instead of Fenway Park so more fans could be accommodated. The National Commission approved the arrangement and charged players 60 percent of the $1,000 the Red Sox paid to the Braves for the use of their field, rationalizing that the players gained the most by the larger attendance.

Ernie Shore took the mound for the Red Sox against the veteran Rube Marquard, with Meyers behind the bat. Shore was something of a surprise. Most expected Boston manager Bill Carrigan to start his sensational young pitcher, George "Babe" Ruth, who was in his third year with the Red Sox. For the 1916 season Ruth's record had been 23–12, with a 1.75 ERA.

The Boston Royal Rooters, dressed in bright red, were once again ready to rouse the Red Sox fans, as they had in the 1912 Series with the Giants. Before the game they marched around the field behind a band that played their trademark song "Tessie" three times. However, the fans wouldn't sing. It was as though they were settling in for a hard-fought contest, and that is what it would be.

In the bottom of the second inning Meyers threw out speedy Red Sox shortstop Everett Scott on a bunt attempt, a play crucial to keeping the Boston team off the scoreboard. Meyers led off the next inning and took two balls from Shore before hitting an easy grounder to the pitcher. With no outs in the fourth the Robins scored on a single by Casey Stengel, followed by a triple off the bat of Zack Wheat. Meyers drove a ball deep into center in the fifth inning that Tilly Walker lost in the sun. It rolled to the scoreboard for a three-base hit. However, the Robins were not able to drive the Cahuilla catcher in from third.

The Red Sox plated two runs of their own and were up 2–1 through six innings with neither pitcher flinching. That proved to be the calm before the storm. In the seventh the Red Sox knocked Marquard out with a three-run surge. The Robins lefty was lifted for Jeff Pfeffer, who allowed one Red Sox run in the eighth.

The game went into the ninth with the Red Sox holding a commanding 6 to 1 lead. Red Sox fans began to stream out of the stands, sure their team had taken the first game of the Series. However, the Robins were not ready to go quietly. They staged a sensational rally, closing to within one run, but the surge fell short, and the game ended with the Red Sox winning, 6 to 5.

Meyers came to bat in the ninth, during the rally, but fouled out. The *New York Times* described the scene: "Meyers, the redskin catcher who dwelt in McGraw's wigwam in times past took two strikes and then fouled out."[52] The Brooklyn catcher was an eight-year major league veteran, who had earned a well-deserved reputation as a skilled and astute ballplayer, yet he was still being portrayed with the same demeaning clichés as at the beginning of his career.

## Game Two (Monday, October 9)

George Herman "Babe" Ruth participated in one game of the 1915 World Series, but as a Red Sox pinch-hitter rather than a pitcher. In the second game of the 1916 Series, also played in Boston on a dark and dreary day, before a crowd of 41,373 fans, Ruth made his second World Series appearance, this time as a starting pitcher. It was the only game during the 1916 Series in which the Babe played. With Otto Miller catching for the Robins, Meyers was able to watch the Red Sox sensation from the bench. It would be the longest World Series game ever — a 14-inning marathon — until the record was tied during the 2005 World Series.

Through 13 innings in a game known as the "double masterpiece" or "hitters nightmare" the Robins' "Sherry" Smith, a six-year veteran, was a match for Ruth. Some observers thought he pitched better than the young Red Sox hurler. In the first inning Ruth gave up a run on an inside-the-park homer by Hy Myers. Smith surrendered a tally in the third when Ruth drove in a run, grounding out with a man on third base.

In the fifth inning a fight broke out between Red Sox third base coach Heinie Wagner and Robins shortstop Ivy Olson when Olson tripped Chet Thomas as he rounded second. Thomas was awarded third by the umpires but was stranded when Ruth struck out to end the inning. Each team threatened, but the score remained tied at a run apiece through 13 innings with both starting pitchers still on the mound.

With darkness descending Ruth retired the Giants on nine pitches in the top of the 14th inning. In the bottom of the frame Dick Hoblitzell walked, Duffy Lewis sacrificed Hoblitzell to second, and pinch-hitter Del Gainer drove in the winning run.

Had Gainer's hit not ended the marathon, the umpires were prepared to stop the game due to darkness and declare it a tie. A tie would have meant an extra game (which would have brought in $80,000), with an additional $20,000 because the game would have been played in Boston. Gainer's single therefore became known as the "$100,000" hit, for that was the amount lost to the World Series coffers. After the game the ever-confident Ruth told his teammates, "I told you I could handle those National League sons of bitches!" Two years later, in the 1918 Series, he would extend his streak of World Series scoreless innings to 29⅔, a record that stood until 1961.[53]

John Tortes Meyers recalled Babe Ruth as a strong left-hander with plenty of speed and a "great curve that broke under your chin." When asked as an old-timer what he thought about Ruth, Meyers told a reporter, "I liked Babe; he was a fine fellow."[54] One of Meyers's prized possessions was a bat Ruth had traded to him. In his later years he placed the Ruth bat in a corner

**Meyers and Babe Ruth were reunited in San Diego during the Bambino's barnstorming tour after the 1927 season. The two sluggers had first met in the 1916 World Series, when Ruth was a pitcher for the Boston Red Sox and Meyers was on the Brooklyn Dodgers (San Diego History Center).**

of his living room, along with one of his own, which carried a John T. Meyers signature. He would often take the bats out to talk with visitors about the "science of hitting." Though both were much heavier than modern bats, Meyers's was the weightier of the two. According to Meyers, when they traded bats, Ruth said the catcher's stick was too heavy for him.[55] In fact, Meyers, who always took short, compact swings, was known, along with Bill Sweeney (who played for the Cubs and Braves between 1907 and 1914), to wield the heaviest bat during the Deadball Era.[56]

## Game Three (Tuesday, October 10)

Meyers also sat out the third contest, the first World Series game ever played at Ebbets Field. It was a cold but bright day, with only 21,087 fans in attendance. The Robins management had raised the price of lower grandstand seats to $5.00, and many remained unoccupied.

Wilbert Robinson turned to Jack Coombs, another World Series veteran, to start the game. With relief help from Jeff Pfeffer, Coombs led the Robins to a 4–3 win, halving the Red Sox Series lead.

After the game Brooklyn fans marched around the field, while Boston's

Royal Rooters who made the trip fell in behind their band. The Rooters were in a festive mood despite their team's loss. The Brooklyn faithful then "borrowed" the Boston band and rendered their own version of "Tessie," to the delight of the Rooters.

## Game Four (Wednesday, October 11)

With Rube Marquard tapped by Robinson as the starting pitcher, Meyers caught the fourth game of the 1916 World Series, also played at Ebbets Field. Though many of the $5.00 seats were still empty, a slightly larger crowd of 21,662 hopeful fans gathered on a warm day. Boston called upon Hubert "Dutch" Leonard to pitch.

With the Robins leading 2 to 0, the tide turned when Boston's Larry Gardner added his second home run in two days with a three-run blast in the second. *The Sporting News* coverage of the game included a picture of Gardner completing the inside-the-park home run by sliding under a tag by Meyers, who was attempting to block the plate with his left knee.[57] The Red Sox scored three more runs and rode Leonard's five-hitter to a decisive 6–2 victory.

Meyers was not a factor offensively, going 0-for-3 in the game. In the second inning he walked but was left stranded. The Brooklyn catcher did work Leonard to a full count in the fourth, and fouled off several more pitches, but then flied out. He popped out in the sixth and reached on a fielder's choice in the ninth. Robinson then inserted Casey Stengel to run for him. Defensively, Meyers was charged with his second passed ball of the Series, but he did throw out two runners on steal attempts.

## Game Five (Thursday, October 12)

On a bright, but cool Columbus Day, a World Series record crowd of 42,620 gathered at Braves Field in Boston for the fifth game. The Red Sox starter in the first game, Ernie Shore, returned to the mound. The Robins countered with Jeff Pfeffer. Meyers was behind the bat.

Shore held the Robins to just three singles and a solitary run. The Red Sox scored four runs to win the game and end the 1916 World Series. The *New York Times* lamented that, if the score had been 40 to 1, "it would have represented more accurately the relative merits of the two contending teams." The Dodgers, the *Times* crowed, were like a patient who provided his own anesthetics so a surgeon could work on him.

The Robins' lone run came without a hit in the second, when George Cutshaw scored on a passed ball while Meyers was batting. The Brooklyn catcher's single in the fifth was the first hit for the Dodgers, spoiling Shore's bid for a no-hitter. It was an infield single that glanced off Shore's glove. With runners on second and third in the top of the seventh, Meyers hit a ball off the handle and was thrown out by Shore. The *Times* commented that Meyers had a number of such chances in the Series, but he "was not 'there' in the pinches."[58]

After the game, Boston fans took the field by storm and the Royal Rooters band played their well-worn song, "Tessie," one last time. The large crowd following the progress of the game on the mammoth outdoor scoreboard in Times Square quietly dispersed when the final out was made.

Meyers played in three games in the five-game series. He recorded only two hits, a single and a triple in ten at-bats, for a .200 average. He received one walk and did not strike out. Behind the bat, he made 21 putouts and had 8 assists and no errors, but he did allow the two passed balls.

The 1916 Series set a per-game attendance record, drawing an average of 32,572 spectators. The players' pool of $162,927.45 also set a record, as did the loser's share of $2,645 per player.

Meyers and a number of other members of the Robins and Red Sox appeared in a documentary in four reels entitled *World Series 1916, Boston vs. Brooklyn,* released soon after the Series ended. The players did not receive any of the film's box office receipts.[59]

After the Series Meyers was once again involved in a dispute with baseball management. He joined other Robins and Red Sox players in challenging the attendance count on which the players' pool was determined. His involvement may have been a factor in his being let go by the Brooklyn club the next year. *Sporting Life* claimed "Chief Meyers [was] in disfavor for his World's Series protest."[60] As reported in another article entitled "Indian Jack is Done," published after the 1916 Series, Brooklyn owner Charles Ebbets was acknowledging that the Cahuilla catcher was on the market. If a trade could not be not made, Meyers would be released. In response to a reporter's question, Ebbets claimed rather unconvincingly that Meyers's role in the recent labor-management dispute was not a factor. Rather, he said, Manager Wilbert Robinson "does not consider that he will be of value as a player."[61]

## Indian Major Leaguers and the Myth of the "Vanishing American"

Before and during the 1917 season a number of sports journalists continued to address the decline of Indian major leaguers by appealing to the increasingly popular myth of the "vanishing American." According to one wire service story, the principal reason so few Native Americans had become baseball stars was mental, not physical. "Strong, healthy, quick, drilled in outdoor sports by inherited rivalries, the Indian never has been able to completely fathom the white man's game of baseball. Many hundreds of the copper-skinned men have been called, but few of them have reached the pinnacle of perfection in the majors."[62]

About the same time, Grantland Rice wrote in his syndicated column, "The Spotlight," that with the fading of Bender, Meyers, and Thorpe, "the ancient curse seems to be following the first American. His baseball shadow seems to be cast in the sunset of a fading day. The old stars are passing and there are no new stars in sight to take their place."[63]

While Rice's claim that Meyers was an example of the last gasp of a dying race gained national attention, the Cahuilla catcher's remarkable achievements on the field received only limited notice. One report listed active players' batting averages in their careers through 1916. The author found "Chief Meyers of the Superbas" had the highest mark among catchers. Meyers had compiled a .297 average after 879 games, with 2,634 at-bats, 264 runs, and 781 hits. The next highest average for a catcher was Lew McCarty of the Giants, with an average of .272 after 234 games.[64]

The narrative of the fading away of Native American major leaguers was rooted in a myth that had originated centuries earlier. Ever since Europeans arrived on the American continent, a dominant image of Native Americans embraced by the newcomers was that of the "vanishing American," a once proud people whom history had consigned to oblivion, to be replaced by the superior European civilization.[65] During the late nineteenth and early twentieth centuries the theme was especially prominent, as scholars in the new discipline of anthropology rushed to preserve evidence of Indian cultures in the belief they were about to disappear. Some, like Seth Humphrey, assured whites they need not worry at the vanishing of the Indian because "the Indian had little in his inheritance to benefit the Aryan stock, and much to encumber it."[66]

Popularization of the myth of the vanishing American coincided with Meyers's major league career. For example, in 1915 American sculptor James Earle Fraser, who had designed the famous Indian head-buffalo nickel two years earlier, created a sculpture of "a forlorn warrior slumped forward on his pony" for the Panama-Pacific International Exposition held in San Francisco. A guidebook described the statue, entitled *The End of the Trail*: "Before you is the end of the Indian race. The poor Indian, following his long trail, has at last come to the end." Small replicas were sold throughout the country: bookends; ashtrays; postcards; paperweights; as well as garish prints in sepia and color, showing the rider silhouetted against a dying sunset. Today Fraser's iconic statue is prominently displayed in the National Cowboy and Western Heritage Museum in Oklahoma City.[67]

## The 1917 Season: Brooklyn and Boston — Last Season in the Majors

Despite reports of the demise of Native American athletes, John Tortes Meyers was still playing in the major leagues in 1917. However, Meyers and other key players took steep cuts in pay. With the expiration of the contract Meyers had signed with the Giants, Ebbets lopped off $2,700 in Meyers's new contract with Brooklyn, about the amount he had received as his loser's share for the 1916 World Series. While Zack Wheat and Casey Stengel held out, all three of the former Giants on the Robins (Meyers, Marquard, and Merkle) signed their reduced contracts.[68]

The portion of the 1917 season Meyers spent with the Robins was dispiriting for him, and the press magnified his frustration. For example, in a May game against Christy Mathewson's Cincinnati Reds, Meyers hit a pop fly to pitcher Fred Toney. When the Cahuilla catcher failed to run out the play, Toney grinned, purposely dropped the ball and tossed it to first. The Reds first baseman then tagged out the Robins runner who had stepped off the bag, and doubled Meyers by tagging the base.[69]

About the same time, an article on the impact of age on players featured a photograph of a seemingly disoriented Meyers staring straight ahead, with a caption that described a "strained, almost wild, look in his eyes." Chief Meyers "is practically through," the report concluded, attributing the decline in his batting average to "damaged eye sight."[70]

Meyers appeared in only 47 games, with 132 at-bats, for the Robins in 1917. His average slipped to .212, with 28 hits (three doubles, but no triples or home runs) and only eight runs and three RBI. His slugging percentage was a weak .235 (less than half that of his 1912 high) and his on-base percentage was only .283.[71]

In noting his release from the Robins, to be effective at the end of August, the United Press called Meyers "the most famous Indian ever to play baseball" and noted that Chief Bender and Jim Thorpe were now "the only representatives of his race play[ing] major league ball."[72] However, Meyers's career in the majors had not quite ended. On August 17, 1917, he signed with the Boston Braves as a potential replacement for Hank Gowdy, who had left the team to become the first major leaguer to enlist for service in World War I.[73] Meyers played in only 25 games, with 68 at-bats, for the Braves. He had 17 hits, including four doubles and four triples, but no home runs. His batting average was .200, his on-base percentage .311, and his slugging percentage .426. He had only four RBI and no stolen bases.[74]

As his major league career moved toward a frustrating conclusion, Meyers demonstrated he could still draw on the wry humor he employed throughout his career. In an August 1917, article an anonymous writer reported, "'Chief' Meyers, though a righthanded thrower and batsman, and righthanded in golf, tennis, etc. writes lefthanded, and fluently, too, while he can hardly imitate a letter 'M' righthanded." According to the author, the chief claimed most Indians write left-handed, saying, "When we were signing treaties with the white man, we had to hold the pen in the left hand and a tomahawk in the right, or they would whack us on the dome in their treacherous paleface fashion. With the right hand armed, we were ready to meet their wickedness half way, and that was how we got into the habit of writing lefthanded."[75]

Meyers tripled in an October 3 game against the Brooklyn Robins. The next day he took the field for the last time in a major league uniform, catching the first game of a season-ending doubleheader against the Robins at Ebbets Field. He was 1-for-4 in a 5 to 1 loss.

John Tortes Meyers's major league career officially ended on October 16, 1917, when the Braves unconditionally released him. It seemed inevitable that the last article about him during his years in the majors included an "Indian pun" in its title: "Chief Meyers a Brave No Longer."[76]

Despite his disappointing final season, the 1918 Spalding Baseball Record again named Meyers as its catcher on the Grand National All America Baseball Team, which selected the top players from 1871, the start of major league baseball, to 1917. A point total based on combining fielding and batting averages determined the selection for position players. In his later years the 1918 Spalding Baseball Record was "[o]ne of Chief Meyers's most treasured remembrances," with a "page blown up and framed in his bedroom."[77]

## The 1918 Season: Buffalo Bisons

In late April 1918, Meyers signed to play with the Buffalo Bisons of the International League. Fellow ex–Giant George "Hooks" Wiltse was the Bisons manager. Meyers was with the team when they opened the season in May.[78]

The 1918 the Bisons struggled to a sixth-place International League finish. Meyers, however, played well, appearing in 65 games in a shortened season that ended in July, with 204 at-bats and a batting average of .328. He had 67 hits (including 14 doubles and one triple), scored 28 runs, and stole two bases.[79]

## Serving in the U.S. Marine Corps (1918–1919)

After his season with the Buffalo Bisons ended, Meyers joined the U.S. Marine Corps on October 31, 1918. The press could not resist the temptation to portray Meyers's enlistment as "Indian on the War Path," as one headline exclaimed. The article urged "Chief" Meyers to get some "German scalps."[80] However, Meyers's reason for enlisting was not some "savage instinct." Nor was it primarily "patriotic fervor," as he later liked to say, regaling reporters through the years with the story of how he was moved to enlist by the dramatic appeals of actress Lillian Russell.[81]

Meyers's principal motivation for becoming a leatherneck was more personal. Meyers's friend and teammate, Eddie Grant, the Harvard-educated lawyer who had played for the Giants during the 1913–1915 seasons, was one of the first Americans to enlist when the United States entered World War I in April 1917. Grant was also the first major league ballplayer to be killed in action during the war, dying on October 5, 1918. After leaving the Bisons Meyers intended to settle down with his wife Anna on a farm he had just purchased in New Canaan, Connecticut, near New Haven. However, after

learning that his Giants teammate, with whom he had enjoyed discussing philosophy and literature, had been killed in action, Meyers decided to enlist to avenge his friend's death.[82] Less than a month after Grant was killed, John Tortes Meyers joined the Marines at a recruitment center in New York and immediately left for his basic training at Parris Island, South Carolina.[83]

In addition to avenging Grant's death, there may have been a more practical reason for Meyers's enlistment. In the spring of 1918 a "work-or-fight" order was issued, mandating that draft-age men engaged in non-productive work be subject to induction even if previously deferred. Soon pro-

One of Meyers's closest friends during his later years with the New York Giants was Harvard-educated Eddie Grant, who joined the team during the 1914 season. In 1918 Grant became the first major leaguer killed in action while serving in World War I. His friend's death was one factor in Meyers's decision to enlist in the U.S. Marine Corps in October 1918 (Library of Congress, Prints & Photographs Division, LC-DIG-ggbain-13622).

fessional ballplayers were being drafted into the armed forces. Despite the common view that ballplayers were slackers who ducked service in the military if they could, 253 major leaguers (142 American League and 111 National League) served in the U.S. Armed Forces during the Great War.[84]

Finally, Meyers may also have been motivated to join the Marines by the response of his fellow Native Americans to the call to serve in the defense of the nation. American Indians have a long history of serving in the armed forces at the highest ratio of any ethnic group. One in four Indian men and women are serving in the armed services at any given time. In World War I that included as many as 17,000 Native Americans. Ten Indians were awarded the Croix de Guerre by the French government for their heroism in combat; 150 won awards for valor.

Stories of the self-sacrifice of Indian soldiers circulated in the press. As one editorial asked, shortly after the Armistice, "If the red man can fight, why can't he vote?"[85] Congress responded in 1919 by passing an act granting citizenship to all honorably discharged Indian veterans. The law was part of the federal government's goal of making all Indians citizens, in order to speed their assimilation into the mainstream society. It would take five more years before Congress extended citizenship rights to all Native Americans.

Despite their service in World War I, Indians were not receiving fair treatment in American society. When they returned from the War, Indian veterans encountered signs in towns near reservations reading, "No Dogs or Indians Allowed!"[86]

Since the Armistice had been signed soon after he enlisted, Private Meyers did not deploy to Europe. Instead, he remained on the east coast of the United States during his service with the Marines. He was honorably discharged on March 17, 1919.

## The 1919 Season: Managing the New Haven Weissmen

About six weeks after leaving the Marine Corps, Meyers decided to return to baseball. George Weiss (who was only 24 at the time) signed him to be player/manager of Weiss's New Haven club, which he had named the Weissmen. Meyers took charge of the team about May 10, 1919.[87] He appeared in 84 games during the 1919 season, batting .301, with 276 at-bats, 39 runs, 114 total bases, and 83 hits (including 18 doubles, two triples, and three home runs), but, as would be expected of a 39-year-old catcher, no stolen bases.[88]

However, managing the Weissman did not go well for Meyers. As one report put it, "Chief Meyers wasn't a howling success as a manager" and became "discouraged."[89] Danny Murphy, former Philadelphia A's player and Meyers's opponent in the 1911 World Series, replaced him as New Haven manager at midseason. Meyers did honor his contract with Weiss by playing for the rest of the 1919 season for the New Haven team. The Weissmen finished the 1919 season in seventh place in the Eastern League, with a disappointing record of 47 wins and 62 losses.

## The 1920 Season: Headed Home

On January 1, 1920, George Weiss announced the signing of Charles Albert Bender to pilot the New Haven club during the 1920 season. If John Tortes Meyers could be convinced to return to the team, the Weissmen would have the most famous pair of Indians in baseball as their battery, Weiss proclaimed. Although Meyers told Weiss at the end of the 1919 season he intended to retire from baseball to tend to his New Canaan farm, the New Haven owner was convinced he could change the catcher's mind, especially with the signing of Bender as the new manager.[90]

However, the "all–Indian battery" Weiss hoped to advertise as a way to promote the New Haven team in 1920 was not to be. Meyers abruptly left the New Haven team before the season started. A month after signing with Bender to play for New Haven, the aging catcher decided to leave the team and devote himself to the apple orchards on his New Canaan farm instead.

Meyers may have owed George Weiss an apology for leaving the New Haven team without offering an explanation, but it was not to enlist in the Marine Corps as he would later claim.

He left the New Haven team intending to live on his farm in New Canaan. However, before long he had disposed of his Connecticut property and returned to southern California where he took a job as a construction foreman for the San Diego Consolidated Gas and Electric Company. According to the 1920 Census he and Anna lived in a rented house at 450 20th Street in San Diego.[91]

Throughout his major league career John Tortes Meyers had maintained a farm in California near Riverside. Except for the 1910–1911 off-season, when he was on the vaudeville circuit with Christy Mathewson, Meyers spent winters in southern California with Anna. It may have been the prospect of moving away permanently from his family and his Cahuilla homeland gradually sinking in that awakened a longing to return to his roots. His grandniece Michele Meyers Cornejo believes a sense of family responsibility was the principal reason her Uncle Jack left the east coast to return to California. His mother, Felcité Tortes, had died in 1916 of ptomaine poisoning, and his sister, Mary Christine, became a single mother of two small boys a few years later, about the time Meyers left Connecticut.[92]

Long before the phrase became popular, Meyers likely knew a "sense of place" that drew him back to his Cahuilla homeland.

# NINE

# Life After Baseball (1921–1971)

## Changes in Indian Policy (1921–1945)

From 1887, when John Tortes Meyers was a seven-year-old, until the 1920s, after he had finished his professional baseball career, federal Indian policy was dominated by a two-pronged assimilationist ideology. From the Dawes Allotment Act of 1887 to the 1920s the policy was to allot tribal lands to individuals in order to shift Indians from the communalism of their traditional communities to the individualism and self-dependency of Euroamerican society. Land allotment was combined with an approach to the education of Native Americans that emphasized encouraging, and often forcing, Indians to leave behind traditional ways and become fully functioning participants in the dominant society.

About the time Meyers returned to his Cahuilla homeland, the failure of these assimilation programs was becoming increasingly apparent. According to the Merriam Report, released in 1928, the two goals of assimilation — absorption and cultural extinction — were a "tragic blunder." Instead, the Report maintained, the U.S. Government's Indian Service should seek social and economic advancement for Indians, with "more understanding of and sympathy for the Indian point of view." Indian policy should seek to build on and encourage rather than "crush out all that is Indian."[1]

At the center of the revolution in federal Indian policy during this period was John Collier, who, after experiencing Indian culture and spirituality at the Taos, New Mexico, pueblo, devoted himself to seeking justice for Indians. President Franklin D. Roosevelt appointed Collier Commissioner of Indian Affairs in 1933, and he served in that key post until his retirement in 1945. Before becoming Commissioner, Collier had already attacked the policy of assimilation, focusing on the Bureau of Indian Affairs and particularly Indian boarding schools as the most egregious symbols of the government's campaign to destroy the identities and cultures of Indians.[2]

Not long after taking office, Collier was instrumental in the passage in the U.S. Congress of the Wheeler-Howard Indian Reorganization Act. The law implemented sweeping reforms in Indian policy. It stressed local self-government and economic independence. The feature of the new policy that would prove fortuitous for John Tortes Meyers was Collier's directive to hire more Indians in administrative positions on Indian agencies.

## Gone But Not Forgotten (1921–1931)

In early 1921 John Tortes Meyers was reportedly "wintering" in San Diego "as usual." According to one reporter who saw him playing with a semi-pro team in San Diego, "The big Indian can still smite the pill a wicked lick with his war club."[3] However, his skills had in fact waned considerably. He quit the San Diego team in disgust after being heckled by fans who shouted he was too old and slow to play.[4] Meyers told a reporter years later, "They laughed at me and booed because I was not so fast and maybe not so good. 'You are getting old, Chief,' I finally told myself. 'Those fellows [who] could not carry your glove are laughing at you. Maybe you had better quit forever. And I did quit—forever.'"[5] It would be his last appearance in a professional or even semi-professional league, although not the last time he played baseball to earn money.

Meyers may have left professional baseball, but he was by no means forgotten. Each time a new Indian ballplayer reached the major leagues in the decade after he retired, articles appeared comparing the player to Meyers, as well as Bender and Thorpe. One noted, "The first Indian on the Boston Braves' roster since Chief Meyers and Jim Thorpe did a fade-out has moccasined his way into the camp at St. Petersburg, Fla., and will be given a trial.... He is Ozmun Winters, said to be a full-blooded Cayuga, and is a catcher."[6]

Meyers was also remembered for his part in the great New York Giants teams of the Deadball Era. Writers invariably praised Meyers when recalling those clubs. For example, an article written in 1928 described the New York Giants between 1903 and 1914 as one of the greatest teams in baseball history. Although claiming they were "misfits," except for Christy Mathewson, the report recalled Giants players in that period were almost magically molded together by John McGraw. Although there were few famous players on the teams—no Lajoies, Wagners, Cobbs, or Hornsbys—they were "smart players, men who knew baseball." Among them, the writer noted, was Chief Meyers.[7]

The same year sports journalist Bozeman Bulger, who had penned the vaudeville skit for Mathewson and Meyers in 1910, heralded Chief Meyers as "one of the few Indians to attain real greatness in baseball," during a time when it was a "fad" to engage Indians as well as "Italians, Frenchmen, and Swedes." Bulger clearly wanted to show that Chief did not fit what he took to be people's stereotypes of Indian athletes. Meyers was not the "fleet-footed, untiring redskin we are wont to picture," but rather was heavy and slow-footed. And he was not the uneducated "son of the forest." Bulger noted that Chief was a cultured man who attended Dartmouth College. Bulger recalled an occasion in Chicago when a respected journalist asked Meyers his opinion on "the Indian question." Showing the indignation he felt throughout his life at the treatment of Native Americans, Meyers responded curtly, "To me it is merely a question of the survival of the most unscrupulous."[8]

Bulger was not the only writer who heralded John Tortes Meyers for his intellect and noted his awareness of the injustices directed against Indians. After a conversation with the Cahuilla catcher, Irvin Cobb described Meyers in a wire service report as a well-informed lover of the arts. He also noted the former major leaguer had a finely honed wit and knew how to use ironic humor. On one occasion a curious fan asked Meyers why he had taken the name "John Meyers." "Because," Meyers responded, with a deadpanned expression, "it sounds so Indian." According to Cobb, when asked to name his favorite painting, Meyers invariably listed two: "The Quest for the Holy Grail" in the Boston Public Library and "Custer's Last Stand." Asked why he named the latter, a common painting that had been given away as an advertisement and appeared in countless saloons, Meyers responded, "Well, it's no Rembrandt, but it tells a beautiful story. It's the only picture done by a white man that I ever saw where my crowd is getting as good as an even break."[9]

In 1928 Jack and his wife Anna purchased a home at 617 Del Mar Avenue in Chula Vista, just south of San Diego.[10] According to the 1930 Census Meyers was living in the house and still employed as a foreman for the San Diego gas company.[11]

Like many other Americans, Meyers suffered a devastating financial collapse during the Great Depression. He lost much of the money he had saved from his baseball career and apparently also his farm near Riverside as well as his home in Chula Vista.[12] In 1931, after losing his gas company job in San Diego due to cutbacks, Meyers was hired as a boxing inspector for the California State Athletic Commission, but it was a part-time position, and he held it for only two years.[13]

Though remembered by major league veterans still in the game in the early 1930s, Meyers was fast becoming an unknown to younger players. In March 1932, Meyers made an appearance at the Giants spring training camp in Los Angeles, where it had been moved from Marlin, Texas. A writer who was present described one of the Giants rookies being introduced to Chief Meyers and asking of what fire department he was chief. Overhearing the remark, John McGraw remarked philosophically that fame on the baseball diamond is fleeting.[14]

However, Meyers was still held in esteem by his Giants manager and others who remembered his playing days. In his syndicated column Will Rogers noted that Chief Meyers, "who hit home runs when the ball wasn't rubber," was one of the guests at a Beverly Hills dinner hosted by John McGraw during the Giants' 1932 spring training. Although Meyers and the other former Giants present had, in Rogers's words, "pass[ed] over the horizon of popular clamor" they were on this night greeted with cheers that would make "present day celebrities envious."[15]

## Returning to Baseball and to the Santa Rosa Reservation (1932–1933)

In 1932 Meyers participated in the first of the many "old timers" games in which he played during his retirement. In late June he was on the roster for a charity baseball game at Wrigley Field in Los Angeles. The proceeds of

Throughout his retirement years, Meyers (center) enjoyed participating in old timers games and reunions with his Giants and Dodgers teammates and other greats of baseball history (National Baseball Hall of Fame Library, Cooperstown, New York).

the contest were designated for the Association of Professional Baseball Players, which supported retired players who were most in need.[16]

As the Depression deepened, like millions of other Americans, Meyers took jobs wherever he could find them. Drawing on his name recognition, he secured employment in 1932 as a car salesman for the Richards and Bowman Ford dealership in National City, California, just south of San Diego. He also picked up some work umpiring in San Diego and across the border in Mexico. About this time Meyers lent his name to the Marigold Gardens Restaurant in the Los Angeles suburb of Duarte. The restaurant "invited customers to eat and dance at the 'Chief Meyers's New York Giants' Marigold Gardens,' which also featured free psychic readings."[17]

Also in 1932, through the influence of John McGraw, Meyers signed on as a part-time scout for the Cincinnati Reds organization, a position he held at least until 1955. His assignment was to look for talent in southern California.[18] Meyers would often say, had there been a scouting system in his day, he would probably have gone directly from Dartmouth to the major leagues rather than knocking around the minor leagues before signing with the Giants.[19]

Meyers also maintained his involvement in the sport by coaching amateur baseball as a volunteer. In 1932 he helped coach an American Legion team called the "Fighting Gobs." He would continue his interest in youth baseball for the rest of his life. Several decades later, in his 80s, he was still attending games in San Bernardino.

Late in 1932 Meyers signed on with the National Baseball School in Los Angeles. Jess Orndorff, who once played briefly for the Boston Braves, was the school's owner.[20] In addition to the Los Angeles School, Orndorff was assembling an old-timers team for a tour of the United States. Beginning on the west coast the team was scheduled to play against organized clubs as well as semiprofessional teams. The plan was for a group of former major league stars to spend an hour or two teaching young people how to play baseball before appearing in old-timers games.

For Meyers the tour was "a missionary rather than a mercenary baseball pilgrimage," as he put it. He said he was excited at the prospect of making his first visit to New York since he had been mustered out of the Marine Corps 13 years earlier.[21] In the publicity churned out to promote the tour Orndorff called Meyers "an effective wielder of the willow" and claimed, incorrectly, that Meyers was a product of the Carlisle Indian school. He may have been confusing Meyers with Jim Thorpe, who also signed to play on the team, giving the two Giants teammates the opportunity to renew their friendship.

In April 1933, the barnstorming old-timers began the tour with an ambitious plan to play as many as 90 games in cities as they traveled to the east coast. However, after compiling a record of 18 wins and only 2 losses, the team, unable to take in enough money to pay expenses, disbanded in Salt Lake City, Utah.[22]

After the collapse of the tour the Cahuilla catcher fell on even harder times. Three decades later he told a reporter he "went down with a bang. But I didn't jump off any building to end it all. I had a Lincoln automobile, I traded it for a Ford.... I went back to the reservation and slept under a big pine tree. It was a far different life than I had known — pampered by masseurs and the easy life in the country's best hotels. The ground was hard."[23] According to Michele Meyers Cornejo, about this time her Uncle Jack built and moved into a small house on the Santa Rosa Reservation.[24] It was likely a traditional, dirt-floored Cahuilla home, shaded by the pine trees that grew in the mountains.

Meyers later recalled, "On the third morning, I woke up and told myself a few facts. 'You're not the only Indian that went broke,' I said. 'Get up and go out and get to work.'" He went to the Mission Indian Agency in Riverside and asked for a job. The timing was serendipitous. John Collier, new Commissioner of Indian Affairs, had just directed Indian agents to hire more Native Americans to administrative positions in the Indian Service. Meyers was offered and readily accepted the position of head of law enforcement for the Indian reservations of southern California.[25]

What gave Meyers the resolve to pick himself up and take the initiative to address the personal crisis he faced? Some might argue it was the competitiveness he learned in athletics or the free enterprise system to which he had been exposed in major league baseball, when, before the era of sports agents, he had to negotiate his own contracts. Or perhaps it was the drive and determination he had developed under the tutelage of John McGraw.

In addition, as a Cahuilla, Meyers was rooted in a culture that taught him the values of industriousness, hard work, integrity, and dependability. The traditional Cahuilla worldview also recognized that because life is uncertain humans must learn to adapt to changing circumstances. When his life fell apart he drew inspiration from his Cahuilla heritage, returning to the Santa Rosa Reservation, his Cahuilla home, to start over.

## Serving as a Real Chief (1933–1945)

On September 4, 1933, Meyers began his career as Chief of Police for the Mission Indian Agency of Southern California, a position he held until his retirement in 1945. Chief Meyers's enforcement duties covered all 30 reservations from San Diego to Santa Barbara.[26] He also carried the titles of Over-

seer in the Indian Service of the Interior Department and Assistant Superintendent for Law Enforcement. In addition to supporting his family, he was
fulfilling the desire he had expressed in 1912, to return to his homeland after
his baseball career ended and be of service to his people.[27]

Several years after he began his tenure with the Bureau of Indian Affairs,
Meyers told a reporter the job "really makes me a chief now. I'm entitled to
the name. My real name, in Indian, is Tortes, but I was never a chief among
my people."[28] After being labeled Chief stereotypically for nearly four decades,
it was now appropriate to call John Tortes Meyers by that title.

Within a few months of beginning his new career in law enforcement,
Meyers also signed to appear in a Hollywood movie. An Associated Press dis-
patch announced his first and only role in a feature film[29]:

> Chief Myers [sic], noted Indian baseball player ... has been signed to play a
> role in the film "Laughing Boy," which portrays Indian life on an Arizona
> desert. He is putting on his war paint and ceremonial beads for his first scene
> before the camera on a Navajo reservation near Tuba City, Arizona.

The movie was based on the 1929 Pulitzer Prize–winning novel *Laughing
Boy: A Navajo Love Story,* written by noted anthropologist Oliver LaFarge. It
is the story of two young lovers, Laughing Boy and Slim Girl, who each
become tainted by the vices of white society before rediscovering their Navajo
roots.[30]

Meyers played the uncredited role of "Crooked Nose," one of a number
of such parts in the film taken by Native Americans.[31] On the set of *Laughing
Boy,* shot on location on the Navajo reservation, Meyers laid out a baseball
diamond with a desert butte as a backstop. There he taught the Navajos working as extras on the film how to play the game he loved, while waiting for the
few scenes in which they appeared.

By 1936 Meyers had largely faded into baseball obscurity. He was, in one
reporter's estimation, "aged and fat and gray." If he was no longer widely
remembered as a baseball star, his spirits and demeanor were apparently not
affected. The picture accompanying the article calling him a "has been" shows
a smiling Meyers nattily dressed in a three-piece suit and bowler hat.[32]

The last known reference to Meyers living with his wife Anna is a brief
note published in November 1938. Meyers had been appointed the week before
as official custodian of a mansion on Wilshire Boulevard in Los Angeles. It
was a home from which Anna Laura Barnett, identified as widow of "the
wealthy Indian Johnson Barnett," had recently moved. According to the note,
"Mr. and Mrs. Meyers will occupy the house and supervise rehabilitation
work." The cost of the renovations was to be paid from the four million dollar
estate left by Mr. Barnett.[33]

Jackson Barnett was a Creek Indian whose Oklahoma land allotment sat on top of one of the largest oil deposits in the country. Because of his wealth Barnett was declared a "reserved Indian" by the Bureau of Indian Affairs. That is, he was deemed too wealthy to be able to manage his own affairs. Trustees were appointed, and Barnett was given only a small monthly stipend. However, when he married, his wife Anna challenged the government-appointed guardians for control of his business affairs, including substantial real estate holdings in Los Angeles. When Barnett died in 1934, the government sued Mrs. Barnett for control of her husband's estate. It was likely in his role as an Indian Service law enforcement supervisor that Meyers was appointed custodian of the mansion. In any event, the Barnett case is a sordid example of the mismanagement of Indians' affairs by the government and the culture of greed that victimized many. Ironically, Chief Meyers was now part of the system of government exploitation he so frequently denounced.[34]

Another passing reference to Meyers circulated by the Associated Press in 1939 claimed that John McGraw made "Chief Meyers, a college graduate, and a cultured Injun, sit in front of hotels every night and say 'how' to passers by."[35] That McGraw would have tried such a stunt, or, if he had, Meyers would have gone along, is farfetched. That a writer would make up the story and the Associated Press send it across the nation reflects the racism that was still dominant nearly 20 years after Meyers retired from baseball.

By 1940 Jack Meyers seems to have fully recovered from the financial and personal turmoil he had experienced during the 1930s. On March 1, 1940, he appeared at the Philadelphia Athletics training camp in Anaheim, California. He was, a reporter on the scene noted, wearing "a big sombrero and had a most prosperous look." The old catcher had come to visit Connie Mack.[36]

After a 13-year career Meyers retired as Chief of Law Enforcement for the Mission Agency in Southern California in 1945. He briefly took a job in Riverside as a guard at the Food Machinery Corporation, which during World War II had shifted production to amphibious tanks. A sportswriter who interviewed him in 1945 noted "Chief Meyers" was gray but "straight as an arrow ... a cultured man, who spends his spare time reading poetry and philosophy."[37]

## Enjoying Retirement (1945–1964)

It took an Act of Congress to prove John Tortes Meyers was eligible for a Social Security pension when he turned 65 in 1945. Throughout his baseball career Meyers always said he was born in 1882 (or 1883) rather than 1880. Now, in retirement, he wanted his true birth date, July 29, 1880, recognized so that he could receive Social Security payments. However, since he had no documentation, he turned to his congressman, who succeeded in having Congress officially establish the 1880 date for his birth. For the rest of his life Meyers carried a miniature photocopy of the congressional act in his wallet.[38]

After retiring from his security job when the war in the Pacific ended, Meyers began what would be a long and fulfilling retirement, during which he remained very much involved in the game he loved. In February 1947, Grantland Rice once again interviewed Meyers and described him as "looking hale, hearty, and happy."[39] When he attended the Pacific Coast League All-Star Game in Los Angeles that August, a reporter noted Chief Meyers was rubbing "his gnarled right hand, the fingers bent and bumpy like old twigs, off a tree; every one of them broken perhaps a half dozen times in a long career." When the reporter suggested the pitches in the Chief's day must have been hard to hold, pointing to the old catcher's hands, Meyers responded, with a cagey grin, "No, I got these playing the piano. Never could hit the keys right, you know."[40]

During a spring training trip a year later, the Giants stopped at San Bernardino, where Meyers was now living at 4468 N. Acacia Ave, and he showed up for the game.[41] In addition to dropping in at spring training camps, attending minor league and youth league games, and participating in old-timers programs, Meyers also enjoyed going to dinners where he knew he would see other ballplayers whom he had played with or against. On occasion, he was invited to speak.

In March 1949, he was in the NBC radio studio in Hollywood to take part in an episode of Ralph Edwards' *This is Your Life*. The old Giants catcher offered his reminiscences of the 1912 World Series during a program honoring Tris Speaker. He recalled the infamous dropped foul ball hit by Speaker in the tenth inning of the decisive eighth game of the Red Sox victory over Meyers and the Giants.[42]

As a member of the 1916 Dodgers team, Meyers attended the 1949 World Series in New York pitting Brooklyn against the Yankees. The old ballplayers were guests of Branch Rickey, then Dodgers president, who two years earlier had broken the "color barrier" in major league baseball by signing Jackie Robinson to a contract. Casey Stengel, who was managing the Yankees in the 1949 Series, introduced his 1916 Brooklyn teammates before a game at Ebbets Field. Meyers and the others, among them Zack Wheat, shook hands with the Dodgers and Yankees players, including Robinson, and formed an arc around Stengel. They walked off the field to the strains of *Auld Lang Syne*.[43]

During his retirement years Meyers also enjoyed getting together with fellow Dartmouth alumni. For example, he attended a "Dartmouth Night" dinner in Los Angeles on October 20, 1950. In a 1962 letter to the Dartmouth

Alumni Office Meyers expressed "fond memories of my days at the school where 'Once a Dartmouth always a Dartmouth.'" He said he would love to go back to the Polo Grounds, where the New York Mets were just beginning the first of the two seasons they would spend in the old Giants field, and return to the Dartmouth campus in Hanover "for one last look see."[44] Just a few years before his death, Meyers was keeping up with Dartmouth through reading the college's alumni magazine.[45]

Meyers (right) and famed Giants and Dodgers manager Leo "the Lip" Durocher at one of the many baseball functions the old Giants catcher enjoyed attending during his retirement years (National Baseball Hall of Fame Library, Cooperstown, New York).

However, as Meyers was remembering his days at Dartmouth, the school apparently did not have the same attachment to him. When asked in a 1958 interview what had happened to "Chief Tortes" (as he was called during his year at the college), Dartmouth president emeritus Ernest Martin Hopkins said simply, "He's dead now."[46]

At a dinner in Pasadena on September 20, 1951, Meyers performed for the first time in public his rendition of "Casey at the Bat."[47] He clearly enjoyed reciting the famous poem, which had been popular while he was in the major leagues and was making a comeback in the 1950s.[48] Word about his rendition spread and Meyers was invited the next year to perform "Casey at the Bat" at the annual dinner of the Association of Professional Ball Players of America.[49] During his last two decades Meyers performed the poem often. His grandnephew and grandnieces remember him reciting it before children, including groups on the Santa Rosa Reservation.[50]

During the 1950s Meyers worked to raise funds to restore the old mission chapel on the Santa Rosa Reservation. His ties to the Santa Rosa Band and his Cahuilla heritage grew even stronger when in 1955 his sister Mary Christine died. Her death made him Felicité Tortes's last surviving child, with the responsibility of keeping alive a connection to the family's Cahuilla roots that had been so important to both his mother and sister.[51]

While attending a Dodgers–White Sox game in Los Angeles during the 1959 World Series, Meyers pointed out to a reporter that a winner's share ($11,231.18) that year was more than the total he received for playing in four World Series ($10,001.90). The reporter, Ed McAuley, made the case in a follow-up article that modern owners and top players should be willing to come to the aid of old timers who had fallen on hard times. There was no retirement system in organized baseball into the 1950s, and a number of players, including some stars, were living in near squalor. With new riches pouring in, thanks to television and personal appearance fees, the reporter argued that major league owners and stars could afford to help the old timers who were struggling.[52]

Two weeks later another article listed some old timers who needed help. One was Sam Crawford, who had been eking out a meager living in the California desert a few years earlier when he was notified he had been elected to the Hall of Fame at Cooperstown. The article also mentioned Chief Meyers, claiming, "His salary was never over $5,000 [sic]," and now he is "living with relatives in San Bernardino, Calif., with only a soldier's pension."[53]

Two years later Meyers *was* barely getting by financially. Much of his pension went to pay rent and for the support he needed in order to remain in his own home. He was well aware the top players of his era never received anywhere near the level of compensation the stars in 1961 earned. He told a reporter, "I was born 50 years too soon. I hit .358 one year with the Giants for a salary of $6,000. I read where a modern player who hit .248 signed for $40,000. I missed the big money in baseball."[54]

Well into his 80s Meyers showed he was still an astute student of the game, offering cogent analysis of bunting and situational hitting. He complained that modern players did not know how or when to bunt and tried so hard to hit home runs they struck out too much. He also commented on the intensity with which ballplayers in his day approached the game and by implication contrasted the attitude of contemporary players. "You know, those fellows back there," the Cahuilla catcher said, "they *thought,* they used their head in baseball, a whole lot. They talked baseball morning, noon, and night. Baseball was their whole life."[55]

Meyers wanted it understood he was not blindly disparaging modern ballplayers, saying they were every bit as talented as the players of his era. However, the improvements in equipment gave contemporary players an advantage his generation lacked. He pointed out that in his day a baseball glove was like "a motorman's mitt" while now a glove is like "a lacrosse net."[56]

What bothered Meyers the most about major league baseball in the 1960s was that the "inside game" was no longer played. While listening to the Dodgers' games on the radio he would get so upset when a runner on third with no one out was stranded, he would shut the radio off and storm around the room. Such a thing, he said, would not have happened in the "scientific game" he learned from John McGraw.[57]

For obvious reasons Meyers especially enjoyed attending games between the Giants and Dodgers. Late in the 1964 season, he sat through every inning of a Dodgers–Giants series in San Francisco as the guest of Giants owner Horace Stoneham. There he reminisced with his old friend, the Giants' secretary, Eddie Brannick. A sportswriter who witnessed the exchange remarked the old Giants catcher "has the vocabulary of a college prof."[58]

## Returning to the National Stage: *The Glory of Their Times* (1964–1967)

John Tortes Meyers was interviewed in San Bernardino by Lawrence Ritter on March 24, 1964, for what many have called the best baseball book ever written, *The Glory of Their Times: The Story of the Early Days of Baseball Told by the Men Who Played It.* In the enlarged edition, Ritter ultimately published edited versions of interviews with 26 of the pioneers of the game, most of them from the Deadball Era. They were all, he claimed in the Introduction, men who transformed a game that lacked social respectability into America's national game.[59]

Ritter later commented on his interview with Meyers, indicating the difficulty he had in initiating the conversation[60]:

> [S]ome conversations were harder to get started than others. Chief Meyers, for example. The Chief resented white society, but once he accepted you, he was as warm and open an individual as you're ever likely to meet. He never forgot he was an Indian, and he made no bones about his resentment, but he wouldn't let that come between you.

Meyers also told Ritter, in a section of the interview not included in *The Glory of Their Times,* that the "thieving government" was "supporting the world and neglecting us poor Indians around here."[61]

Throughout his life, like the trickster, Meyers often used wry humor to challenge injustices and expose absurdities. Now, however, knowing his interview with Ritter would be published and read by fans of the national pastime, he addressed head-on the way Indians were treated in baseball. The old catcher clearly wanted Ritter to know the bitterness he harbored toward the society that so often objectified him and treated him as a foreigner. Even as an old

man, he still felt and expressed that resentment. While it was no longer accept-
able to stereotype other minorities, he pointed out that Indians were still
belittled constantly.[62]

Within a month of Meyers's interview with Ritter, *Baseball Digest* provided an example of the continued stereotyping of Indian ballplayers with
an article entitled "They Heard the Indian Glove Song." Ostensibly intending
to write a tribute to Meyers, Bender, and other Native American baseball
greats, the author could not avoid invoking well-worn clichés, calling Meyers
and the others "a genuine copper-plated All American baseball team." Even
"half–Indians" like Meyers deserve to be considered "warriors" who "found
enduring success on the baseball warpath." "Alas," the article concluded,
drawing on the myth of the vanishing American, "the noble red man is the
forgotten man in baseball lore."[63]

Despite his ongoing bitterness at being a "stranger in a strange land,"
John Tortes Meyers did not wear a chip on his shoulder. As Lawrence Ritter
experienced, the Cahuilla catcher did not take his resentment toward white
society out on individuals, nor, it should be added, did he try to deaden the
pain he felt as many in such circumstances have done.

*The Glory of Their Times* was rejected by a string of publishers until
Macmillan purchased the rights. Since its first publication in 1966, the book
has sold more than 400,000 copies in printed and audio editions. For many
years Ritter split the profits from the book with the elderly players and their
survivors. Each player, including Meyers, received about $10,000 over the
years.[64]

The popularity of the book brought new fame to John Tortes Meyers
and the other largely forgotten players from the early decades of baseball.
After the book's publication, the Veterans Committee of the National Baseball
Hall of Fame tapped several of those interviewed, including Meyers's Giants
battery mate Rube Marquard. Their selection was, many believe, influenced
by the recognition Ritter had given them.

As an effect of his new notoriety Meyers began to receive requests almost
daily for his autograph. If the sender included a prepaid return envelope, the
old catcher always obliged, even if it was a baseball. However, he would only
sign one item per request. "No ball player likes to be traded," he would joke.
"I know I'm being traded in the Bronx, because those fellows got their relatives
to write to me. I wonder what I bring."[65]

Late in the 1965 season, at the instigation of Riverside Elks Lodge No.
643 where Meyers had long been a member, Dodgers owner Walter O'Malley
agreed to fly the old catcher to New York on the team jet for a series with the
New York Mets. Although still vilified by Brooklyn Dodgers fans who have
never forgiven O'Malley for moving their beloved team to Los Angeles, the

Dodgers' owner has a deserved reputation as one of the leaders among owners in treating ballplayers of all races equally. He supported the signing of Jackie Robinson in 1947 and continued the progress initiated by Branch Rickey in race relations.[66] Lawrence Ritter served as Meyers's host in New York and accompanied him wherever he went. This was the trip during which Meyers performed the two "ceremonies" described in the Prologue.

A year later Meyers returned to New York, with all expenses paid by Macmillan, as part of the launch of *The Glory of Their Times.* Meyers told a reporter, probably with a gleam in his eye, he had read the book before the trip and was eager "to settle some scores."[67]

The main event of the visit was a dinner at Toots Shor's restaurant, long a hangout for major league ballplayers. Present were Meyers's Giants teammates Rube Marquard, Fred Snodgrass, and Al Bridwell. Meyers was in rare form, telling the story of how Casey Stengel won the 1916 pennant for the Dodgers by keeping the old players on the team "pepped up." He also repeated his defense of Fred Snodgrass, making sure that all present knew neither McGraw nor his fellow Giants blamed Snodgrass for his infamous "muff" in the 1912 Series. At that point Snodgrass thanked Meyers and shook his "gnarled right hand."[68]

By this time Meyers was signing autographs ("Chief Meyers, 1880–1966") with his left hand, because his right hand was so crippled. Meyers noted when asked about the injuries that the fingers "never bother me, but you should see my legs. They're all scarred from all the base runners coming into me. If you had any white feathers you wouldn't last long in those days. They used to sit on the bench and sharpen their spikes."[69]

For Meyers the 1966 trip was the culmination of his long odyssey toward full acceptance and recognition. On September 25 he appeared with other ballplayers featured in *The Glory of Their Times* on the *Ed Sullivan Show*, at a time when the variety show was a "must watch" on Sunday evening for millions of Americans.

Although Meyers did not fulfill his dream of returning to the Dartmouth campus in Hanover, New Hampshire, Ritter did take him to the Dartmouth Club in New York. There he met representatives of the College, including Dartmouth alumni who had played baseball, although not any from the year Meyers had spent on campus. He presented to them a signed copy of *The Glory of Their Times.*

In his 87th year, now a national figure again, John Tortes Meyers returned one last time to New York for the Mets' opening game of the 1967 season.[70] *The Glory of Their Times* had lifted him to a level of fame he had not experienced since his years with the Giants and the Dodgers more than a half-century earlier. On this trip he appeared on NBC-TV's popular *Today*

**Meyers (center) presents a signed copy of *The Glory of Their Times* to representatives of Dartmouth College at the Dartmouth Club in New York in 1966 (courtesy Dartmouth College Library).**

*Show,* where, for a national television audience, he recited "Casey at the Bat." An article in *The Indian Reporter,* a publication by and for southern California Indian tribes, described the occasion[71]:

> To thousands of baseball fans, he will always be Chief. We're talking about Chief Meyers, who was the great New York Giants catcher when Christy Mathewson was the best pitcher in the National League. The chief, who now lives in Rialto, not too far from his native Santa Rosa Mountains, was on television the other day to recite "Casey at the Bat." He's now 87 but appears to be in good health.

## Final Years (1967–1971)

In his final years Meyers lived in a mobile home development at 442 East First Street in Rialto, between Riverside and San Bernardino. He was cared for by a housekeeper and nurse named Rose, and, after Rose died, by another live-in nurse. His grandnephew, Colonel John V. Meyers, remembers Rose kept a close rein on his great-uncle. "My father would bring Uncle Jack cigars," he said, "which he very much enjoyed, but Rose would only let him have a stoke or two before taking them away."

"I do remember Uncle Jack telling us stories about the 'old times' in baseball," his grandnephew also recalled. "One I vividly remember is about a player who slid hard into him at the plate. Uncle Jack's insteps were all cut up from being spiked so often. Later in the game the player did not see Uncle Jack catch the ball at home. He hid the ball behind his back until the player reached home. 'I tagged him good,' Uncle Jack said, 'broke a couple of his ribs.'"

Reflecting the pride his descendants have in their uncle, Colonel Meyers pointed out that John Tortes Meyers "holds at least one record, most assists for a catcher in a World Series." The record to which he was referring was for throwing out 12 runners in a six-game series, a mark for assists set by Meyers in the 1911 Series that is still unequalled. Colonel Meyers also believes his great-uncle would have been selected for the National Baseball Hall of Fame at Cooperstown had he played one more year and met the minimum of a ten-year major league career in order to be considered.

While living in Rialto, Meyers attended his grandnephew's high school football games as often as he could. At the games the announcer often acknowledged the old major leaguer's presence.[72] When he visited his great-uncle's home, Colonel Meyers remembers seeing the "treasures" his Uncle Jack liked to show visitors. He notes with frustration that his great-uncle's favorite, the watch fob given to him by his Giants manager, John McGraw, disappeared along with most of his Uncle Jack's mementos. They are, he said, probably spread out now among baseball collectors.

"Uncle Jack had a flowery way of speaking," his grandnephew recalled. "He valued education. What I know about Cahuilla history and culture came from my father and Uncle Jack. Uncle Jack in particular was very proud of our Cahuilla heritage and very much respected the tribal morés. When I knew him he was certainly respected as an elder in our family and in the community."[73]

According to Michele Meyers Cornejo, her Uncle Jack's pride in Cahuilla culture came principally from his mother, Felcité, and sister, Mary Christine. Both, she said, were very active in Cahuilla affairs and fluent in their traditional language.[74]

Michele's cousin, Shanna Meyers, who lives near the house her great-uncle built on the Santa Rosa Reservation and raises cattle there, said her great-uncle expressed his pride in being Cahuilla by agreeing to serve as an elected leader of the Santa Rosa Band and taking a key role in the Band's earning federal recognition as a tribe.[75]

She remembers her Uncle Jack as a "snappy dresser." "Whenever he went out," she said, "he wore a three-piece suit and shiny shoes. He was always very conscious of his appearance." Michele Cornejo also remembers her Uncle Jack always wearing a diamond pinky ring.

Today John Tortes Meyers's descendants remain active in the affairs of the Santa Rosa Band of the Cahuilla. Colonel Meyers is on the tribal council. Shanna Meyers and Michele Meyers Cornejo are members of the Band's enrollment committee.

During interviews with John Tortes Meyers in June 1969, for a three-part series commemorating the 100th anniversary of major league baseball, Jim Dawson of the *Riverside Press-Enterprise* found his "handshake is firm, his brown eyes full of humor, and his wit ... keen." As he neared the end of his life, Meyers told Dawson, "The Giants are still my team. Once a Giant, always a Giant." He did, however, acknowledge keeping up with the Dodgers by listening to Vin Scully's broadcasts. He also regularly read *The Sporting News.*

During the interview Meyers shared with Dawson the secret of his longevity. He said when he retired from baseball he had a physical examination. When the doctor asked him what he planned to do now, Meyers responded, "Just rest and relax, I guess." The doctor gave him some advice: "Chief, you're like a racing car. Your motor has been running since 1898. You just keep pulling a little load mentally and physically. Don't pull over to the curb."

According to Dawson, Meyers said, "I've found that to be pretty good advice. My grandfather died at 113 and several of my relatives have lived between 100 and 115 years."[76]

The last time Lawrence Ritter heard from his old friend was in a 1970 Christmas letter. "I am not any too well," Meyers wrote. "My eyesight is failing, getting quite dim. Just read the headlines now. No fine print. It is quite some chore for me to write, as you can see by my handwriting. It looks like the sun is getting down pretty low on the old Chief. Maybe Bresnahan got a bad finger and soon Mr. McGraw will be calling for a catcher. Who knows what is going on up there. Don't let this disturb you, my good friend. I am not a quitter."[77]

Seven months later, on Sunday, July 25, 1971, after an illness of several months that sent him to the Community Hospital in San Bernardino a number of times, John Tortes Meyers died. The short obituary in the *New York Times* was titled "Chief Meyers dies; Stengel Teammate"[78]:

> Chief Meyers was one of Casey Stengel's teammates on the Brooklyn Dodgers of 1916. In 1965 the Chief made a road trip with the Los Angeles Dodgers and visited Shea Stadium a few days before Stengel retired as manager of the Mets....
>
> A statistical compilation made in 1917 showed that Meyers led all major league catchers in batting over a stretch of years. In eight years through the 1916 season he batted .297. At the end of his last year in baseball, 1917, he had a .291 lifetime record. In World Series play he batted .290.

The obituary in *The Sporting News* mistakenly identified Meyers as a "full-blooded Indian from one of California's Mission tribes," but it correctly called him "a cultured and witty man," who spent a year at Dartmouth before turning professional. Quoting *The Glory of Their Times*, *The Sporting News* pointed out that when he played, "Indians were looked upon as foreigners" and noted, "The Chief was always sensitive about the sub-standard place the Indians were given in American history."[79]

John Tortes Meyers was laid to rest on Friday, July 30, 1971, after a 10:00 A.M. funeral service in the chapel of Ralph W. Allen Mortuary in Rialto. The Riverside Elks Club made the arrangements for the service.[80] The Cahuilla catcher was buried in Green Acres Memorial Park in Bloomington, California, near Rialto.[81]

When Lawrence Ritter received the call informing him that his friend had passed away, Ritter said his mind went back to what Meyers had said during their first meeting seven years earlier[82]:

> I guess ... I am like an old hemlock. My head is still high but the winds of close to a hundred winters have whistled through my branches, and I have been witness to many wondrous and many tragic things. My eyes perceive the present, but my roots are imbedded deeply in the grandeur of the past.

.

# Honors, Ongoing Challenges, and Legacy (1972–2011)

## Honors

### Ranking John Tortes Meyers
### Among the Best Catchers

How does John Tortes Meyers compare with other outstanding catchers in the history of baseball? It may be a question that cannot, in the final analysis, be answered objectively. William McNeil has made one of the first serious attempts at developing a statistical method for determining the best catchers in baseball history. However, he omits from consideration catchers of the Deadball Era (including Meyers) because "their statistics, particularly their defensive statistics, could not confidently be measured and converted to the same basis as modern catchers."[1]

The limited evidence has not kept some baseball enthusiasts from speculating on how to rate Meyers in relation to the best catchers. In particular, they have asked whether the Veterans Committee should consider Meyers for induction into the National Baseball Hall of Fame at Cooperstown, New York.[2]

Those who believe Meyers should receive Hall of Fame consideration make the following case. First, they point to his outstanding offensive performance. His .291 lifetime batting average is the highest among *all* catchers of the Deadball Era.[3] In fact, Meyers's lifetime batting average is higher than that of eight of the 13 National and American League catchers in the Hall of Fame: Ray Schalk (.253), Gary Carter (.262), Johnny Bench (.267), Carlton Fisk (.269), Roy Campanella (.276), Roger Bresnahan (.279), Rick Ferrell (.281), and Yogi Berra (.285). Only five Hall of Fame catchers compiled higher career batting averages: Mickey Cochrane (.320), Bill Dickey (.313), Ernie Lombardi (.306), Buck Ewing (.303), and Gabby Hartnett (.297). Meyers's 1912 average of .358 places him fourth on the list of the best single season batting averages for a major league catcher, behind only Joe Mauer (.365 in 2009), Bill Dickey (.362 in 1936) and Mike Piazza (.362 in 1997).

In other offensive categories Meyers ranks among the top 25 of past and current major league catchers who caught at least 800 games: On-Base Percentage — .3668 (15th) and Batting Contribution Measured in Runs Per Game — 5.380 (24th). In the offensive category of Total Player Wins, he ranks first.[4]

Despite the lack of objective comparative data, his advocates also contend Meyers was an excellent defensive catcher. At a time when catchers were emerging as "field generals," Meyers, they assert, was one of the best strategists and tacticians of his era. Because of his ability to make the right defensive decisions in the heat of battle, Meyers's manager John McGraw called him "a quick thinker." McGraw always compared Meyers's defensive skills favorably with those of Hall of Famer Roger Bresnahan, whom he also managed. After observing him for seven years McGraw considered Meyers to be "one of the best catchers in the National League," a team leader, and "all around a very valuable man."[5] In particular, Meyers earned a well-deserved reputation for his ability to determine when runners were about to steal and cut them down on the base paths.

Moreover, Meyers's role in working effectively with the Hall of Fame pitchers on the Giants staff deserves recognition, his proponents argue. Christy Mathewson once said, "The Chief understands my style so well, that we hardly need signs to communicate."[6] Meyers was also instrumental in helping Rube Marquard prepare for games and caught virtually every one of Marquard's record-setting 19 consecutive victories during the 1912 season.

His supporters further contend that in addition to his stellar performance on the diamond, Meyers's contributions to the game off the field deserve Hall of Fame consideration. Decades before the creation of the players' union, they point out, Meyers was a strong advocate for players' rights, chosen by his teammates to represent them in disputes with management. More than once during the World Series in which he played, he was selected to press the case for fair compensation of players to league officials.

Also under the category of "impact on the game," advocates of Meyers claim, is his groundbreaking role as one of the first Native Americans to achieve the status of legitimate major league star. He overcame significant obstacles to reach and sustain the highest level of performance. Albert Bender was on the margin of Hall of Fame eligibility when the Veterans Committee selected him for Cooperstown, those making the case for Meyers point out, but Bender's impact as the first Native American major league pitcher both to excel and to endure were appropriately weighed by the Veterans Committee.[7] Meyers was also one of the first Native American major leaguers to reach the pinnacle of success and to remain at that level for a number of years.

Finally, Meyers's proponents point to the fact that before there was a National Baseball Hall of Fame, John Tortes Meyers was selected for the top honors in major league baseball. They include the 1913 Spalding Guide Hall of Fame for his performance in the 1912 season, and the Grand National All-America Baseball Team in 1912 (ranking players for the single best season at their position since 1871). He continued to be listed on the Grand National Team through the rest of his career. He was also listed as the top catcher in the 1912 Reach Guide.

Over the years Meyers has shown up consistently in lists of the best major league catchers. For example, in 1973 *Baseball Digest* gave honorable mention to Meyers in its compilation of baseball's all-time greatest catchers.[8]

In addition, STATs, Inc. has named Meyers to its National League all-star teams for 1911, 1912, 1913, and 1914.[9] Finally, in choosing the top 50 players of the Deadball Era (1901–1919) the Deadball Committee of the Society for American Baseball Research (SABR), in a poll conducted by Steve Constantelos in 2002, named Chief Meyers, along with Roger Bresnahan and Johnny Kling, as the catchers on the list.[10]

On the basis of all of these factors, his supporters believe the Veterans Committee should give John Tortes Meyers renewed consideration for induction into the National Baseball Hall of Fame. However, others make a compelling counter-argument that his on-field record leaves him significantly short of realistic Hall of Fame consideration. Bill James, for example, selected Meyers for his 1910–1919 Major League All-Star Team but considered the Cahuilla catcher only the 60th best among the top 100 catchers in baseball history on the basis of his Win Shares method of evaluation.[11]

In the final analysis, whether or not Meyers receives renewed consideration by the Veterans Committee for induction into the National Baseball Hall of Fame, he does merit recognition as one of the very best catchers of the Deadball Era and among the best of all time.

## Other Honors

In 1969, two years before he died, word reached the Santa Rosa Reservation that John Tortes Meyers would be inducted into a planned all–Indian Athletic Hall of Fame at Haskell Indian Nations University in Lawrence, Kansas. Identified in *The Indian Reporter* as the former Santa Rosa spokesman, Meyers was, according to the newsletter, one of the first mentioned for this new Hall of Fame.[12] Unfortunately, he died a year before his induction in 1972.

The stated purpose of the all–Indian Athletic Hall of Fame is "to recognize the great athletes of American Indian heritage and to serve as a model for the Indian youth to strive for their own physical greatness."[13] Nearly a hundred athletes have been selected and recognized in a Hall of Heroes on the Haskell Indian Nations University campus. John Tortes Meyers was among 14 in the first class of inductees, alongside several other major league ballplayers: Charles Albert Bender, Allie Reynolds, and Jim Thorpe.

Meyers's page on the Hall of Fame's website names him as John T. Meyers (called "Chief"). It identifies him as a member of the Cahuilla Band, born in Riverside, California, and then lists his baseball achievements. In citing various tributes to and stories about Meyers, the Hall of Fame page intentionally does not refer to him as "Chief," "out of respect for John T. Meyers."

One of the more unusual settings in which Meyers has been recognized for his accomplishments as a ballplayer was a U.S. Supreme Court ruling. In his majority opinion in the famous baseball anti-trust case (Flood v. Kuhn, 1972), Supreme Court Justice Harry Blackmun offered his list of the best players in major league history. According to Justice Blackmun, Chief Meyers belongs in the elite group of baseball players who "sparked the diamond" through the national pastime's first century.[14]

In 1984 John Tortes Meyers was among the first Dartmouth College alumni to be inducted into the Wearers of the Green, the College's athletic honor society.[15]

On May 24, 2004, members of the Meyers family were present when their Uncle Jack was inducted into the Riverside, California, Sport Hall of Fame. Created in 2003, the Hall's mission is "to honor those athletes, athletic administrators and community leaders who have brought fame and honor to the City of Riverside through participation in their chosen sport." The Riverside Hall of Fame plaques are displayed on a Wall of Distinction located on the exterior of the Community Medical Group building at the corner of 14th Street and Magnolia Avenue in Riverside. The plaque honoring John "Chief" Meyers notes his background, his accomplishments in baseball, and successful career after his days in baseball ended.[16]

## Ongoing Challenges

### Prejudice Against Native Americans
### in Major League Baseball

As he approached the end of his life, John Tortes Meyers was well aware of the prejudice still directed against Native Americans. Unfortunately, some of the stereotyping and bias he experienced during his career, and which remained at the end of his life, are still present in major league baseball today.

The Cleveland Indians still use as a prominent symbol the grinning Chief Wahoo in a mock Indian headdress. Fans of the Indians and Atlanta Braves rock their stadiums with the same war whooping and chants that greeted the first Native American players. To these have been added the stereotypical "tomahawk chop," supposedly a gesture, team officials claim unconvincingly, of respect for the Native American warrior tradition.[17]

Philip Deloria has placed the modern stereotyping of Indian athletes in the context of the politics of representation. Just as was the case during Meyers's career, at the beginning of the twenty-first century white Americans still tend to define Native American athletes in terms of biased expectations of how Indians "should be."[18]

A contrast may be drawn between the recognition given to African Americans who have excelled in major league baseball and the lack of acclaim afforded Native American stars. Although both groups have had to overcome racism in their quest to reach the top of their professions, African Americans like Jackie Robinson were considered self-sacrificing pioneers, leading the way for other African Americans. By contrast, Native Americans like Albert Bender and John Tortes Meyers, who took the same kind of abuse on the baseball diamond and overcame it to rise to stardom, were most often portrayed as oddities acting out their innate warrior instincts on the baseball diamond. As Deloria has pointed out, "Jackie Robinson has imprinted on our culture with vastly more force than Chiefs Bender or Meyers. As a trailblazer rather than an anomaly, he carries far more cultural weight than even Jim Thorpe."[19]

Unfortunately, even Ken Burns' acclaimed PBS-TV documentary "Baseball" reflects this imbalance. A segment in the series entitled "Fair and Equal" explores in depth the contradiction between the claim that baseball was a melting pot and the reality of the exclusion of Black ballplayers from the major leagues until 1947. It also documents vividly the racism Jackie Robinson and other Blacks experienced when they entered the game. However, the segment almost entirely ignores the similar challenges faced by Native American major leaguers like Meyers and Bender a half-century earlier and the important contributions they made to the game.

Ironically, a photo of John Tortes Meyers in his New York Giants catching gear appears in one scene in the "Fair and Equal" segment of the documentary film, but he is not identified in the narrative. Instead, while Meyers's picture is on the screen, the story of John McGraw's attempt to pass off African American second baseman Charlie Grant as a Cherokee Indian named "Chief Tokahoma" so he could play for the Giants is being told. Viewers are left with the impression that the athlete being shown them is Charlie Grant, not one of the first Native American heroes of the game. The confusion was surely not intentional, but an opportunity to highlight the important role Native Americans played in the early history of baseball and the racism and prejudice they experienced and overcame was missed. There is only one passing reference made to Indian ballplayers in "Baseball," and that is to Albert Bender "who like other Native Americans was called 'Chief.'"[20]

As Jeffrey P. Beck has observed, "While the number of Jackie Robinson (#42) has been retired in every major league stadium, there is no tribute to those courageous Native Americans who overcame racial abuse to have stellar careers."[21] Each year major league baseball honors the contributions of African Americans to baseball with Jackie Robinson Day in April and also the contributions of Latino players with Roberto Clemente Day in September. Why are the contributions and achievements of Native American ballplayers like John Tortes Meyers not honored by the major leagues, Beck asks? Apparently, the stereotype of the "invisible Indian" in major league baseball continues in the twenty-first century.

## Native Americans at Dartmouth College

Another issue deserving attention in a discussion of ongoing challenges is the status of Native Americans at Dartmouth since 1905-1906, the year John Tortes Meyers spent at the College. It is a mixed story of admirable progress and pockets of continuing prejudice.

By 1969 Dartmouth had graduated a total of only 19 Native Americans throughout its history. The mandate of the College's charter two centuries earlier to educate Indians remained largely unfulfilled. That finally began to change in the aftermath of the national movement to reassert Native American rights during the 1960s. In 1970 Dartmouth President John Kemeny reaffirmed the College's commitment to Native American education and directed the Admissions Office to recruit Indian students actively. He announced a goal of 15 Native American students in the class of 1974. He also established the college's Native American Program (NAP) to provide cultural and academic support for Indian students, intending it to be a program "run by Indians for Indians." In 1972 a Native American Studies Program was added.[22]

The absence of Native Americans prior to 1970 had not kept Dartmouth from developing its own version of Indian traditions. The College had an unofficial Indian symbol and mascot, and Dartmouth sports teams were called the "Indians." Students chanted war whoops at athletic contests and engaged in the breaking of "Indian peace pipes" in pre-graduation celebrations. A mural in Thayer Dining Hall painted by *Saturday Evening Post* cover artist Walter B. Humphrey of the Class of 1914 depicted drunken and half-naked Indian men and women in an imaginary rendition of the College's founding.

In 1971 Indian students and faculty took the initiative to end the stereotyping of Native Americans at Dartmouth. They claimed that throughout its history the College had "nourished only a romantic notion of being an 'Indian' school through the creation and retention of ... assorted caricatures of Indian Americans" and called on Dartmouth to remove all such symbols. In 1974 the Dartmouth Board of Trustees voted to change the College's nickname from "Indians" to "Big Green," and banned the display of representations of the "Dartmouth Indian" in college-sponsored settings. The "Indian pipe-breaking" ceremony was discouraged (though many graduating seniors continued it) and the offensive mural was kept covered except for special occasions.

In response to these actions a group of angry alumni objected to what they considered an unwarranted attack on Dartmouth's traditions. Some Dartmouth students joined them. In 1979 two non-native students skated across the ice rink dressed as "Dartmouth Indians" between periods of a Dartmouth intercollegiate hockey game. The conservative student journal *Dartmouth Review* took the lead in defending their action, arguing removal of the Indian symbols at Dartmouth was misguided. In one article, then–Dartmouth student Laura Ingraham (now a nationally known conservative commentator and author) argued that if Samson Occom, the Native American who played a pivotal role in founding Dartmouth as a school dedicated to the education of Indians, "were alive today, he would have chanted loudly our College cry, 'Wah-hoo-wah.'"[23]

In recent decades elected Dartmouth student leaders have taken the lead in challenging this perspective. For example, in 1992 the Senior Class Executive Committee voted unanimously to abolish the pipe-breaking ritual at graduation, responding to the concerns expressed by Dartmouth's Native American students that it was a desecration of the sacred pipe rituals of a number of Indian nations.[24]

The enrollment of Native American students gradually increased. By 1996 300 Native Americans from 120 tribes had graduated from Dartmouth College. The undergraduate population of 4,000 at Dartmouth was 3.3 percent Native American, while only 180 of the country's 3,000 colleges and universities had achieved as much as a two percent enrollment of American Indians. Seventy-five percent of Native students at Dartmouth were graduating, compared with a national graduation rate of only 15 percent for Indian students.

In the nearly four decades since its establishment, Dartmouth's Native American Studies Program has gained international recognition as one of the finest of its kind. It provides undergraduates "with a wide array of course offerings, as well as research and internship opportunities, designed to expose students to Native history, cultures, and contemporary issues."[25]

One modern Dartmouth student who represents well John Tortes Meyer's legacy is Robert (Bob) Antoine Bennett, a member of the Rosebud Sioux (Sicangu Lakota) tribe and a 1994 graduate of the College. Bennett overcame the same sort of prejudice and stereotyping Meyers endured to have a successful professional baseball career and then pursue a career in law enforcement in order to serve Indian people.[26]

The conflict over the kind of stereotypical representations Meyers encountered during his year at Dartmouth and that continued through the years flared up again as recently as 2006. At the beginning of the 2006-07 academic year concern was expressed about incidents on campus. *Dartmouth Review* again distributed T-shirts with the banned "Dartmouth Indian" to incoming freshmen. In addition, "a group of fraternity pledges interrupted a Native American ceremony by clapping, dancing, and then running through the center of a drum circle." One of the rowing teams "chose 'Cowboys, Indians, and Barnyard Animals' as its unofficial theme."

In November 2006, Dartmouth President James Wright issued a call in the student newspaper, *The Dartmouth,* to denounce these actions. The conservative *Dartmouth Review* responded with an edition featuring a cover "depicting a scalp-wielding Native American and the headline 'The Natives Are Getting Restless!'"[27] The magazine continues to maintain an on-line "Indian store," selling t-shirts, ties, bags, mugs, and other items with the Dartmouth Indian symbol, and even a cane with an Indian head, which, a description next to the item claims, has been "a Dartmouth Commencement tradition since 1899."[28]

Despite the ongoing controversies, by 2009 over 700 Native Americans from more than 160 tribes had attended Dartmouth since the College recommitted itself to its original charter. In the fall of 2009 more than 50 Indian students were members of Dartmouth's freshman class.

As Colin Calloway, former chair of the Native American Studies Program, has written, "Native American students are not just statistics to show that Dartmouth is finally living up to its historic mission. They connect Dartmouth to Native worlds and worldviews that are lost to most of modern America, to tribal communities and concerns that seem far removed from a privileged Ivy League college."[29]

Dartmouth College is today providing a microcosm of how the larger American culture should be responding to five centuries of failure and neglect in relating to Native Americans. One Dartmouth man, John Tortes Meyers, would surely be very proud.

## John Tortes Meyers in the Contemporary Popular Imagination

How is John Tortes Meyers remembered and represented in the popular imagination today? One indication is found in an essay by award-winning writer Adam Gopnik, first published in *The New Yorker* and anthologized in a collection entitled *Paris to the Moon*. In the essay Gopnik describes a bedtime story he made up for his three-year-old son Luke, who was growing up in Paris with no understanding of baseball.[30] "The Rookie," is the story of "a small boy in Anywhere, U.S.A., in the spring of 1908." His parents discovered their son had an uncanny ability to throw stones at things, so they sent him off to New York to try out with the Giants manager, John J. McGraw.

When the boy arrived McGraw called the great Christy Mathewson out of the dugout to watch him pitch, along with "Chief Meyers, the great American Indian catcher." In the story the Chief came out, "with a weary, crippled, long-suffering gait, and squatted." After watching the three-year old Rookie pitch, Meyers shouted, "Hey, Mr. McGraw! I ain't never seen speed like that, and ain't he got movement on it too!"

Impressed by the Rookie's velocity, McGraw decides to have him pitch an exhibition game against the Detroit Tigers the next Sunday. In the game Ty Cobb tries to bait the Rookie by calling him "Baby!" but he strikes out the Georgia Peach after doctoring the ball with milk.

From then on Gopnik told Luke a story about the Rookie every night. In the stories "the Chief was always blustery and honest, wanting nothing more than to settle in with his copy of the *Police Gazette* and have a peaceful afternoon at McSorley's." He also serves as the Rookie's babysitter.

Although Gopnik said he was drawing on *The Glory of Their Times*, the Meyers he created in the stories he told Luke was certainly not the player of that interview. The old catcher Lawrence Ritter met was witty and cultured. The Meyers Gopnik created was ungrammatical and coarse, more interested in the *Police Gazette* than Shakespeare. The Meyers we have met in these pages visited museums and art galleries throughout his life. Gopnik's Meyers spent his afternoons in an Irish tavern. The one similarity is that the actual Meyers did reach out to those whom he sensed were having trouble fitting in.

In "The Rookie," Chief Meyers is not an unsympathetic character, but he is a considerably distorted version of the ballplayer and person John Tortes Meyers was. Unfortunately, nearly four decades after his death, as was the case throughout his life, the Meyers too many readers encounter is a caricature rather than the actual, much more interesting man he was.

# Legacy

## Native American Participation
## in Major League Baseball

In the decades after Meyers retired from the Boston Braves in 1917, Native American ballplayers did reach the major leagues, but in declining numbers.

The list included Moses "Chief" Yellowhorse (Pawnee), who pitched for Pittsburgh in 1921-22; Pepper Martin (Osage), known as "The Wild Horse of the Osage," a member of the famed St. Louis Cardinals "Gashouse Gang," who played for the Cardinals between 1928 and 1944[31]; Roy Johnson (Cherokee), who played in the American League between 1929 and 1938; his brother Bob "Indian Bob" Johnson, whose career (mostly with the Philadelphia Athletics) spanned 1933 through 1945; and Rudy York (Cherokee), who played from 1934 through 1948, mostly with Detroit.

Why did American Indian participation in professional baseball decline during the 1930s and fall precipitously after World War II? Writing in 1940, one commentator gave the racist interpretation still common over two decades after Meyers left the major leagues, attributing the "red man's fall from the pinnacle he once enjoyed" in the athletic world to "an admixture of other races and the thinning of the [fullblooded] stock."[32]

More recently, and more accurately, Joseph Oxendine has suggested the reasons for the decline in the number of Native American players in professional baseball included the closing of Indian boarding schools like Carlisle where baseball and other sports were stressed, the scarcity of opportunities for Indians in other institutions of higher education, the poor quality of reservation and local schools, federal policies of termination and relocation, and, in general, depressed social conditions for Indians on and off the reservations.[33] To the list should be added the racial bigotry that "undoubtedly unnerved many a [Native American] player."[34]

A telling statistic is that, "[w]hile American Indians make up about one percent of the country's population, according to the 2000 Census, they account for only four-tenths of a percent of the scholarship athletes at the major college level."[35]

In the decade after World War II the most prominent Native American major leaguer was Allie Pierce "Super Chief" Reynolds (1917–1994). An enrolled member of the Creek Nation and graduate of Oklahoma State University, Reynolds played for the Cleveland Indians and New York Yankees from 1942–1954, experiencing the same kind of racial stereotyping Meyers faced.[36] *Sports Illustrated* named Reynolds the nation's top professional athlete one year, yet in addition to carrying the nickname "Superchief," he was described in other publications as "A Good Indian Who Delivers Goods" and "Chief or Medicine Man?"[37]

Inspired by the example of John Tortes Meyers and other Native American pioneers in baseball, Allie Reynolds did not let the prejudice he experienced defeat him. Like Meyers he took an active role standing up for his fellow ballplayers. For example, he was chosen as an American League player representative in the groundbreaking negotiations with owners that led to the creation of the major league players' pension fund.[38] After his retirement, Reynolds went on to a successful career in the oil business and remained active in baseball, serving as president of the American Association.[39]

For the next half-century after Allie Reynolds, there were few Native American major leaguers. Most notable were Gene Locklear (Lumbee), Bucky Dent (Cherokee), and Dwight Lowry (Lumbee) in the 1970s and 1980s, and Jayhawk Owens (Cherokee) and Bobby Madritsch (Lakota Sioux) in the 1990s and early 2000s.

### Contemporary Native American Major Leaguers: Taking Responsibility

In the second decade of the twenty-first century the participation of Native Americans in major league baseball is increasing. In 2011 three American Indian major leaguers are top-caliber players: Joba Chamberlain, Jacoby Ellsbury, and Kyle Lohse. Chamberlain, a pitcher for the New York Yankees, is a member of the Ho Chunk (Winnebago) Tribe of Nebraska. Ellsbury, an outfielder for the Boston Red Sox, belongs to the Navajo (*Diné*) Nation of Arizona and New Mexico. He was selected to play in the 2011 Major League All-Star game. Lohse, who pitches for the St. Louis Cardinals, is a member of northern California's small Nomlaki Wintun tribe.

According to Royse Parr of the Society for American Baseball Research, "All three players are fiercely proud of their heritage. They focus their energies on trying to be positive role models for America Indian youth. Chamberlain frequently returns to the Winnebago reservation to encourage kids. Lohse and Ellsbury have often spoken to American Indian youth groups."[40]

Another major leaguer not normally identified as a Native American because his tribal ancestry is Central American rather than North American is also taking responsibility in making the opportunity he has had available to other Indian youth. Journeyman pitcher Miguel Batista is a descendant of the Carib Indians of the present Dominican Republic who were decimated by Columbus and the Europeans who followed him. Between 1992 and 2011 Batista played in the major leagues for Pittsburgh, Florida, the Chicago Cubs, Montreal, Kansas City, Arizona (twice), Toronto, Seattle, Washington, St. Louis and the New York Mets.

While an Arizona Diamondback in 2001, Batista visited the Navajo Reservation and decided to make the game he loved available to young people there. He committed $50,000 of his own money to building a baseball field, renewing what Meyers had done during the filming of *Laughing Boy* in the 1930s. Like Meyers, Batista is a cultured man who has published a novel and a book of poetry. In addition to the baseball field he has worked to build a library and get books into the hands of Navajo children.[41]

Despite the efforts of current Native American major leaguers, the challenges facing American Indians who might aspire to become professional baseball players remain significant. While Major League Baseball has instituted an R.B.I. program (Reviving Baseball in the Inner Cities) there is no comparable program for reservations or off-reservation native communities. Because they think Indian athletes given scholarships to play baseball and other sports at colleges and universities drop out at a higher rate than other students, coaches are reluctant to recruit them.[42]

If John Tortes Meyers were still with us, he would certainly be supporting the efforts of contemporary Native American major leaguers to encourage talented Indian youth to strive to compete at the highest levels in their chosen professions. He would be in the stands urging young ballplayers on, offering advice on "scientific hitting" and the art of catching to those who asked him how it was done in his day.

Meyers died just as Dartmouth College was finally following through on the commitment of its charter to Native American education. We can be sure that if he were alive today, he would be one of the most enthusiastic promoters of Dartmouth's Native American Program, encouraging Indian young people to apply for scholarships at Dartmouth and other colleges and universities with similar opportunities.

One thing is certain. By the example of his baseball career and his life of service to his people, John Tortes Meyers showed young Native Americans and all who face the challenges of overcoming discrimination and prejudice how to walk with their heads held high.

Describing the rookie Cahuilla catcher in 1909, a journalist penned words that are just as fitting as an epitaph[43]:

> A strong love of justice, a lightning sense of humor, a fund of general information that runs from politics to Plato, a quick, logical mind, and the self-contained, dignified poise that is the hallmark of good breeding — he is easily the most remarkable ballplayer in the big leagues.

# Chapter Notes

## Prologue

1. Lawrence Ritter, "Chief Meyers," *Baseball's Finest: The Greats, the Flakes, the Weird, and the Wonderful*, ed. Danny Peary (New York: Simon & Schuster, 1990), 151; Donald Honig, "The Author Meets a Baseball Lion And a Few Celebrated Pussycats," *Sports Illustrated*, October 17, 1983.

2. Tom Simon, ed., *Deadball Stars of the National League* (Washington, D.C.: Brassey's, 2004), 17.

3. *The Sporting News*, December 6, 1923; see also Fred Lieb, "Baseball — The Nation's Melting Pot," *Baseball Magazine*, August 1923, 393–95.

4. "Chielf [sic] Myers [sic] Sole Ambition to 'Make Good' in New York Team," *Nebraska State Journal*, May 2, 1909, C7; Lawrence Ritter, "Chief Meyers," *The Glory of Their Times: The Story of the Early Days of Baseball Told by the Men Who Played It, Enlarged Edition* (New York: HarperCollins Perennial, 2002), 170. In 1969 Meyers told another reporter, "Being an Indian in baseball was difficult. You felt like a foreigner sometimes" (*Riverside [California] Press-Enterprise*, June 25, 1969).

5. Simon, *Deadball Stars*, 71.

6. Honig, "The Author Meets a Baseball Lion."

7. Lawrence Ritter, *The Glory of Their Times*, 184.

## Chapter One

1. Jack McDonald, "One for the Chief," *San Francisco Examiner*, August 30, 1966, 52. Reprinted as "Catching Up with Matty's Catcher," *Baseball Digest*, 25, no. 10 (1967), 55.

2. Kevin Nelson, *Golden Game: The Story of California Baseball* (Berkeley, CA: Heyday Books, 2004), 87.

3. Undated, unattributed article in John Tortes Meyers File, National Baseball Hall of Fame Library, Cooperstown, New York.

4. Tom Patterson, *A Colony for California: Riverside's First Hundred Years* (Riverside: Press-Enterprise, 1971), 135.

5. Personal Interview with Colonel John V. Meyers (September 22, 2008). Marion's World War I draft registration card, dated 1918, confirms that he was a plasterer who worked for the Cresmer Manufacturing Company (Riverside County Draft Records, Roll 1531275, Draft Board 1). According to Michele Meyers Cornejo (personal interview, July 16, 2010), Marion owned cattle on the Santa Rosa reservation before dying in the 1930s.

6. Personal Interview with Shanna Meyers (September 29, 2008).

7. Henry C. Koerper, "The Catcher Was a Cahuilla: A Remembrance of John Tortes Meyers," *Journal of California and Great Basin Anthropology* 24, no. 1 (2004), 21–22.

8. For example, 1911 U.S. Indian Census, California Special Census 1907–11, Cahuilla Agency, Roll M595-12, Image 504.

9. Jim Dawson, "Meyers' Memory Bridges Baseball's Generation Gap," *Riverside* (*California*) *Press-Enterprise*, June 24, 1969, 1.

10. Undated, unattributed article, John Tortes Meyers File, National Baseball Hall of Fame Library, Cooperstown, New York.

11. Lawrence Ritter, "Chief Meyers," *The Glory of Their Times: The Story of the Early Days of Baseball Told by the Men Who Played It, Enlarged Edition* (New York: HarperCollins Perennial, 2002), 170.

12. Koerper, "The Catcher Was a Cahuilla," 21.

13. Dawson, "Meyers' Memory," 1. On Spring Rancheria, see John D. Goodman, "Spring Rancheria: Archaeological Investigations of a Transient Cahuilla Village in Early Riverside, California," (unpublished Master's Thesis, University of California, Riverside, June 1993).

14. Patterson, *A Colony for California*, 135.

15. Personal Interview with Shanna Meyers (September 29, 2008).

16. Don Watson, "Famed Indian Ball Player Dies at 91," *The Daily Enterprise: A Newspaper for Riverside County* (July 27, 1971), B-1.

17. Frederick C. Hoxie, *A Final Promise: The Campaign to Assimilate the Indians, 1880–1920* (New York: Cambridge University Press, 1989), ix–x.

18. For comprehensive overviews of the attempt to assimilate Indians to white society through education, see Jon Reyhner and Jeanne Eder, *American Indian Education: A History* (Norman: University of Oklahoma Press, 2004); and David Wallace Adams, *Education for Extinction: American Indians and the Boarding Schools Experience* (Lawrence: University of Kansas Press, 1995).

19. On the role of baseball and other sports at Carlisle Indian School and other Indian boarding schools, see John Bloom, *To Show What an Indian Can Do: Sports at Native American Boarding Schools* (Minneapolis: University of Minnesota Press, 2000) and Sally Jenkins *The Real All Americans: The Team That Changed a Game, a People, a Nation* (New York: Doubleday, 2007).

20. Matthew Sakiestewa Gilbert, *Education Beyond the Mesas: Hopi Students at Sherman Institute* (Lincoln: University of Nebraska Press, 2010), 48, 163.

21. Nelson, *Golden Game*, xi.

22. Earl L. Buie, "He Put the Indian 'Sign' on Baseball," *San Bernardino (California) Sun-Telegram*, April 5, 1961, E-1; Dawson, *"Meyers' Memory,"* 1; Ritter, *The Glory of Their Times*, 170.

23. John T. Meyers, "Greatest Catcher Believes he 'Booted' Life's Chance by Choosing Diamond Career," *New York American*, June 16, 1912, L, 4.

24. Koerper, *The Catcher Was a Cahuilla*, 22.

25. Dawson, *"Meyers' Memory,"* 2.

26. Buie, "He Put the Indian 'Sign' on Baseball," E-1.

27. Bob Ryan, "The First Name in Fireballing: Any Discussion of Heat Begins with Walter Johnson," *The Boston Globe*, March 31, 2000, E7.

28. Watson, "Famed Indian Ball Player Dies at 91," B-1.

29. Joe Blackstock, "For 'Chief' Meyers, Hitting the Ball Was the Easy Part," *Inland Valley Daily Bulletin (Ontario, CA)*, July 9, 2005.

30. Koerper, *The Catcher Was a Cahuilla*, 23; Nelson, *The Golden Game*, 83.

31. Buie, "He Put the Indian 'Sign' on Baseball," E-1.

32. Ritter, *The Glory of Their Times*, 170.

33. Meyers, "Greatest Catcher," L, 4; *El Paso Herald*, December 7, 1907.

34. Meyers, "Greatest Catcher," L, 4.

35. Ralph Glaze and Rolfe Humphries, "How Chief Made the Major Leagues," *Empire Magazine*, August 20, 1967, 32–34.

36. "'Chief' Meyers Shanghaied" (unattributed and undated, John Tortes Meyers File, National Baseball Hall of Fame Library, Cooperstown, New York).

37. Grantland Rice, "A Talk with Chief Meyers," February 14, 1947 (John Tortes Meyers File, National Baseball Hall of Fame Library, Cooperstown, New York). See also Meyers, *Greatest Catcher*, L, 4 and McDonald, "One for the Chief," 52.

38. Lawrence Ritter, "Chief Meyers," *Baseball's Finest: The Greats, the Flakes, the Weird, and the Wonderful*, ed. Danny Peary (New York: Simon & Schuster, 1990), 151.

39. Brian McDonald, *Indian Summer: The Forgotten Story of Louis Sockalexis—the First Native American in Major League Baseball* (Emmaus, PA: Rodale Press, 2003), vii, 54, 65, 71, 94, 107, 109. See also David Fleitz, *Louis Sockalexis: The First Cleveland Indian* (Jefferson, NC: McFarland, 2002); Ellen J. Staurowsky, "Sockalexis and the Making of the Myth at the Core of Cleveland's 'Indian' Image, C. Richard King and Charles Fruehling Springwood, ed. *Team Spirits: The Native American Mascots Controversy* (Lincoln: University of Nebraska Press, 2001), 82–106.

40. Jeffrey P. Beck, *The American Indian Integration of Baseball* (Lincoln: University of Nebraska Press, 2004), 4.

41. Kate Buford, *Native Son: The Life and Sporting Legend of Jim Thorpe* (New York: Alfred A. Knopf, 2010), 87.

42. Joseph B. Oxendine, *American Indian Sports Heritage* (Lincoln: University of Nebraska Press, 1995), x; James Skipper, *Baseball Nicknames: A Dictionary of Origins and Meanings*, Jefferson, NC: McFarland, 1992; Frank DeFord, *The Old Ball Game: How John Mc Graw, Christy Mathewson, and the New York Giants Created Modern Baseball* (New York: Atlantic Monthly Press, 2005), 134–35.

43. Tom Swift, *Chief Bender's Burden: The Silent Struggle of a Baseball Star* (Lincoln: University of Nebraska Press, 2008), 6–7. Another Bender biographer, Robert Peyton Wiggins, concludes that while Bender at first avoided using "Chief" when he signed autographs, he "did not state publicly that he disliked the nickname and ... would eventually accept it for his professional identity" (*Chief Bender: A Baseball Biography* [Jefferson, NC: McFarland, 2010], 58).

44. Stephen I. Thompson, "The American Indian in the Major Leagues," *Baseball Research Journal* 12 (1983), 1; John. P. Rossi, *The*

*National Game: Baseball and American Culture* (Chicago: Ivan Dee, 2000), 82.

45. Beck, *American Indian Integration of Baseball*, 5, 72.

46. Cited in Beck, *American Indian Integration of Baseball*, 5.

47. "Chielf [sic] Myers [sic] Sole Ambition to 'Make Good' in New York Team," *Nebraska State Journal*, May 2, 1909, C7.

48. George Ringwald, "Former Major Leaguer 'Chief' Meyers: Old-timer Analyzes Today's Baseball," *Riverside (California) Press Enterprise*, August 23, 1964.

49. Ray Robinson, *Matty: An American Hero— Christy Mathewson of the New York Giants* (New York: Oxford University Press, 1994), 91; Wiggins, *Chief Bender*, 139.

50. Personal Interview with Shanna Meyers (September 29, 2008).

## Chapter Two

1. John T. Meyers, "Greatest Catcher Believes he 'Booted' Life's Chance by Choosing Diamond Career," *New York American*, June 16, 1912, L, 4.

2. Personal Interviews with Shanna Meyers (September 29, 2008), Colonel John V. Meyers (September 22, 2008), and Michele Meyers Cornejo (July 16, 2010).

3. Personal interview with Shanna Meyers (September 29, 2008). In July 2011, the Bureau of Indian Affairs web site (*http://www.bia.gov*) still listed the tribe as the Santa Rosa Band of Mission Indians.

4. George Ringwald, "Former major leaguer 'Chief' Meyers: Old-timer analyzes today's baseball," *Riverside (California) Press Enterprise*, August 23, 1964.

5. William A. Phelon, "The Indian Players," *Baseball Magazine*, October 1913, 21.

6. Lowell John Bean, "Cahuilla," *Handbook of North American Indians, Volume 8: California*, ed. Robert F. Heizer (Washington: Smithsonian Institution, 1978), 575.

7. Harry Clebourne James, *The Cahuilla Indians: The Men Called Master* (Tucson, AZ: Westernlore Press, 1960), 22.

8. Lowell John Bean. *Mukat's People: The Cahuilla Indians of Southern California* (Berkeley: University of California Press, 1972), 24; Bean, "Cahuilla," 575–576, fig. 1. By the time of Meyers's birth in 1880 more than half of the Cahuilla homeland had been lost as a result of the European and Euroamerican invasion.

9. Personal Interview with Colonel Meyers (September 22, 2008).

10. James, *The Cahuilla Indians*, 41.

11. William Duncan Strong, "Cahuilla," *University of California Publications in American Archaeology and Ethnology, Volume 26: Aboriginal Society in Southern California* (Berkeley: University of California Press, 1929), 36.

12. Bean, *Mukat's People*, 15–16.

13. Lowell John Bean, Lisa J. Bourgeault, Frank W. Porter, III, *The Cahuilla* (New York: Chelsea House, 1989), 19–23; Strong, "Cahuilla," 130–43; see also James, *The Cahuilla Indians*, 68–75.

14. This summary of the Cahuilla worldview is drawn from Bean et al, *The Cahuilla*, 18–19, 47–48; Bean, *Mukat's People*, 160–82; Bean, "Cahuilla," 582–83; and Lowell John Bean, principal investigator, *Tahquitz Report: A report of a cultural survey of the Tahquitz Canyon and mitigation efforts on the impact of a planned flood control project on the Tahquitz Creek, affecting sites associated with the Agua Caliente Band of the Cahuilla nation*, 1996, Ch. 5–7.

15. Bean, *Mukat's People*, 163.

16. Bean, *Mukat's People*, 97–98.

17. This summary of Cahuilla values is based on the descriptions by Lowell John Bean in several sources: Bean, et al, *The Cahuilla*, 48, 57–59; Bean, *Mukat's People*, 124–29, 173–180; Bean, "Cahuilla," 583; Bean, *Tahquitz Report*, Ch. 5–7.

18. Personal Interview with Colonel Meyers (September 22, 2008).

19. Bean *et al*, "Cahuilla," 583.

20. Robert F. Heizer and Albert L. Hurtado, eds., *The Destruction of California Indians* (Lincoln, NE: Bison Books, 1993), 201–202.

21. James, *The Cahuilla Indians*, 124–25.

22. Helen Hunt Jackson and Abbot Kinney, *On the Condition & Needs of the Mission Indians of California* (Washington: Government Printing Office, 1883), 18. Lawrence Ritter used this story to introduce his interview with Chief Meyers in *The Glory of Their Times*. Late in life Meyers said he guided Jackson during her tour of the Cahuilla homeland, although he would only have been a few years old at the time (e.g., Don Watson, "Famed Indian Ball Player Dies at 91," *The Daily Enterprise: A Newspaper for Riverside County*, July 27, 1971, B-1). It was likely another example of his use of ironic humor.

23. Tom Patterson, *A Colony for California: Riverside's First Hundred Years* (Riverside: Press-Enterprise), 119, 138.

24. Bean, *Mukat's People*, 18.

25. Meyers, "Greatest Catcher," L, 4.

26. Francisco Patencio, *Stories and Legends of the Palm Springs Indians as Told to Margaret Boynton* (Los Angeles: Times-Mirror Press, 1943).

27. James, *The Cahuilla Indians*, 139.

28. In 2000 the highest native population of

the Cahuilla reservations was Morengo with 543 (56.9 percent of the reservation's total population), followed by Soboba—433 (83 percent), Torres-Martinez—195 (4.7 percent), Agua Caliente—176 (.8 percent), Cahuilla—106 (68.8 percent), Los Coyotes—56 (80 percent), Santa Rosa—56 (80 percent), and Cabazon—15 (1.9 percent) (*http://factfinder. census.gov*, accessed 2/8/10). Augustine and Ramona Village had no census returns recorded.

29. Bean, *Tahquitz Report.*

## Chapter Three

1. Dartmouth College web site (*www.dartmouth.edu/~govdocs/case/*charter.htm, accessed 4/22/09); Colin Calloway, *The Indian History of an American Institution: Native Americans and Dartmouth* (Hanover, NH: Dartmouth College Press, 2010), 22.

2. Lawrence Ritter, "Chief Meyers," *The Glory of Their Times: The Story of the Early Days of Baseball Told by the Men Who Played It, Enlarged Edition* (New York: HarperCollins Perennial, 2002), 171. See also John T. Meyers, "Greatest Catcher Believes He 'Booted' Life's Chance by Choosing Diamond Career," *New York American* (June 16, 1912), L, 4.

3. Calloway, *The Indian History of an American Institution*, xiv.

4. Andrew Garrod and Colleen Larimore, ed., *First Person, First Peoples: Native American College Graduates Tell Their Life Stories* (Ithaca, NY: Cornell University Press, 1997), 7–8; Calloway, *The Indian History of an American Institution*, 26–28.

5. Wilder Dwight Quint, *The Story of Dartmouth* (Boston: Little, Brown, 1914), 55–57.

6. Jon Reyhner and Jeanne Eder, *American Indian Education: A History* (Norman: University of Oklahoma Press, 2004), 34.

7. Meyers, "Greatest Catcher," L, 4.

8. Calloway, *The Indian History of an American Institution*, 115.

9. Charles Eastman, *From the Deep Woods to Civilization* (Norwood, MA: Norwood Press, 1916), 65.

10. Raymond Wilson, *Ohiyesa: Charles Eastman, Santee Sioux* (Urbana: University of Illinois Press, 1983), 33.

11. Eastman, *From the Deep Woods to Civilization*, 67–68.

12. Eastman, *From the Deep Woods to Civilization*, 97–98, 68, 74, 67.

13. For an analysis of Eastman's writings and his role as an important Indian intellectual during the early twentieth century, see Lucy Maddox, *Citizen Indians: Native American Intellectuals, Race, and Reform* (Ithica, NY: Cor-

nell University, 2005), 126–41; David Martinez, *Dakota Philosopher: Charles Eastman and American Indian Thought* (St. Paul: Minnesota Historical Society Press, 2009).

14. Maddox, *Citizen Indians*, 30, 128–9. For a picture of Eastman in a feathered headdress, carrying a bow and arrows while a student at Dartmouth and in the dress of a Dakota warrior at the fortieth anniversary of his graduation from Dartmouth in 1927, see Wilson, *Ohiyesa*, 104.

15. Calloway, *The Indian History of an American Institution*, 126–27.

16. Meyers, *Greatest Catcher*, L, 4.

17. Ibid.

18. Calloway, *The Indian History of an American Institution*, 133.

19. Quint, *The Story of Dartmouth*, 214–15, 226–27. The use of manufactured Indian symbols was not, of course, unique to Dartmouth. As historian Philip Deloria has demonstrated, "playing Indian" is older even than the Boston Tea Party, with "imagined Indians" taking the place of real ones, and the created image used to represent what are claimed as distinctly American traits. See Philip Deloria, *Playing Indian* (New Haven: Yale University Press, 1999).

20. Calloway, *The Indian History of an American Institution*, 133.

21. Ralph Glaze and Rolfe Humphries, "How Chief Made the Major Leagues," *Empire Magazine*, August 20, 1967, 33.

22. Ibid.

23. Unidentified, unattributed, undated article, John Tortes Meyers File, National Baseball Hall of Fame Library, Cooperstown, New York.

24. Transcript of an interview with Ernest Martin Hopkins, February 21–March 14, 1958. Hanover, NH: Rauner Special Collections Library, Dartmouth College, 26 (*www.dartmouth.edu/~library/rauner/archives/oral.../EMHReelsl_9.pdf*, accessed March 25, 2011).

25. John Tortes Meyers File, National Baseball Hall of Fame Library, Cooperstown, New York.

26. Hopkins Interview, March 28–April 4, 1958, 81. (*www.dartmouth.edu/~library/rauner/archives/oral.../EMHReelsl0-22.pdf*, accessed March 25, 2011).

27. Glaze and Humphries, "How Chief Made the Major Leagues," 33; Lawrence Ritter, "Chief Meyers," *Baseball's Finest: The Greats, the Flakes, the Weird, and the Wonderful*, ed. Danny Peary (New York: Simon & Schuster, 1990), 152.

28. Meyers, "Greatest Catcher," L, 4.

29. Hopkins Interview, February 21–March 14, 1958, 27.

30. Glaze and Humphries, "How Chief Made the Major Leagues," 34.

31. Meyers, "Greatest Catcher," L, 4.

32. *The Sporting News*, August 24, 1949, 22.

33. On the incredible success of the Carlisle Indian School football team, see Sally Jenkins, *The Real All Americans: The Team That Changed a Game, a People, a Nation* (New York: Doubleday, 2007).

34. Meyers, "Greatest Catcher," L, 4.

35. Hopkins Interview, February 21–March 14, 1958, 26.

36. John Tortes Meyers File, Dartmouth College Alumni Archive, Hanover, New Hampshire. Another article, probably also from *The Dartmouth*, dated January 13, 1906, written after the end of his first semester at the college, has the title "Redskin Athlete." The title is followed by the statement in bold "Tortes, a Coahuila [sic] Mission Indian, Is Progressing in His Studies and Training for Track and Baseball." It ran with the same picture of Meyers in a football uniform as the earlier article.

37. Unattributed article, John Tortes Meyers File, Dartmouth College Alumni Archive, Hanover, New Hampshire.

38. Calloway, *The Indian History of an American Institution*, 133–34.

39. Unattributed article, John Tortes Meyers File, Dartmouth College Alumni Archive, Hanover, New Hampshire.

40. Glaze and Humphries, "How Chief Made the Major Leagues," 34. See also Hopkins Interview 1958, 27.

41. Ritter, *Baseball's Finest*, 152.

42. Meyers, "Greatest Catcher," L, 4.

43. Hopkins Interview, February 21–March 14, 1958, 27. Hopkins was elderly when he recalled the incident, which was likely a creation of his imagination, since it does not fit with the chronology of Meyers's minor league career.

44. John Lenkey, "Chief Meyers Hale and Hearty at 86," *The Sporting News*. January 14, 1967, 40.

45. Meyers, "Greatest Catcher," L, 4.

46. Ritter, *The Glory of Their Times*, 172.

47. George Ringwald, "Former major leaguer 'Chief' Meyers: Old-timer Analyzes Today's Baseball," *Riverside (California) Press Enterprise*, August 23, 1964.

48. Meyers, "Greatest Catcher," L, 4.

49. *St. Louis Globe-Democrat*, August 29, 1909.

50. Ritter, *The Glory of Their Times*, 172.

51. Jeffrey P. Beck, *The American Indian Integration of Baseball* (Lincoln: University of Nebraska Press, 2004), 80. Baseball historian Peter Morris also cites this incident as an indication of how members of racial minorities overcame prejudice to succeed in baseball, comparing Meyers's response to the attempt to cross him up with a similar experience of the famed African American catcher of the late nineteenth century, Fleetwood Walker (*Catcher: How the Man Behind the Plate Became and an American Folk Hero* [Chicago: Ivan R. Dee, 2009], 272).

52. Henry C. Koerper, "The Catcher Was a Cahuilla: A Remembrance of John Tortes Meyers," *Journal of California and Great Basin Anthropology* 24:1(2004), 26.

53. Meyers, "Greatest Catcher," L, 4.

54. Lenkey, "Chief Meyers Hale and Hearty at 86," 40.

55. Koerper, "The Catcher Was a Cahuilla," 26–27; Kevin Brass, "Our Own Field of Dreams," *San Diego Magazine*, July 1992, 70.

56. Bill Swank, *Baseball in San Diego: From the Plaza to the Padres*. (Mount Pleasant, SC: Arcadia, 2005), 45–46.

57. Ringwald, "Former major leaguer 'Chief' Meyers." The reference is to Act 1, Scene 5 of *Hamlet*.

58. Meyers, "Greatest Catcher," L, 4.

59. Ibid.

60. *St. Louis Globe-Democrat*, August 29, 1909.

61. Meyers, "Greatest Catcher," L, 4.

62. Koerper, "The Catcher Was a Cahuilla," 26.

63. www.cwcfamily.org/wj/cc6.htm, accessed 2/25/09.

64. Swank, *Baseball in San Diego*, 46–47; Koerper, "The Catcher Was a Cahuilla," 26–27; Kevin Nelson, *Golden Game: The Story of California Baseball* (Berkeley, CA: Heyday Books, 2004), 85.

65. Unidentified, unattributed, undated article, John Tortes Meyers File, National Baseball Hall of Fame Library, Cooperstown, New York.

66. Meyers, "Greatest Catcher," L, 4.

67. Koerper, "The Catcher Was a Cahuilla," 31.

68. 1920 Census for San Diego, California (Roll T625=132, Page 6A, Enumeration District 336, Image 248) and 1930 Chula Visa, California Census (Roll 190, Page 6a, Enumeration District 33, Image 707.0).

69. *Pittsburgh Post-Gazette*, December 6, 1939, 18.

70. Personal Interviews with Colonel John V. Meyers (September 22, 2008), Shanna Meyers (September 29, 2008), and Michele Meyers Cornejo (July 16, 2010).

71. Unidentified, unattributed, undated article, John Tortes Meyers File, National Baseball Hall of Fame Library, Cooperstown, New York.

72. Unidentified, unattributed article, dated 1909 (John Tortes Meyers File, National Base-

ball Hall of Fame Library, Cooperstown, New York).

73. Koerper, "The Catcher Was a Cahuilla," 26–27.

74. *The Sporting News*, February 5, 1947, 13.

75. John McGraw, "Making a Pennant Winner," *Pearson's Magazine*, November 1912, 121.

## Chapter Four

1. John McGraw, "Making a Pennant Winner," *Pearson's Magazine* (November 1912), 121.

2. Basic information on the Deadball Era was drawn from Thomas Gilbert, *Dead Ball: Major League Baseball Before Babe Ruth* (New York: Franklin Watts, 1996) and the website of the Deadball Era Committee of the Society for American Baseball Research (http://world.std.com/~pgw/Deadball, accessed 2/11/09).

3. Lawrence Ritter, "Chief Meyers," *The Glory of Their Times: The Story of the Early Days of Baseball Told by the Men Who Played It, Enlarged Edition* (New York: HarperCollins Perennial, 2002), 172.

4. Cited in Cait N. Murphy, *Crazy '08: How a Cast of Cranks, Rogues, Boneheads, and Magnates Created the Greatest Year in Baseball History* (San Francisco: HarperCollins, 2008), 183.

5. Earl L. Buie, "He Put the Indian 'Sign' on Baseball," *San Bernardino (California) Sun-Telegram* (April 5, 1961), E-1, E-5.

6. Ray Robinson, *Matty: An American Hero — Christy Mathewson of the New York Giants* (New York: Oxford University, 1995), 8; Philip Seib, *The Player: Christy Mathewson, Baseball, and the American Century* (New York: Four Walls Eight Windows, 2003), xi.

7. Ritter, *The Glory of Their Times*, 96.

8. John Lenkey, "Chief Meyers Hale and Hearty at 86," *The Sporting News*, January 14, 1967, 29, 40.

9. Jack McDonald, "One for the Chief," *San Francisco Examiner*, August 30, 1966, 52. Reprinted as "Catching Up with Matty's Catcher," *Baseball Digest*, 25, no. 10 (1967), 55–56.

10. Frank DeFord, *The Old Ball Game: How John McGraw, Christy Mathewson, and the New York Giants Created Modern Baseball* (New York: Atlantic Monthly Press, 2005), 176.

11. Robinson, *Matty*, 140.

12. *The Sporting News*, April 9, 1952, 13.

13. Paul Zimmerman, "Sportscripts," *Los Angeles Times*, August 13, 1947, 10.

14. Ritter, *The Glory of Their Times*, 175–76.

15. Christy Mathewson, *Pitching in a Pinch: Or Baseball from the Inside* (Cleveland: L. Van Oeyen, 1912), 158–59.

16. Ed A. Goewey, "The Old Fan Says," *Leslie's Illustrated Weekly*, August 21, 1913, 182.

17. Charles Alexander, *John McGraw* (Lincoln: University of Nebraska, 1995), 3–4.

18. *Los Angeles Times*, February 26, 1934, 10; cited in Richard Adler, *Mack, McGraw and the 1913 Baseball Season* (Jefferson, NC: McFarland, 2008), 39.

19. Geoffrey Ward and Ken Burns, *Baseball: An Illustrated History* (New York: Knopf, 1996), 68.

20. Tom Simon, ed., *Deadball Stars of the National League* (Washington, D.C.: Brassey's, 2004), 39.

21. DeFord, *The Old Ball Game*, 158.

22. Mike Vacarro, *The First Fall Classic: The Red Sox, the Giants, and the Cast of Players, Pugs, and Politicos Who Reinvented the World Series in 1912* (New York: Doubleday, 2009), 114.

23. Francis J. Powers, "Matty Great at Irking M'Graw, Too," *Chicago Daily News*, January 12, 1945, 24.

24. Zimmerman, "Sportscripts," 10; see McDonald, "One for the Chief," 52 and Jeffrey P. Beck, *The American Indian Integration of Baseball* (Lincoln: University of Nebraska Press, 2004), 85–86.

25. Jim Dawson, "McGraw Rescinded Fine After Talk with Chief," *Riverside (California) Press-Enterprise*, June 25, 1969.

26. Powers, "Matty Great At Irking M'Graw, Too," 24; see McDonald, "One for the Chief," 52.

27. Ritter, *The Glory of Their Times*, 172.

28. Grantland Rice, "A Talk with Chief Meyers," February 14, 1947 (John Tortes Meyers File, National Baseball Hall of Fame Library, Cooperstown New York).

29. McGraw, "Making a Pennant Winner," 121.

30. "Best Batteries— McGraw Rates Combinations," *The Sporting News*, February 8, 1934, 4.

31. Unidentified, unattributed, undated article, John Tortes Meyers File, National Baseball Hall of Fame Library, Cooperstown, New York.

32. Brian McDonald, *Indian Summer: The Forgotten Story of Louis Sockalexis — the First Native American in Major League Baseball* (Emmaus, PA: Rodale Press, 2003), 131.

33. Kate Buford, *Native Son: The Life and Sporting Legend of Jim Thorpe* (New York: Alfred A. Knopf, 2010), 215.

34. Ritter, *The Glory of Their Times*, 174.

35. Alexander, *John McGraw*, 5.

36. Personal interview, September 29, 2008.

37. Ritter, *The Glory of Their Times*, 174–75.

38. Simon, *Deadball Stars*, 15.

39. Peter Morris, *Catcher: How the Man Be-*

*hind the Plate Became and an American Folk Hero* (Chicago: Ivan R. Dee, 2009), 266–67, 229–30.

40. Lenkey, "Chief Meyers Hale and Hearty at 86," 29.

41. John Drebinger, "Eddie Brannick, Polo Grounds Fixture Since His Boyhood," *The Sporting News*, July 2, 1942, 3A.

42. Unidentified, unattributed, undated article, John Tortes Meyers File, National Baseball Hall of Fame Library, Cooperstown, New York.

43. "Handling the Big Guns in Baseball," *San Francisco Call*, September 10, 1911.

44. Robinson, *Matty*, 95–97.

45. This account of the "Merkle Game" and its aftermath is based on the retellings found in Murphy, *Crazy '08*, 182–98; DeFord, *The Old Ball Game*, 138–49; Simon, *Deadball Stars*, 21, 23; David W. Anderson, *More Than Merkle: A History of the Best and Most Exciting Baseball Season in Human History* (Lincoln: University of Nebraska Press, 2000), 172–3, 177–9; Robinson, *Matty*, 97–101; and Ward and Burns, *Baseball: An Illustrated History*, 92–95.

46. Ritter, *The Glory of Their Times*, 180.

47. Frank Graham, *The New York Giants: An Informal History of a Great Baseball Club* (Carbondale: Southern Illinois University Press, 2002 [1952]), 60; Robinson, *Matty*, 84–85.

48. "Gossip and Pictures from the World of Sports," *Leslie's Illustrated Weekly*, February 25, 1909, 186. Calling him "Big Chief Meyers," *Sporting Life* reported on March 13, 1909 (p. 1) that in a spring training game the new Giants catcher "banged the ball so hard it would have cleared the center field fence at the Polo Grounds."

49. John T. Meyers, "Greatest Catcher Believes he 'Booted' Life's Chance by Choosing Diamond Career," *New York American* (June 16, 1912), L, 4.

50. Powers, "Matty Great At Irking M'Graw, Too," 24.

51. Cited in Morris, *Catcher*, 248.

52. *New York Times*, March 5, 1909.

53. *New York Times*, March 7, 1909.

54. Beck, *American Indian Integration of Baseball*, x.

55. "Chielf [sic] Myers [sic] Sole Ambition to 'Make Good' in New York Team," *Nebraska State Journal*, May 2, 1909, C7.

56. Exodus 2:22.

57. Robinson, *Matty*, 115.

58. *New York Times*, April 16, 1909.

59. *New York Times*, April 18, 1909.

60. "Side Lights of Giants' Victory," *New York American*, April 18, 1909, B, 1; cited in Beck, *American Indian Integration of Baseball*, 82.

61. *Sporting Life*, May 1, 1909, 9.

62. *The Arizona-Journal Miner*, May 8, 1909.

63. *Sporting Life*, May 17, 1909, 1.

64. *New York Times*, June 17, 1909.

65. *New York Times*, August 25, 1909.

66. Powers, "Matty Great At Irking M'Graw, Too," 24.

67. Lenkey, "Chief Meyers Hale and Hearty at 86," 40.

68. Henry C. Koerper, "The Catcher Was a Cahuilla: A Remembrance of John Tortes Meyers," *Journal of California and Great Basin Anthropology* 24:1(2004), 26.

69. Meyers, "Greatest Catcher," L 4.

70. Personal Interview (September 29, 2008).

71. For a full account, see Mel H. Bolster, *Crazy Snake and the Smoked Meat Rebellion* (Boston: Brandon Press, 1976).

72. J. W. McConaughy, "Indian Most Remarkable Player in Game: M'Graw Picks Meyers for Chief Catcher," August 5, 1909 (John Tortes Meyers File, National Baseball Hall of Fame Library, Cooperstown, New York); cited in Beck, *American Indian Integration of Baseball*, 78.

73. Vacarro, *The First Fall Classic*, 39.

74. *New York Times*, March 19, 1910; *The Sporting News*, February 18, 1943, 5.

75. *New York Times*, June 14, 1910.

76. *New York Times*, June 15, 1910.

77. *New York Times*, July 12, 1910.

78. Koerper, "The Catcher was a Cahuilla," 26.

79. Unidentified, unattributed article, John Tortes Meyers File, National Baseball Hall of Fame Library, Cooperstown, New York.

80. Robinson, *Matty*, 118.

81. Alexander, *John McGraw*, 150; Robinson, *Matty*, 118–20; *New York Times*, September 15, 1910.

82. Simon, *Deadball Stars*, 72.

83. *New York Times*, November 6, 1910.

84. *New York Times*, November 13, 1910.

85. *Sporting Life*, December 3, 1910, 6; Koerper, "The Catcher was a Cahuilla," 34.

86. DeFord, *The Old Ball Game*, 130.

87. Seib, *The Player*, 70.

88. Henry C. Koerper, "John Tortes Meyers: A Cahuilla in the Big Leagues," *News from Native California: An Inside View of the California Indian World*, 10, no. 4 (Summer 1997), 4. A number of the cards with Meyers's likeness are available for viewing in the Library of Congress Prints and Photographs online catalogue (www.loc.gov/pictures).

## Chapter Five

1. *New York Times*, February 26, 1911.

2. Frank Graham, *The New York Giants: An*

*Informal History of a Great Baseball Club* (Carbondale: Southern Illinois University Press, 2002 [1952]), 67–68.

3. Joel Zoss and John Bowman, "Native Americans at Bat," *Diamonds in the Rough: The Untold History of Baseball* (New York: Macmillan, 1989), 142; Geoffrey Ward and Ken Burns, *Baseball: An Illustrated History* (New York: Knopf, 1996), 86.

4. Kate Buford, *Native Son: The Life and Sporting Legend of Jim Thorpe* (New York: Alfred A. Knopf, 2010), 173.

5. Ray Robinson, *Matty: An American Hero—Christy Mathewson of the New York Giants* (New York: Oxford University, 1994), 123.

6. Frank DeFord, *The Old Ball Game: How John McGraw, Christy Mathewson, and the New York Giants Created Modern Baseball* (New York: Atlantic Monthly Press, 2005), 108; Harold and Dorothy Seymour, *Baseball: The Golden Age, Vol. II* (New York: Oxford University Press, 1971), 115–16.

7. Robinson, *Matty*, 65.

8. *The Sporting News*, April 6, 1911, 1.

9. Damon Runyon and Jim Reisler, *Guys, Dolls, and Curveballs* (Carroll & Graf, 2005), 4 (www.books.google.com/books?id=HCsGgh CRBBgC, accessed 2/23/09).

10. John Tortes Meyers File, Dartmouth College Alumni Archive, Hanover, New Hampshire.

11. Charles Alexander, *John McGraw* (Lincoln: University of Nebraska, 1995), 152; Robinson, *Matty*, 121.

12. DeFord, *The Old Ball Game*, p. 154; Robinson, *Matty*, 122.

13. *New York Times*, April 18, 1911.

14. *New York Times*, May 21, 1911.

15. W. A. Phelon, "Who Will Win the Pennant?" *Baseball Magazine*, June 1911, 18, 28.

16. *New York Times*, June 10, 1911.

17. Christy Mathewson, *Pitching in a Pinch: or Baseball from the Inside* (Cleveland: L. Van Oeyen, 1912), 158–59.

18. Alexander, *John McGraw*, pp. 155–6; Lawrence Ritter, "Chief Meyers," *The Glory of Their Times: The Story of the Early Days of Baseball Told by the Men Who Played It, Enlarged Edition* (New York: HarperCollins Perennial, 2002), 102–104. For the full story of "Victory" Faust, see Gabriel Schechter, *Victory Faust: The Rube Who Saved McGraw's Giants* (Los Gatos, CA: Charles April Publications, 2000).

19. Robinson, *Matty*, 124–25.

20. *New York Times*, September 13, 1911.

21. *New York Times*, September 6, 1911.

22. Brian W. Dippie, *The Vanishing American: White Attitudes and U.S. Indian Policy* (Middletown, CT: Wesleyan University Press, 1982), 207–208. See also Orin Starn, *Ishi's Brain: In Search of America's Last "Wild" Indian* (New York: W. W. Norton, 2005); and Theodora Kroeber, *Ishi in Two Worlds: A Biography of the Last Wild Indian in North America* (Berkeley: University of California Press, 2002 [1961]).

23. "Handling the Big Guns in Baseball," *San Francisco Call*, September 10, 1911.

24. *New York Times*, September 18, 1911.

25. *New York Times*, September 24, 1911.

26. Gabriel Schechter, "Charlie Faust," *The Baseball Biography Project* (http://bioproj.sabr.org/bioproj.cfm?a=v&v=l&pid=4309&bid=217, accessed 5/23/10).

27. DeFord, *The Old Ball Game*, 160; Robinson, *Matty*, 121–22.

28. *The Sporting News*, February 21, 1962, 4.

29. Henry C. Koerper, "The Catcher Was a Cahuilla: A Remembrance of John Tortes Meyers," *Journal of California and Great Basin Anthropology* 24:1(2004), 26.

30. *Sporting Life*, December 16, 1911, 1.

31. Tom Simon, ed., *Deadball Stars of the National League* (Washington, D.C.: Brassey's, 2004), 17.

32. Lucy Maddox, *Citizen Indians: Native American Intellectuals, Race, and Reform* (Ithica, NY: Cornell University Press, 2005), 9. On Charles Eastman's role in the SAI see Raymond Wilson, *Ohiyesa: Charles Eastman, Santee Sioux* (Urbana, IL: University of Illinois Press, 1983), 154–63.

33. Donald Fixico, *Daily Life of Native Americans in the Twentieth Century* (Westport, CT: Greenwood Press, 2006), 77.

34. Philip Deloria, *Indians in Unexpected Places* (Lawrence: University Press of Kansas, 2006), 227–8, 234.

35. Ritter, *The Glory of Their Times*, 180.

36. Nathan Aaseng, "Athletes," *American Indian Lives Series* (New York: Facts on File, 1995), 13.

37. Today many Chippewa, also called Ojibwe, prefer to be known as the *Anishinaabeg* (singular, *Anishinaabe*), a self-designation in their own language that means "original people."

38. Ritter, *The Glory of Their Times*, 180.

39. Norman Macht, *Connie Mack and the Early Years of Baseball* (Lincoln: University of Nebraska Press, 2007), 314–15.

40. Tom Swift, *Chief Bender's Burden: The Silent Struggle of a Baseball Star* (Lincoln: University of Nebraska Press, 2008), 252. Two other recent biographies of Bender also document the prejudice he endured throughout his baseball career: William C. Kashatus, *Money Pitcher: Chief Bender and the Tragedy of Indian Assimilation* (University Park: Pennsylvania State University Press, 2006), and Robert Peyton Wiggins, *Chief Bender: A Baseball Biography* (Jefferson, NC: McFarland, 2010).

41. Swift, *Chief Bender's Burden*, 251.

42. Swift, *Chief Bender's Burden*, 241–2; Wiggins, *Chief Bender*, 106.

43. Wiggins, *Chief Bender*, 59–60. Wiggins describes a number of other examples of the bigoted stereotyping Bender endured, including incidents when, like Meyers, he was assumed to be an African American because of his dark complexion.

44. Kashatus, *Money Pitcher*, ix–x.

45. Aaseng, "Athletes," 1.

46. Macht, *Connie Mack*, 314.

47. Buford, *Native Son*, 173.

48. Stephen I. Thompson," The American Indian in the Major Leagues," *Baseball Research Journal* 12 (1983), 4; Kashatus, *Money Pitcher*, 57.

49. Swift, *Chief Bender's Burden*, 60.

50. Jeffrey P. Beck, *The American Indian Integration of Baseball*. (Lincoln: University of Nebraska Press, 2004), 75–76. For example, a reporter described Chief Bender as "taciturn and non-talkative to a fault, and having all the unemotional qualities of his race" (Wiggins, *Chief Bender*, 65).

51. Kashatus, *Money Pitcher*, xiii, xv.

52. Wiggins, *Chief Bender*, 152.

53. Ward and Burns, *Baseball: An Illustrated History*, 126.

54. Macht, *Connie Mack*, 518.

55. Alexander, *John McGraw*, 156–57; Robinson, *Matty*, 126–27.

56. Ritter, *The Glory of Their Times*, 111.

57. W. A. Phelon, "Mack vs. McGraw: When Giants Meets While Elephant," *Baseball Magazine*, November 1911, 4–5.

58. (*Rochester*) *Union and Advertiser*, as reprinted in *The Arrow*, December 1, 1911; cited in Buford, *Native Son*, 105.

59. "Giants Great Backstop Predicts Series Victory," *Syracuse Herald*, October 15, 1911; cited in Wiggins, *Chief Bender*, 140–41.

60. *New York Times*, October 15, 1911.

61. DeFord, *The Old Ball Game*, 163.

62. Ibid.

63. Macht, *Connie Mack*, 523–24; Grantland Rice, *The Tumult and the Shouting* (New York: A. S. Barnes, 1954), 227.

64. *New York Times*, October 15, 1911.

65. Kashatus, *Money Pitcher*, 97.

66. George Ringwald, "Former major leaguer 'Chief' Meyers: Old-timer analyzes today's baseball," *Riverside* (*California*) *Press Enterprise*, August 23, 1964.

67. *New York Times*, October 15, 1911.

68. *New York Times*, October 17, 1911.

69. Ibid.

70. DeFord, *The Old Ball Game*, 164–65; Robinson, *Matty*, 128.

71. Mathewson, *Pitching in a Pinch*, 151.

72. Peter Morris, *A Game of Inches: The Stories Behind the Innovations That Shaped Baseball, Vol. 1: The Game on the Field* (Lanham, MD: Ivan R. Dee, 2006), 347.

73. Swift, *Chief Bender's Burden*, 187–88, 190.

74. Grantland Rice, "The Greatest Pitcher," January 10, 1939 (John Tortes Meyers File, National Baseball Hall of Fame Library, Cooperstown, New York).

75. *New York Times*, October 18, 1911.

76. Ritter, *The Glory of Their Times*, 114.

77. *New York Times*, October 18, 1911.

78. *The Sporting News*, November 2, 1944, 17.

79. *New York Times*, October 25, 1911.

80. DeFord, *The Old Ball Game*, 167.

81. *New York Times*, October 25, 1911.

82. *New York Times*, October 26, 1911.

83. *New York Times*, October 27, 1911.

84. Alexander, *John McGraw*, 158.

85. *New York Times*, October 27, 1911.

86. Frank Graham, *The New York Giants: An Informal History of a Great Baseball Club* (Carbondale: Southern Illinois University Press, 2002 [1952]), 70; Robinson, *Matty*, 130.

87. Swift, *Chief Bender's Burden*, 162.

88. *New York Times*, October 28, 1911.

89. *New York Times*, November 14, 1911.

90. Unidentified, unattributed, undated article, John Tortes Meyers File, National Baseball Hall of Fame Library, Cooperstown, New York.

## Chapter Six

1. Mike Vaccaro, *The First Fall Classic: The Red Sox, the Giants, and the Cast of Players, Pugs, and Politicos Who Reinvented the World Series in 1912* (New York: Doubleday, 2009), 16.

2. *New York Times*, March 1, 1912.

3. *New York Times*, March 17, 1912.

4. *Boy's Life*, March 1912, 31,

5. Vaccaro, *The First Fall Classic*, 18–19.

6. Ray Robinson, *Matty: An American Hero — Christy Mathewson of the New York Giants* (New York: Oxford University, 1994), 134–35.

7. *New York Times*, April 21, 1912.

8. Unidentified, unattributed, undated article, John Tortes Meyers File, National Baseball Hall of Fame Library, Cooperstown, New York.

9. *The New York American*, June 1, 1912.

10. Jim Dawson, "McGraw Rescinded Fine After Talk with Chief," June 25, 1969.

11. *The New York American*, June 5, 1912.

12. *The New York American*, June 13, 1912.

13. *The New York American*, June 15, 1912.

14. John T. Meyers, "Greatest Catcher Be-

lieves he 'Booted' Life's Chance by Choosing Diamond Career," *New York American*, June 16, 1912, L, 4.

15. Lawrence Ritter, "Chief Meyers," *The Glory of Their Times: The Story of the Early Days of Baseball Told by the Men Who Played It, Enlarged Edition* (New York: HarperCollins Perennial, 2002), 172.

16. Jack McDonald, "One for the Chief," *San Francisco Examiner*, August 30, 1966, 52. Reprinted as "Catching Up with Matty's Catcher," *Baseball Digest*, 25, no. 10 (1967), 55–56.

17. *New York Times*, June 30, 1912.

18. Ritter, *The Glory of Their Times*, 179.

19. *The New York American*, July 14, 1912.

20. Ed A. Goewey, "The Old Fan Says That the Case of Chief Myers [sic] Proves That the Live Redskin Can be a Good Indian," *Leslie's Illustrated Weekly*, July 11, 1912, 32.

21. *New York Times*, July 28, 1912.

22. Grantland Rice, "A Talk with Chief Meyers," February 14, 1947 (John Tortes Meyers File, National Baseball Hall of Fame Library, Cooperstown, New York).

23. Grantland Rice, "The Greatest Pitcher," January 10, 1939 (John Tortes Meyers File, National Baseball Hall of Fame Library, Cooperstown, New York).

24. *The New York American*, July 14, 1912.

25. Jim Dawson, "Chief Picks Honus Wagner as Baseball's Greatest Player," *Riverside (California) Press-Enterprise*, June 26, 1969, B-10.

26. *New York Times*, August 23, 1912.

27. *New York Times*, September 18, 1912.

28. *The Sporting News*, October 20, 1921, 4.

29. Ed A. Goewey, "The Old Fan Says," *Leslie's Illustrated Weekly* August 21, 1912, 182; cited in Jeffrey P. Beck, *The American Indian Integration of Baseball* (Lincoln: University of Nebraska Press, 2004), 82–83.

30. Henry C. Koerper, "The Catcher Was a Cahuilla: A Remembrance of John Tortes Meyers," *Journal of California and Great Basin Anthropology* 24 no. 1 (2004), 26.

31. memory.loc.gov/cgibin/query/r?amme m/spalding:@field(DOCID+@lit(spalding0015 8div11), accessed 10/4/08.

32. Koerper, "The Catcher Was a Cahuilla," 28.

33. Bill James, *The New Bill James Historical Baseball Abstract* (New York: Free Press, 2001), 409.

34. Unidentified, unattributed article, John Tortes Meyers File, National Baseball Hall of Fame Library, Cooperstown, New York.

35. Tom Simon, ed., *Deadball Stars of the National League* (Washington, D.C.: Brassey's, 2004), 7.

36. Vaccaro, *The First Fall Classic*, 6.

37. Frank DeFord, *The Old Ball Game: How John McGraw, Christy Mathewson, and the New York Giants Created Modern Baseball* (New York: Atlantic Monthly Press, 2005), 179–80.

38. Vaccaro, *The First Fall Classic*, 32–33.

39. Robinson, *Matty*, 140–41; Vaccaro, *The First Fall Classic*, 73.

40. Vaccaro, *The First Fall Classic*, 78.

41. Vaccaro, *The First Fall Classic*, 87.

42. *New York Times*, October 10, 1912.

43. Vacarro, *The First Fall Classic*, 103–105.

44. Vacarro, *The First Fall Classic*, 110, 114.

45. Vacarro, *The First Fall Classic*, 131.

46. *The Sporting News*, October 17, 1912, 3.

47. Vacarro, *The First Fall Classic*, 159.

48. *The Sporting News*, October 17, 1912, 3.

49. Vacarro, *The First Fall Classic*, 155.

50. *The Sporting News*, October 18, 1975, 19.

51. Vacarro, *The First Fall Classic*, 198.

52. DeFord, *The Old Ball Game*, 181.

53. *New York Times*, October 16, 1912.

54. Vacarro, *The First Fall Classic*, 234.

55. *The Sporting News*, October 18, 1975, 19.

56. *The Sporting News*, February 10, 1968, 20.

57. *The Sporting News*, October 18, 1975, 22.

58. Vacarro, *The First Fall Classic*, 9, 257.

59. *New York Times*, October 17, 1912.

60. *The Sporting News*, March 24, 1956, 6.

61. *St. Louis Post-Dispatch*, October 31, 1991, 4D; see also *The Sporting News*, October 18, 1975, 19, 22.

62. DeFord, *The Old Ball Game*, 185.

63. This account of the historic eighth game is based on the retellings in Vacarro, *The First Fall Classic*, 220–65; DeFord, *The Old Ball Game*, 182–85; Robinson, *Matty*, 143–50; *The Sporting News*, October 24, 1912, 3; Bob Broeg, "'12 W.S. Rated Most Thrilling," *The Sporting News*, October 18, 1975, 19, 22; Hugh Fullerton, "Giants, With Title in Grasp, Muffed Chance in '12 Series," *The Sporting News*, January 29, 1942, 7.

64. Ritter, *The Glory of Their Times*, 91; DeFord, *The Old Ball Game*, 186; Charles Alexander, *John McGraw* (Lincoln: University of Nebraska, 1995), 165; Frank Graham, *The New York Giants: An Informal History of a Great Baseball Club* (Carbondale: Southern Illinois University Press, 2002 [1952]), 73

65. Robinson, *Matty*, 149.

66. *New York Times*, October 17, 1912.

67. DeFord, *The Old Ball Game*, 187–88.

68. Ritter, *The Glory of Their Times*, 181–82.

69. John Lenkey, "Chief Meyers Hale and Hearty at 86," *The Sporting News*, January 14, 1967, 40. Two years later he was more specific in telling reporter Jim Dawson, "Merkle or Matty could have caught it. I couldn't get to

the ball at all. I had run down there to try and back up the play" ("Meyers' Memory Bridges Baseball's Generation Gap," *Riverside (California) Press-Enterprise*, June 24, 1969, 1).

70. Benjamin Spillman, "Fall Classic Stirs Family Memories of Player," *The Desert Sun*, November 4, 2001, B1.

71. *The Sporting News*, October 24, 1912, 3.

72. *Sioux City [Iowa] Journal*, September 15, 1912.

73. David L. Fultz, "The Baseball Players Fraternity," *Baseball Magazine*, August 1914, 88.

74. Geoffrey Ward and Ken Burns, *Baseball: An Illustrated History* (New York: Knopf, 1996), 121.

75. *www.mlbplayers.mlb.com/pa/info/history.jsp*, accessed 5/12/09.

76. William McNeil, *The California Winter League: America's First Integrated Professional Baseball League* (Jefferson, NC: McFarland, 2002), 13.

77. F. C. Lane, "The Greatest of All Catchers," *Baseball Magazine*, February 1913, 1.

78. "The Real Who's Who in Baseball," *Baseball Magazine*, August 1913, 78.

## Chapter Seven

1. *New York Times*, March 12, 1913.

2. *The Sporting News*, February 27, 1913.

3. *The Sporting News*, April 3, 1913, 6.

4. *New York Times*, March 19, 1913.

5. *Baseball Magazine*, August 1913, 118.

6. Frank Graham, *The New York Giants: An Informal History of a Great Baseball Club* (Carbondale: Southern Illinois University Press, 2002 [1952]), 75; Ray Robinson, *Matty: An American Hero — Christy Mathewson of the New York Giants* (New York: Oxford University, 1994), 154.

7. Charles Alexander, *John McGraw* (Lincoln: University of Nebraska, 1995), 168.

8. John T. Meyers, "Meyers Lauds Jim Thorpe, Olympic Hero," *New York American* (May 25, 1913), 3, L, 5.

9. Ed A. Goewey, "Three Noted Indian Baseball Players, *Leslie's Illustrated Weekly Newspaper*, November 13, 1913, 474.

10. *Baseball Magazine*, July 1913, 84.

11. William A. Phelon, "The Indian Players," *Baseball Magazine*, October 1913, 20.

12. Jeffrey P. Beck, *The American Indian Integration of Baseball* (Lincoln: University of Nebraska Press, 2004), 2.

13. Bill Crawford, *All-American: The Rise and Fall of Jim Thorpe* (Hoboken, NJ: John Wiley & Sons, 2004), 211–12.

14. *Los Angeles Times*, February 2, 1913. Cited in Kate Buford, *Native American Son: The Life and Sporting Legend of Jim Thorpe* (New York: Alfred A. Knopf, 2010), 175.

15. Graham, *New York Giants*, 72; Joseph B. Oxendine, *American Indian Sports Heritage* (Lincoln: University of Nebraska Press, 1995), 227.

16. Rob Neyer, *Rob Neyer's Big Book of Baseball Lineups: A Complete Guide to the Best, Worst, and Most Memorable Players to Ever Grace the Major Leagues* (New York: Fireside, 2003), 269.

17. Tom Simon, ed., *Deadball Stars of the National League* (Washington, D.C.: Brassey's, 2004), 81; Grantland Rice, *The Tumult and the Shouting: My Life in Sport* (New York: A. S. Barnes, 1954), 231–32, 228.

18. Jane R. Smith, "Triumph and Tragedy," *American History*, May/June 1997; cited in Buford, *Native Son*, 181.

19. Oxendine, *American Indian Sports Heritage*, 227; Crawford, *All-American*, 213.

20. Blanche McGraw, *The Real McGraw*, ed. Arthur Mann (New York: David McKay, 1953), 241. Cited in Buford, *Native Son*, 181.

21. Charles Springwood, "Playing Indian and Fighting (for) Mascots: Reading the Complications of Native American and European Alliances," *Team Spirits: The Native American Mascots Controversy*, ed. C. Richard King and Charles Springwood (Lincoln: University of Nebraska Press, 2001), 310–14; Crawford, *All-American*, 227. See also Buford, *Native Son*, 233–38 and Robert Whitman, *Jim Thorpe and the Oorang Indians: N.F.L.'s Most Colorful Franchise* (Defiance, OH: Hubbard, 1984); and Charles Springwood, "Playing Football, Playing Indian: A History of the Native Americans Who Were the NFL's Oorang Indians," *Native Athletes in Sport and Society: A Reader*, ed. C. Richard King (Lincoln: University of Nebraska Press, 2005), 132.

22. Buford, *Native Son*, 261–309.

23. Gerald R. Gems, "Negotiating a Native American Identity Through Sport: Assimilation, Adaptation, and the Role of the Trickster," King 2005, 15–16.

24. Tom Swift, *Chief Bender's Burden: The Silent Struggle of a Baseball Star* (Lincoln: University of Nebraska Press, 2008), 202.

25. At a televised event during the re-election campaign of California governor Earl Warren in October 1950, Meyers and Thorpe were chosen to appear on camera together (*Los Angeles Times*, October 26, 1950; cited in Buford, *Native Son*, 349).

26. Buford, *Native Son*, 369.

27. Lawrence Ritter, "Chief Meyers," *The Glory of Their Times: The Story of the Early Days of Baseball Told by the Men Who Played It, Enlarged Edition* (New York: HarperCollins Perennial, 2002), 175.

28. Philip Deloria, *Indians in Unexpected Places* (Lawrence: University Press of Kansas, 2006), 135.
29. *New York Times*, April 15, 1913.
30. www.baseball-reference.com/players/t/thorpji01.shtml, accessed April 5, 2011.
31. *New York Times*, May 9, 1913.
32. *New York Times*, May 10, 1913.
33. W. A. Phelon, "The Decline and Fall of the Left-Handed Batter," *Baseball Magazine*, July 1913, 65.
34. John T. Meyers, "Batters Can Be Developed, Says Meyers," *New York American*, May 11, 1913, 3, L, 4.
35. *New York American*, May 31, 1913.
36. Alexander, *John McGraw*, 169; *New York Times*, July 1, 1913.
37. *Baseball Magazine*, June 1913, 8.
38. *New York Times*, July 15, 1913.
39. *New York Times*, July 18, 1913.
40. *New York Times*, August 31, 1913, October 4, 1913; Alexander, *John McGraw*, 169–70.
41. Henry C. Koerper, "The Catcher Was a Cahuilla: A Remembrance of John Tortes Meyers," *Journal of California and Great Basin Anthropology* 24, no. 1 (2004), 26.
42. Simon, *Deadball Stars*, 17.
43. Norman Macht, *Connie Mack and the Early Years of Baseball* (Lincoln: University of Nebraska Press, 2007), 588.
44. *New York Times*, October 4, 1913; for another favorable assessment of Meyers's ranking as a catcher at this point in his career, see F. C. Lane, "The Greatest of All Catchers: Essential Points in a Catcher's Work," *Baseball Magazine*, February 1913, 41–51.
45. *New York Times*, October 13, 1913.
46. *The Sporting News*, September 24, 1925, 24.
47. Macht, *Connie Mack*, 586.
48. Swift, *Chief Bender's Burden*, 203.
49. Philip Seib, *The Player: Christy Mathewson, Baseball, and the American Century* (New York: Four Walls Eight Windows, 2003), 85–86; Robert Peyton Wiggins, *Chief Bender: A Baseball Biography* (Jefferson, NC: McFarland, 2010), 167.
50. Swift, *Chief Bender's Burden*, 203; Wiggins, *Chief Bender*, 163.
51. *Chicago Daily Tribune*, October 9, 1913, 23; cited in Richard Adler, *Mack, McGraw and the 1913 Baseball Season* (Jefferson, NC: McFarland, 2008), 223.
52. Robinson, *Matty*, 156.
53. Adler, *Mack, McGraw and the 1913 Baseball Season*, 271.
54. Macht, *Connie Mack*, 586; Adler, *Mack, McGraw and the 1913 Baseball Season*, 208–11.
55. Adler, *Mack, McGraw and the 1913 Baseball Season*, 248.

56. Rice, *The Tumult and the Shouting*, 227.
57. William C. Kashatus, *Money Pitcher: Chief Bender and the Tragedy of Indian Assimilation* (University Park: Pennsylvania State University Press, 2006), 107–108.
58. Adler, *Mack, McGraw and the 1913 Baseball Season*, 262.
59. Frank DeFord, *The Old Ball Game: How John McGraw, Christy Mathewson, and the New York Giants Created Modern Baseball* (New York: Atlantic Monthly Press, 2005), 191; Alexander, *John McGraw*, 170.
60. James E. Elfers, *The Tour to End All Tours: The Story of Major League Baseball's 1913–1914 World Tours* (Lincoln: University of Nebraska Press, 2003), dust jacket.
61. DeFord, *The Old Ball Game*, 173–74.
62. *The Sporting News*, October 23, 1913, 1.
63. *New York Times*, October 24, 1913.
64. Elfers, *The Tour to End All Tours*, 47–48.
65. Elfers, *The Tour to End All Tours*, 57–58.
66. *The Sporting News*, November 6, 1913, 3.
67. *New York Times*, November 11, 1913.
68. Ibid.
69. "The Tour of the World," *Sporting News*, November 22, 1913, 4.
70. Elfers, *The Tour to End All Tours*, 77–78; Bill Swank, *Baseball in San Diego: From the Plaza to the Padres* (Arcadia Publishers, 2005), 63.
71. Crawford, *All-American*, 214; Sally Jenkins, *The Real All Americans: The Team That Changed a Game, a People, a Nation* (New York: Doubleday, 2007), 289.
72. Elfers, *The Tour to End All Tours*, 82, 87.
73. "Mathewson and Chief Meyers Give Up the Tour," *Winona [Minnesota] Republican Herald*, November 18, 1913, 2.
74. Elfers, *The Tour to End All Tours*, 29.
75. Alexander, *John McGraw*, 175; Simon, *Deadball Stars*, 82.
76. *The Sporting News*, November 27, 1913, 8; Swank, *Baseball in San Diego*, 63.
77. For a definitive account of the Federal League see Robert Peyton Wiggins, *The Federal League of Base Ball Clubs: The History of an Outlaw Major League, 1914–1915* (Jefferson, NC: McFarland, 2008).
78. *New York Times*, May 1, 1914.
79. Brian McDonald, *Indian Summer: The Forgotten Story of Louis Sockalexis— the First Native American in Major League Baseball* (Emmaus, PA: Rodale Press, 2003), viii–ix.

## Chapter Eight

1. *New York Times*, April 5, 1914.
2. *New York Times*, February 23, 1914.
3. Frank Graham, *The New York Giants: An Informal History of a Great Baseball Club* (Carbondale: Southern Illinois University Press,

2002, [1952]), p. 75; Ray Robinson, *Matty: An American Hero — Christy Mathewson of the New York Giants* (New York: Oxford University, 1994), 154.

4. *New York Times*, February 25, 1914; *The Day*, February 24, 1914.

5. *New York Times*, February 27, 1914.

6. *New York Times*, March 9, 1914.

7. Charles Alexander, *John McGraw* (Lincoln: University of Nebraska, 1995), 179; Robert W. Creamer, *Babe: The Legend Comes to Life* (New York: Simon & Schuster, 1974), 81–82.

8. *New York Times*, April 24, 1914.

9. L. G. Moses, *Wild West Shows and the Images of American Indians, 1883–1933* (Albuquerque: University of New Mexico Press, 1996), 168–94, 5–7, 129–32, 150–67, 196.

10. Lucy Maddox, *Citizen Indians: Native American Intellectuals, Race, and Reform* (Ithaca, NY: Cornell University, 2005), 26, 139.

11. Moses, *Wild West Shows*, 168–94.

12. Philip Deloria, *Indians in Unexpected Places* (Lawrence: University Press of Kansas, 2006), 121–22.

13. Lawrence Ritter, "Chief Meyers," *The Glory of Their Times: The Story of the Early Days of Baseball Told by the Men Who Played It, Enlarged Edition* (New York: HarperCollins Perennial, 2002), 183–84.

14. *New York Times*, May 10, 1914.

15. "Afraid of Chief Meyers," *Winona (Minnesota) Republican-Herald*, June 22, 1914, 2.

16. *The Evening Independent*, August 5, 1914, 6.

17. *The Evening Independent*, August 12, 1914, 6.

18. Henry C. Koerper, "The Catcher Was a Cahuilla: A Remembrance of John Tortes Meyers," *Journal of California and Great Basin Anthropology* 24, no. 1 (2004), 26.

19. Tom Simon, ed., *Deadball Stars of the National League* (Washington, D.C.: Brassey's, 2004), 17.

20. William Connelly, "The Greatest Baseball Team of All History," *Baseball Magazine*, May 1914, 33–42.

21. Alexander, *John McGraw*, 182–84.

22. *New York Times*, February 28, 1915.

23. *New York Times*, April 11, 1915.

24. Alexander, *John McGraw*, 186–87.

25. *New York Times*, July 1, 1915.

26. *New York Times*, July 14, 1915.

27. *New York Times*, July 21, 1915.

28. Alexander, *John McGraw*, 187–88.

29. "Some Players Are Unable to Stand Kidding," *Winona [Minnesota] Republican-Herald*, April 15, 1916, 1.

30. The *Sporting News*, December 30, 1915.

31. Koerper, "The Catcher Was a Cahuilla," 26.

32. *New York Tribune*, November 15, 1915. Just two years earlier Ed Goewey had heralded the achievements of Meyers and Chief Bender and the promise of Jim Thorpe as evidence "against the repeated assertion that the Indian is 'dying out,' for though the Indians are decreasing in numbers many of them are showing genius along diversified lines which marks them as the peer of competitors representing other races." ("Three Noted Indian Baseball Players," *Leslie's Illustrated Weekly Newspaper*, November 13, 1913, 474).

33. Donald Fixico, *Daily Life of Native Americans in the Twentieth Century* (Westport, CT: Greenwood Press, 2006), 28, 78–79; Brian W. Dippie, *The Vanishing American: White Attitudes and U.S. Indian Policy* (Middletown, CT: Wesleyan University Press, 1982), 193–94.

34. Unidentified, unattributed article, dated February 1, 1916 (John Tortes Meyers File, National Baseball Hall of Fame Library, Cooperstown, New York).

35. Unidentified, unattributed article, dated February 17, 1916 (John Tortes Meyers File, National Baseball Hall of Fame Library, Cooperstown, New York).

36. William A. Phelon, "A Chapter from Current Baseball History," *Baseball Magazine*, April 1916, 18.

37. Ritter, *The Glory of Their Times*, 179.

38. "Zach Wheat, Most Graceful of Outfielders," *Baseball Magazine*, January 1917, pp. 49–51, 104. Modern historian Glenn Stout has described Wheat as a "full-fledged star of the first order" who was "allegedly half-Cherokee" in *The Dodgers: 125 Years of Dodgers Baseball* (Boston: Houghton Mifflin, 2004), 63.

39. Simon, *Deadball Stars*, 287–90; www.cmgww.com/baseball/wheat/biography.htm, accessed 3/9/09; Harold and Dorothy Seymour, *Baseball: The Golden Age, Vol. II* (New York: Oxford University Press, 1971), 155.

40. Ritter, *The Glory of Their Times*, 179; Robert W. Creamer, *Stengel: His Life and Times* (New York: Simon & Schuster, 1984), 105.

41. *New York Times*, April 9, 1916.

42. Stout, *The Dodgers*, 61–62.

43. *New York Times*, April 20, 1916.

44. W. R. Hoefer, "Cutting the Corners," *Baseball Magazine*, July 1916, 65.

45. Information on the trial is drawn from the following articles: "Sun Worshippers in Alienation Suit," *New York Times*, June 9, 1916; "Chief in Court," *The Washington Post*, June 10, 1916, 7; "Says He Was Like Mrs. Frame's Son," *New York Times*, June 10, 1916; "Loves Weaverson as a Son, She Says," *New York Times*, June 13, 1916; "Weaverson's Love Discussed by Jury," *New York Times*, June 14, 1916;

"Weaverson Jury Disagrees," *New York Times*, June 15, 1916.

46. http://philtar.ucsm.ac.uk/encycloped ia/zorast/mazdaz.html, accessed 3/9/09.

47. Personal interview with Colonel John V. Meyers (September 22, 2008).

48. "'Chief' Meyers Again Idol," *Winona [Minnesota] Republican Herald*, July 16, 1916, 6.

49. *New York Times*, August 16, 1916.

50. *New York Times*, October 6, 1916; Seymour 1971, 287; Creamer, *Stengel*, 109; Stout, *The Dodgers*, 66–67.

51. Koerper, "The Catcher Was a Cahuilla," 26.

52. *New York Times*, October 8, 1916.

53. Creamer, *Babe*, 126–30; Geoffrey Ward and Ken Burns, *Baseball: An Illustrated History* (New York: Knopf, 1996), 155.

54. Koerper, "The Catcher Was a Cahuilla," 28–29.

55. John Lenkey, "Chief Meyers Hale and Hearty at 86." *The Sporting News*, January 14, 1967, 29.

56. Peter Morris, *A Game of Inches: The Stories Behind the Innovations That Shaped Baseball, Vol. 1: The Game on the Field* (Ivan R. Dee, 2006), 410; see also F. C. Lane, "How a Ball Player Grips His Bat," *Baseball Magazine*, October 1917, 482.

57. *The Sporting News*, October 19, 1916, 3.

58. *New York Times*, October 13, 1916.

59. http://www.imdb.com/title/tt0159140/, accessed 2/21/10.

60. *Sporting Life* 68, no. 11 (1916), 1.

61. Unidentified, unattributed article, dated November 9, 1916 (John Tortes Meyers file, National Baseball Hall of Fame Library, Cooperstown, New York).

62. "Chief Bender Leads Race in High Circuit," *Winona [Minnesota] Republican-Herald*, March 15, 1917, 6. Another article published nationally less than two weeks later called Jim Thorpe the "sturdy son of the Sac-and-Fox tribe ... the last of his race to make a fight for a big league berth, for the ray of the Indian in baseball is soon to pass" (*Evening Independent*, March 28, 1917, 15).

63. *Anaconda Standard*, February 10, 1917; cited in Royse Parr, *American Indians in Major League Baseball: Now and Then*, Society of American Baseball Research (www.readex.com/reade x/newsletter.cfm?newsletter=231, accessed 2/12/ 09).

64. *New York Times*, February 25, 1917.

65. See Brian W. Dippie, *The Vanishing American: White Attitudes and U.S. Indian Policy* (Middletown, CT: Wesleyan University Press, 1982); Elizabeth S. Bird, ed., *Dressing in Feathers: The Construction of the Indian in American Popular Culture* (Boulder, CO: Westview Press, 1996).

66. Seth K. Humphrey, *Mankind: Racial Values and Racial Prospect* (New York: Scribner's, 1917), 160; cited in Maddox, *Citizen Indians*, 59.

67. Dippie, *The Vanishing American*, 218–19; www.nationalcowboymuseum.org/educat ion/lesson-plans/Fraser/Fraser.aspx, accessed 10/22/10.

68. *New York Times*, February 25, 1917; *The Sporting News*, March 1, 1917, 6.

69. *The Sporting News*, May 24, 1917, 3.

70. F. C. Lane, "How a Ballplayer's Eyes Grow Old," *Baseball Magazine* May 1917, 244.

71. Koerper, "The Catcher Was a Cahuilla," 26.

72. H. C. Hamilton, "Famous Indian Passes," *The Pittsburgh Press* August 16, 1917, 21; *Winona [Minnesota] Republican-Herald*, August 17, 1917, 6.

73. *New York Times*, August 18, 1917; Simon, *Deadball Stars*, 72; Unidentified, unattributed article, John Tortes Meyers file, National Baseball Hall of Fame Library, Cooperstown, New York.

74. Koerper, "The Catcher Was a Cahuilla," 26.

75. "Clippings and Cartoons," *Baseball Magazine*, August 1917, 451.

76. Unidentified, unattributed article, John Tortes Meyers file, National Baseball Hall of Fame Library, Cooperstown, New York.

77. Lenkey, "Chief Meyers Hale and Hearty at 86," 29.

78. Jack McDonald, "One for the Chief," *San Francisco Examiner* (August 30, 1966), 52. Reprinted as "Catching Up with Matty's Catcher," *Baseball Digest*, 25, no. 10 (1967), 55.

79. Koerper, "The Catcher Was a Cahuilla," 26.

80. *The Sporting News*, November 14, 1918, 2.

81. Grantland Rice, "A Talk with Chief Meyers," February 14, 1947 (John Tortes Meyers File, National Baseball Hall of Fame Library, Cooperstown, New York); Earl L. Buie, "He Put the Indian 'Sign' on Baseball," *San Bernardino (California) Sun-Telegram* (April 5, 1961); Lawrence Ritter, "Interview Transcript" for *The Glory of Their Times*, March 24, 1964, 1–3 (John Tortes Meyers file, National Baseball Hall of Fame Library, Cooperstown, New York); Lenkey, "Chief Meyers Hale and Hearty at 86," 29.

82. Tom Simon, "Eddie Grant," *The Baseball Biography Project* (http://bioproj.sabr.org/bioproj.cfm?a=v&v=l&bid=941&pid=5382, accessed 4/27/09).

83. Unidentified, unattributed, undated ar-

ticle, John Tortes Meyers file, National Baseball Hall of Fame Library, Cooperstown, New York.

84. "Professional Baseball's Roll of Honor," *Baseball Magazine* (1919), 35–36.

85. Dippie, *The Vanishing American*, 94.

86. Fixico, *Daily Life of Native Americans*, xv, 79, 80, 82.

87. *New York Times*, May 3, 1919; *The Sporting News*, February 16, 1933, 3; http://www.baseball-reference.com/minors/team.cgi (accessed 8/28/09).

88. Koerper, "The Catcher Was a Cahuilla," 26.

89. *The Sporting News*, February 16, 1933, 3.

90. *New York Times*, February 18, 1920; *The Sporting News*, February 26, 1920, 7.

91. 1920 Census for San Diego, California (Roll T625=132, Page 6A, Enumeration District 336, Image 248).

92. Personal Interview with Michele Meyers Cornejo (July 16, 2010).

## Chapter Nine

1. Brian W. Dippie, *The Vanishing American: White Attitudes and U.S. Indian Policy* (Middletown, CT: Wesleyan University Press, 1982), 298–300; for the full text of the Merriam Report, see http://www.alaskool.org/native_ed/research_reports/IndianAdmin/Indian_Admin_Problms.html, accessed 3/20/09.

2. Dippie, *The Vanishing American*, 276; see also Lawrence C. Kelly, *The Assault on Assimilation: John Collier and the Origin of Indian Policy Reform* (Albuquerque: University of New Mexico Press, 1983); and James Wilson, *The Earth Shall Weep: A History of Native America* (New York: Atlantic Monthly Press, 1999), 333–58.

3. Jess Puryear, "San Diego Gets Share of Winter Baseball," *The Sporting News*, January 27, 1921, 5–8.

4. Henry C. Koerper, "The Catcher Was a Cahuilla: A Remembrance of John Tortes Meyers," *Journal of California and Great Basin Anthropology* 24, no. 1 (2004), 33; John Lenkey, "Chief Meyers Hale and Hearty at 86," *The Sporting News*, January 14, 1967, 29.

5. Steve George, "Chief Meyers, Unrecognized and Almost Forgotten, Emerges from Out of Game's Early Memory Book," *The Sporting News*, March 26, 1936, 19.

6. *The Sporting News*, March 5, 1931, 5.

7. *The Sporting News*, January 12, 1928, 6.

8. Bozeman Bulger, "Twenty-Five Years in Sports, Part II," *The Saturday Evening Post*, May 12, 1928, 38, 63.

9. Irvin S. Cobb, "The Wise Indian," *Winona [Minnesota] Republican-Herald*, August 8, 1922, 8; see also Jim Dawson, "McGraw

Rescinded Fine After Talk with Chief," *Riverside (California) Press-Enterprise*, June 25, 1969.

10. http://cvhistorichomes.com/no_14.htm, accessed 3/12/09. The house, which is still standing, is notable as one of the first Mission Revival buildings in Chula Vista. It also has a bit of Pueblo Revival influence. Called the Frances Fisher house, it had been built in 1911 and sold to a lawyer named Henry Fisher and his wife Frances in 1919.

11. 1930 Chula Visa, California Census (Roll 190, Page 6a, Enumeration District 33, Image 707.0).

12. Earl L. Buie, "He Put the Indian 'Sign' on Baseball," *San Bernardino (California) Sun-Telegram*, April 5, 1961, E-5; Jim Dawson, "Meyers' Memory Bridges Baseball's Generation Gap," *Riverside (California) Press-Enterprise*, June 24, 1969, 1.

13. Koerper, "The Catcher Was a Cahuilla," 33.

14. *The Sporting News*, March 10, 1932, 4.

15. *Winona [Minnesota] Republican-Herald*, March 25, 1932, 1.

16. *Prescott (Arizona) Evening Courier*, June 24, 1932.

17. Koerper, "The Catcher Was a Cahuilla," 33.

18. *The Sporting News*, January 19, 1933, 1; December 28, 1955, 25.

19. Jack McDonald, "One for the Chief," *San Francisco Examiner*, August 30, 1966, 52. Reprinted as "Catching Up with Matty's Catcher," *Baseball Digest*, 25, no. 10 (1967), 55–56.

20. Unidentified, unattributed, undated article, John Tortes Meyers file, National Baseball Hall of Fame Library, Cooperstown, New York.

21. *World Telegraph*, March 9, 1933 (John Tortes Meyers file, National Baseball Hall of Fame Library, Cooperstown, New York).

22. Koerper, "The Catcher Was a Cahuilla," 33; *The Sporting News*, January 5, 1933, 8; March 16, 1933, 6; April 27, 1933, 3.

23. Buie, "He Put the Indian 'Sign' on Baseball," E-5.

24. Personal interview with Michele Meyers Cornejo (July 16, 2010).

25. Buie, "He Put the Indian 'Sign' on Baseball," E-5.

26. Koerper, "The Catcher Was a Cahuilla," 34.

27. John T. Meyers, "Greatest Catcher Believes he 'Booted' Life's Chance by Choosing Diamond Career," *New York American*, June 16, 1912, L, 4.

28. Steve George, "Chief Meyers, Unrecognized and Almost Forgotten, Emerges from Out of Game's Early Memory Book," *The Sporting News* (March 26, 1936), 19.

29. Unidentified, unattributed, undated, John Tortes Meyers file, National Baseball Hall of Fame Library, Cooperstown, New York.
30. Dippie, *The Vanishing American*, 294.
31. http://www.imdb.com/title/tt0025371/fullcredits#cast, accessed 12/13/08. For a list of Native Americans in the film see Alan Gevinson, *Within Our Gates: Ethnicity in American Feature Films, 1911–1960* (Berkley: University of California Press, 1997), 578, For more on the film see http://www.tcm.com/tcmdb/title.jsp?stid=2245, accessed 3/23/09. This site includes a link to the original trailer for the movie.
32. George, "Chief Meyers, Unrecognized and Almost Forgotten," 19.
33. Unidentified, unattributed, undated article, John Tortes Meyers file, National Baseball Hall of Fame Library, Cooperstown, New York.
34. See Tavis Thorne, *The World's Richest Indian: The Scandal over Jackson Barnett's Oil Fortune* (New York: Oxford University Press, 2003).
35. "Flashes of Sport," *Winona [Minnesota] Republican-Herald*, January 18, 1939, 9.
36. *The Sporting News*, March 7, 1940, 2.
37. *Chicago Daily News*, January 12, 1945, 24.
38. John Lemcey, "Ex-Catcher Chief Meyers Will Mark 86th Birthday," *The Sporting News*, July 23, 1966, 30.
39. Grantland Rice, "A Talk with Chief Meyers," February 14, 1947 (John Tortes Meyers File, National Baseball Hall of Fame Library, Cooperstown, New York).
40. Paul Zimmerman, "Sportscripts," *Los Angeles Times*, August 13, 1947, 10.
41. *The Sporting News*, April 18, 1948, 23.
42. Charles C. Alexander, *Spoke: A Biography of Tris Speaker* (Dallas: Southern Methodist University Press, 2007), 296.
43. Unidentified, unattributed, undated article, John Tortes Meyers File, National Baseball Hall of Fame Library, Cooperstown, New York.
44. John Tortes Meyers File, Dartmouth College Alumni Archive, Hanover, New Hampshire.
45. Jim Dawson, "Chief Picks Honus Wagner as Baseball's Greatest Player," *Riverside (California) Press-Enterprise*, June 26, 1969, B-10.
46. Transcript of an interview with Ernest Martin Hopkins, February 21–March 14, 1958. Hanover, NH: Rauner Special Collections Library, Dartmouth College, 26 (www.dartmouth.edu/~library/rauner/archives/oral.../EMHReels1_9.pdf, accessed 3/25/11).
47. Mannie Pineda, "Stories About Fall Classic Spun by Ex-Participants," *The Sporting News* (October 3, 1951), 18.

48. E.g., Buie "He Put the Indian 'Sign' on Baseball," E-5. Lawrence Ritter taped Meyers reciting "Casey at the Bat" in 1966. The recording is included in the 1998 audio version of *The Glory of Their Times*, so Meyers's sonorous tones and obvious delight in the recitation can still be heard today. See Lawrence S. Ritter, *The Glory of Their Times: The Story of the Early Days of Baseball Told by the Men Who Played It, Audio Version*, HighBridge, 1998.
49. Rube Samuelson, "Del Webb and the Jolter at Game's Aid Society Party," *The Sporting News*, February 20, 1952, 21.
50. Personal Interviews with Colonel John V. Meyers (September 22, 2008) and Michele Meyers Cornejo (July 16, 2010); Tom Simon, ed., *Deadball Stars of the National League* (Washington, D.C.: Brassey's, 2004), 72.
51. Personal interviews with Shanna Meyers (September 29, 2008) and Michele Meyers Cornejo (July 16, 2010).
52. Ed McAuley, "Dodger Bonanza Spotlights Need for Aid to Old-Timers," *The Sporting News*, October 28, 1959, 2, 12.
53. *The Sporting News*, November 11, 1959, 18.
54. Buie, "He Put the Indian 'Sign' on Baseball," E-5.
55. George Ringwald, "Former major leaguer 'Chief' Meyers: Old-timer analyzes today's baseball," *Riverside (California) Press Enterprise*, August 23, 1964.
56. Lawrence Ritter, "Chief Meyers," *The Glory of Their Times: The Story of the Early Days of Baseball Told by the Men Who Played It, Enlarged Edition* (New York: HarperCollins Perennial, 2002), 178.
57. John Lenkey, "Chief Meyers Hale and Hearty at 86," 29.
58. McDonald, "One for the Chief," 52.
59. Ritter, *The Glory of Their Times*, xvi.
60. David Lawrence Reed, "Lawrence S. Ritter, the last New York giant," *The Baseball Research Journal*, Thursday, January 1 2004 (http://www.allbusiness.com/health-care-social-assistance/social-assistance-individual/880357-1.html, accessed 1/12/09).
61. Lawrence Ritter, "Interview Transcript" for *The Glory of Their Times*, March 24, 1964, 32 (John Tortes Meyers file, National Baseball Hall of Fame Library, Cooperstown, New York).
62. Ritter, *The Glory of Their Times*, 183; Dawson, "McGraw Rescinded Fine After Talk with Chief."
63. Bill Bryson, "They Heard the Indian Glove Call," *Baseball Digest* February 1964, 67–73.
64. Myrna Oliver, Obituary of Lawrence Ritter, *Los Angeles Times*, February 20, 2004 (http://articles.latimes.com/2004/feb/20/local/me-ritter20, accessed 3/14/09).

65. Lenkey, "Chief Meyers Hale and Hearty at 86," 40.

66. Michael D'Antonio, *Forever Blue: The True Story of Walter O'Malley, Baseball's Most Controversial Owner, and the Dodgers of Brooklyn and Los Angeles* (New York: Riverhead Books, 2009), 318.

67. *Long Island Press*, October 16, 1966 (John Tortes Meyers File, Dartmouth College Alumni Archive, Hanover, New Hampshire).

68. Lenkey, "Chief Meyers Hale and Hearty at 86," 40.

69. *Long Island Press*, October 16, 1966.

70. *The Sporting News*, April 22, 1967, 29.

71. *The Indian Reporter*, July/August 1967.

72. Benjamin Spillman, "Fall Classic Stirs Family Memories of Player," *The Desert Sun*, November 4, 2001, B1.

73. Personal Interview with Colonel John V. Meyers (September 22, 2008).

74. Personal interview with Michele Meyers Cornejo (July 16, 2010).

75. Personal Interview with Shanna Meyers (September 29, 2008); see also Dawson, "Meyer's Memory," 1.

76. Dawson, "Meyer's Memory," 1.

77. Lawrence Ritter, "Chief Meyers," *Baseball's Finest: The Greats, the Flakes, the Weird, and the Wonderful*, ed. Danny Peary (New York: Simon & Schuster, 1990), 153.

78. *New York Times*, July 28, 1971.

79. *The Sporting News*, August 14, 1971, 46.

80. *The Daily Enterprise: A Newspaper for Riverside County*, Valley Edition, July 27, 1971, B-1.

81. www.baseball-almanac.com/players/player.php?p=meyerch01, accessed 8/13/08.

82. Ritter, "Chief Meyers," 153.

# Epilogue

1. William McNeil, *Backstop: A History of the Catcher and a Sabermetric Ranking of 50 All-time Greats* (Jefferson, NC: McFarland, 2006), 21.

2. For example, see the web site baseballthinkfactory (http://www.baseballthinkfactory.org/files/hall_of_merit/discussion/chief_meyers, accessed 2/22/10). The discussion took place in May 2007.

3. The one exception is Ted Easterly, who batted .300, but Easterly, who played for Cleveland (1909–1912) and Chicago (1912–1913), as well as Kansas City of the Federal League (1913–1915), appeared in only 700 total games (including those in the Federal League), while Meyers played in nearly 1,000 games, all in the National League.

4. http://members.tripod.com/bb_catchers/catchers/8coffops.htm, accessed 3/20/09.

This source also contends that Meyers's career success rate in stealing bases was .917 (44 stolen bases; 4 caught stealing), which would be the highest among past and present catchers. However, he was actually caught stealing fourteen times during his career (http://www.retrosheet.org/boxesetc/M/Pmeyec101.htm, accessed 1/16/11).

5. John McGraw, "Making a Pennant Winner," *Pearson's Magazine*, November 1912, 121.

6. Lawrence Ritter, "Chief Meyers," *Baseball's Finest: The Greats, the Flakes, the Weird, and the Wonderful*, ed. Danny Peary (New York: Simon & Schuster, 1990), 147.

7. Tom Swift, *Chief Bender's Burden: The Silent Struggle of a Baseball Star* (Lincoln: University of Nebraska Press, 2008), 252–55.

8. *Baseball Digest*, June 1973, 60.

9. Tom Simon, ed., *Deadball Stars of the National League* (Washington, D.C.: Brassey's, 2004), 17.

10. http://world.std.com/~pgw/Deadball/honor.roll.html, accessed 4/23/09.

11. Bill James, *The New Bill James Historical Abstract* (New York: Free Press, 2001), 109, 409, 431.

12. *The Indian Reporter*, September–October 1969.

13. http://americanindianathletichalloffame.com, accessed 3/16/09.

14. http://www.annaivey.com/iveyfiles/academia, accessed 1/12/09.

15. http://alumni.dartmouth.edu/Green/WearersoftheGreen, accessed 3/20/09.

16. http://www.rshof.com/inductees/inductees_04/jmeyers.html, accessed 3/21/09.

17. Jeffrey P. Beck, *The American Indian Integration of Baseball* (Lincoln: University of Nebraska Press, 2004), 30; see also David Nevard, "Wahooism in the USA," http://webpages.charter.net/joekuras/bhxi3d.htm, accessed 1/12/09; and Ira Berkow, "Sports of The Times; For Love of Those Braves," *New York Times*, October 23, 1991, B7.

18. Philip Deloria, *Indians in Unexpected Places* (Lawrence: University Press of Kansas, 2006), 31.

19. Deloria, *Indians in Unexpected Places*, 237–38.

20. See the book accompanying the series: Geoffrey Ward and Ken Burns, *Baseball: An Illustrated History* (New York: Knopf, 1996). Ward and Burns are not the only artists and historians to devote little or no attention to the role of Native Americans in the American game. As Thomas Altherr noted in 2003, in most works of fiction or poetry inspired by baseball Indians have largely been ignored, and histories of baseball "barely mention indigenous ballplayers" ("North American Indigenous People and

Baseball: 'The One Thing the White Man Has Done Right," *Above the Fruited Plane: Baseball in the Rocky Mountain West*, ed. Thomas L. Altherr [Cleveland, OH: Society for American Baseball Research], 2003), 650). In response to an inquiry from a reader about Native Americans who played in the major leagues, *The Baseball Digest* lamented in its January 1998 edition, "it's a shame that the contributions of Native Americans to major league baseball have received scant attention" (6).

21. Beck, *American Indian Integration of Baseball*, 30.

22. For a fuller account of the recommitment of Dartmouth to-the education of Native Americans, beginning in 1970 and continuing to the present, see Colin Calloway, *The Indian History of an American Institution: Native Americans and Dartmouth* (Hanover, NH: Dartmouth College Press, 2010), 155–78.

23. James Panero and Stefan Beck, eds., "Indian Wars: The Meaning of a Symbol," *The Dartmouth Review Pleads Innocent: Twenty-five Years of Being Threatened, Impugned, Vandalized, Sued, Suspended, and Bitten at the Ivy League's Most Controversial Conservative Newspaper* (Wilmington, DE: ISI Books, 2006), 72.

24. Calloway, *The Indian History of an American Institution*, 168–69.

25. Andrew Garrod and Colleen Larimore, ed. *First Person, First Peoples: Native American College Graduates Tell Their Life Stories* (Ithaca, N.Y.: Cornell University Press, 1997), 12.

26. Garrod and Larimore 1997, *First Person, First Peoples*, 136–53.

27. Calloway, *The Indian History of an American Institution*, 169–70; Nichola W. Tucker, "Dartmouth Reviewed: Community Protests Anti-Native American Imagery," *The Nation*, December 5, 2006 (http://www.thenation.com/doc/20061218/dartmouth, accessed 2/8/09).

28. http://www.dartreview.com/store/, accessed 2/8/09.

29. Calloway, *The Indian History of an American Institution*, 185–86.

30. Adam Gopnik, *Paris to the Moon* (New York: Random House, 2000), 197–211.

31. See Thomas Barthel, *Pepper Martin: A Baseball Biography* (Jefferson, NC: McFarland, 2003).

32. Jim Hurley, "Lo, Vanishing Athlete," *The American Legion Magazine* August 1940, 30.

33. Joseph B. Oxendine, *American Indian Sports Heritage*. (Lincoln: University of Nebraska Press, 1995), xxi, 261–71; C. Richard King, ed. *Native Athletes in Sport and Society: A Reader* (Lincoln: University of Nebraska Press, 2005), xxii.

34. Altherr, "North American Indigenous People and Baseball," 24–25.

35. Selena Roberts, "Off-Field Hurdles Stymie Indian Athletes, *New York Times*, June 17, 2001, 1.

36. See Bob Burke and Royse Parr, *Allie Reynolds: Super Chief*, Oklahoma City: Oklahoma Heritage Association, 2002; Nathan Aaseng, "Athletes," *American Indian Lives Series* (New York: Facts on File, 1995), 35–44.

37. Beck, *American Indian Integration of Baseball*, 28.

38. Claire Smith, "Allie Reynolds, Star Pitcher For Yankees, Is Dead at 79," *New York Times*, December 28, 1994.

39. Aaseng, "Athletes," 44.

40. Royse Parr, "American Indians in Major League Baseball: Now and Then" (www.readex.com/readex/newsletter.cfm?newsletter=231; accessed 2/12/09).

41. George Castle, "Batista Provides a Helping Hand" (http://mlbplayers.mlb.com/pa/newsarticle.jspymd=20070724&content_id=2105872&vkey=mlbpa_news&fext=.jsp, July 24, 2007, accessed 10/3/08).

42. www.usatoday.com/sports/2007-02-21-native-american-cover_x.htm, accessed 2/23/10.

43. "McGraw's Indian Catcher Started Out to Become a Civil Engineer," *St. Louis Globe-Democrat*, August 29, 1909.

# Bibliography

Note: In addition to the following references, articles from various periodicals (*New York Times*, *New York American*, *The Sporting News* and many others) and from archives (National Baseball Hall of Fame Library [Cooperstown, New York], Rauner Special Collections Library, Dartmouth College [Hanover, New Hampshire], the Society for Baseball Research Lending Library, Agua Caliente Cultural Museum [Palm Springs, California], and Riverside, California, Metropolitan Museum are cited in the Chapter Notes.

Aaseng, Nathan. "Athletes," *American Indian Lives Series.* New York: Facts on File, 1995.

Adler, Richard. *Mack, McGraw and the 1913 Baseball Season.* Jefferson, NC: McFarland, 2008.

Alexander, Charles. *John McGraw.* Lincoln: University of Nebraska, 1995.

_____. *Spoke: A Biography of Tris Speaker.* Dallas: Southern Methodist University Press, 2007.

Altherr, Thomas L. "North American Indigenous People and Baseball: 'The One Thing the White Man Has Done Right,'" *Above the Fruited Plane: Baseball in the Rocky Mountain West*, ed. Thomas L. Altherr, 18–27. Cleveland, OH: Society for American Baseball Research, 2003.

Anderson, David W. *More Than Merkle: A History of the Best and Most Exciting Baseball Season in Human History.* Lincoln: University of Nebraska Press, 2000.

Barrow, Isaac. "The Second Chief: The Story of John 'Chief' Meyers," *Bleacher Report*, October 31, 2008 (http://bleacherreport.com/articles/75963-the-second-chief-the-story-of-john-chief-meyers; accessed 3/3/09).

Barrows, David Prescott. *The Ethnobotany of the Cahuilla Indians of Southern California.* Chicago: University of Chicago Press, 1900.

Bean, Lowell John. "Cahuilla." *Handbook of North American Indians, Volume 8: California*, ed. Robert F. Heizer. Washington: Smithsonian Institution, 1978.

_____. *Mukat's People: The Cahuilla Indians of Southern California.* Berkeley: University of California Press, 1972.

_____, principal investigator. *Tahquitz Report.* A report of a cultural survey of the Tahquitz Canyon and mitigation efforts on the impact of a planned flood control project on the Tahquitz Creek, affecting sites associated with the Agua Caliente Band of the Cahuilla nation, 1996.

Bean, Lowell John, Lisa J. Bourgeault, Frank W. Porter, III. *The Cahuilla.* New York: Chelsea House Publishers, 1989.

Bean, Lowell John, Sylvia Vane, and Jackson Young, *The Cahuilla Landscape: The Santa Rosa and San Jacinto Mountains.* Menlo Park, CA: Ballena Press, 1991.

Beck, Jeffrey P. *The American Indian Integration of Baseball.* Lincoln: University of Nebraska Press, 2004.

Bird, Elizabeth S., ed. *Dressing in Feathers: The Construction of the Indian in American Popular Culture.* Boulder, CO: Westview Press, 1996.

Blackstock, Joe. "For 'Chief' Meyers, Hitting the Ball Was the Easy Part," *Inland Valley Daily Bulletin* (Ontario, CA), July 9, 2005.

Bloom, John. *To Show What an Indian Can Do: Sports at Native American Boarding Schools.* Minneapolis: University of Minnesota Press, 2000.

Bloom, John, and Randy Hanson. "Warriors and Thieves: Appropriations of the Warrior Motif in Representations of Native American Athletes," *Race, Recreation, and Culture,* ed. John Bloom and Michael Willard, 246–63. New York: New York University Press, 2002.

Bloom, John, and Michael Nevin-Willard. "Introduction: Out of Bounds and between the Lines: Race in Twentieth-Century American Sport," *Sports Matters: Race, Recreation, and Culture,* ed. John Bloom and Michael Willard. New York: New York University Press, 2002.

Bolster, Mel H. *Crazy Snake and the Smoked Meat Rebellion.* Boston: Brandon Press, 1976.

Bruchac, Joseph. *Jim Thorpe: Original All-American.* New York: Dial Books, 2006.

Bryson, Bill. "They Heard the Indian Glove Call," *Baseball Digest,* February 1964.

Buford, Kate. *Native American Son: The Life and Sporting Legend of Jim Thorpe.* New York: Alfred A. Knopf, 2010.

Buie, Earl L. "He Put the Indian 'Sign' on Baseball," *San Bernardino (California) Sun-Telegram,* April 5, 1961.

Burke, Bob, and Royse Parr. *Allie Reynolds: Super Chief.* Oklahoma City: Oklahoma Heritage Association, 2002.

Calloway, Colin. *The Indian History of an American Institution: Native Americans and Dartmouth.* Hanover, NH: Dartmouth College Press, 2010.

Churchill, Ward, Norbert Hill, and Maru Jo Barlow. "An Historical Overview of Twentieth-Century Native American Athletics," *The Indian Historian* 12, no. 4 (1979): 22–32.

Cornejo, Michele Meyers. Personal Interview, July 16, 2010.

Crawford, Bill. *All American: The Rise and Fall of Jim Thorpe.* Hoboken, NJ: John Wiley & Sons, 2004.

Creamer, Robert W. *Babe: The Legend Comes to Life.* New York: Simon & Schuster, 1974.

_____. *Stengel: His Life and Times.* New York: Simon & Schuster, 1984.

Curtis, Edward S. "The Cahuilla," *The North American Indian, Vol. XV,* 21–36. Norwood, MA: Plimpton Press, 1926 (http://curtis.library.northwestern.edu/curtis/viewPage.cgi?showp=1&size=2&id=nai.15.book.00000042&volume=15; accessed 8/16/08).

D'Antonio, Michael. *Forever Blue: The True Story of Walter O'Malley, Baseball's Most Controversial Owner, and the Dodgers of Brooklyn and Los Angeles.* New York: Riverhead Books, 2009.

Dawson, Jim. "Chief Picks Honus Wagner as Baseball's Greatest Player." *Riverside Press-Enterprise,* June 26, 1969.

_____. "McGraw Rescinded Fine After Talk with Chief." *Riverside Press-Enterprise,* June 25, 1969.

_____. "Meyers' Memory Bridges Baseball's Generation Gap." *Riverside Press-Enterprise,* June 24, 1969.

DeFord, Frank. *The Old Ball Game: How John McGraw, Christy Mathewson, and the New York Giants Created Modern Baseball.* New York: Atlantic Monthly Press, 2005.

Deloria, Philip. *Indians in Unexpected Places.* Lawrence: University Press of Kansas, 2006.

_____. *Playing Indian.* New Haven: Yale University Press, 1999.

Dippie, Brian W. *The Vanishing American: White Attitudes and U.S. Indian Policy.* Middletown, CT: Wesleyan University Press, 1982.

Eastman, Charles. *From the Deep Woods*

to Civilization. Norwood, MA: Norwood Press, 1916.

_____. *The Indian To-day: The Past and Future of the First American.* Garden City, NY: Doubleday, 1915.

_____. *The Soul of an Indian.* Lincoln: University of Nebraska Press, 1980 [1911].

Elfers, James E. *The Tour to End All Tours: The Story of Major League Baseball's 1913–1914 World Tour.* Lincoln: University of Nebraska Press, 2003.

Fixico, Donald. *Daily Life of Native Americans in the Twentieth Century.* Westport, CT: Greenwood Press, 2006.

Garrod, Andrew, and Colleen Larimore, ed. *First Person, First Peoples: Native American College Graduates Tell Their Life Stories.* Ithaca, NY: Cornell University Press, 1997.

Gems, Gerald R. "Negotiating a Native American Identity Through Sport: Assimilation, Adaptation, and the Role of the Trickster." *Native Athletes in Sport and Society: A Reader*, ed. C. Richard King, 1–21. Lincoln: University of Nebraska Press, 2005.

Gendar, Jeannine. *Grass Games and Moon Races: California Indian Games and Toys.* Berkeley, CA: Heyday Books, 1995.

George, Steve. "Chief Meyers, Unrecognized and Almost Forgotten, Emerges from Out of Game's Early Memory Book," *The Sporting News*, March 26, 1936.

Gilbert, Matthew Sakiestewa. *Education Beyond the Mesas: Hopi Students at Sherman Institute.* Lincoln: University of Nebraska Press, 2010.

Gilbert, Thomas. *Dead Ball: Major League Baseball Before Babe Ruth.* New York: Franklin Watts, 1996.

Glaze, Ralph, and Rolfe Humphries. "How Chief Made the Major Leagues." *Empire Magazine*, August 20, 1967.

Goewey, Ed A. "Three Noted Indian Baseball Players." *Leslie's Illustrated Weekly Newspaper*, November 13, 1913.

Goodman, John D. "Spring Rancheria: Archaeological Investigations of a Transient Cahuilla Village in Early Riverside, California," Master's Thesis, University of California, Riverside, June 1993.

Gopnik, Adam. *Paris to the Moon.* New York: Random House, 2000.

Graham, Frank. *The New York Giants: An Informal History of a Great Baseball Club.* Carbondale: Southern Illinois University Press, 2002 [1952].

Hamelin, Joe. "Meyers Chief Among Catchers: Riverside Sport Hall of Fame Inductee was Lesser-Known Standout," *The Riverside Press-Enterprise*, May 23, 2004, C1.

Heizer, Robert F., and Albert L. Hurtado, eds. *The Destruction of California Indians.* Lincoln, NB: Bison Books, 1993.

Hoffman, Jeane. "Chief Meyers Recalls Catching for Pitching Greats of Giants," Undated, John Tortes Meyers Players File. National Baseball Hall of Fame Library, Cooperstown, New York.

Honig, Donald. "The Author Meets a Baseball Lion and a Few Celebrated Pussycats," *Sports Illustrated*, October 17, 1983 (http://vault.sportsillustrated.cnn.com/vault/article/magazine/MAG1121391/3/index.htm; accessed 9/2/08).

Hooper, Lucile. "The Cahuilla Indians," *University of California Publications in American Archaeology and Ethnology*, Vol. 16, 316–79. Berkeley: University of California Press, 1920.

Hopkins, Ernest Martin. *Transcripts of Interviews, February 21–March 14 and March 28–April 4, 1958.* Hanover, NH: Rouner Special Collections Library, Dartmouth College.

Hoxie, Frederick C. *A Final Promise: The Campaign to Assimilate the Indians, 1880–1920.* New York: Cambridge University Press, 1989 [1984].

Hurley, Jim. "Lo, Vanishing Athlete." *The American Legion Magazine*, August 1940.

Hurtado, Albert L. *Indian Survival on the California Frontier.* New Haven: Yale University Press, 1988.

Jackson, Helen Hunt, and Abbot Kinney. *On the Condition & Needs of the Mission Indians of California.* Washington: Government Printing Office, 1883.

James, Bill. *The New Bill James Historical Baseball Abstract.* New York: Free Press, 2001.

_____. *Whatever Happened to the Hall of Fame? Baseball, Cooperstown, and the Politics of Glory.* New York: Simon & Schuster, 1995.

James, Harry Clebourne. *The Cahuilla Indians: The Men Called Master.* Tuscon: Westernlore Press, 1960.

Jenkins, Sally. *The Real All Americans: The Team That Changed a Game, a People, a Nation.* New York: Doubleday, 2007.

Kashatus, William C. *Money Pitcher: Chief Bender and the Tragedy of Indian Assimilation.* University Park: Pennsylvania State University Press, 2006.

Kelly, Lawrence C. *The Assault on Assimilation: John Collier and the Origin of Indian Policy Reform.* Albuquerque: University of New Mexico Press, 1983.

King, C. Richard, *Native Americans and Sport in North America.* New York: Routledge, 2007.

_____. *Native Americans in Sports.* 2 vols. Armonk, NY: Sharpe Reference, 2003.

_____, ed. *Native Athletes in Sport and Society: A Reader.* Lincoln: University of Nebraska Press, 2005.

King, C. Richard, and Charles Fruehling Springwood, ed. *Team Spirits: The Native American Mascots Controversy.* Lincoln: University of Nebraska Press, 2001.

Koerper, Henry C. "The Catcher Was a Cahuilla: A Remembrance of John Tortes Meyers." *Journal of California and Great Basin Anthropology* 24, no. 1 (2004): 21–40.

_____. "John Tortes Meyers: A Cahuilla in the Big Leagues." *News from Native California: An Inside View of the California Indian World* 10, no. 4 (1997): 4–6.

Kroeber, A. L. *Ethnography of the Cahuilla Indians:* University of California Publications in American Archaeology and Ethnology, *Vol. 8,* 235–269. Berkeley: University of California Press, 1908.

_____. *Handbook of the Indians of California.* Smithsonian Institution. Bureau of American Ethnology, no. 78, 1–990. Mineola, NY: Dover Publications: 1976 [1925].

Lane, F.C. "The Greatest of All Catchers: Essential Points in a Catcher's Work." *Baseball Magazine,* February 1913.

Lemcey, John. "Ex-Catcher Chief Meyers Will Mark 86th Birthday." *The Sporting News,* July 23, 1966.

Lenkey, John. "Chief Meyers, Hale and Hearty at 86." *The Sporting News,* January 14, 1967, pp. 29, 40.

Lesch, R. J. "Chief Meyers." Society of American Baseball Research Biography Project (bioproj.sabr.org/bioproj.cfm?a=v&v=l&pid=9594&bid=991; accessed 8/11/08).

Lieb, Fred. "Baseball — The Nation's Melting Pot." *Baseball Magazine,* August, 1923.

Macht, Norman, *Connie Mack and the Early Years of Baseball.* Lincoln: University of Nebraska Press, 2007.

Maddox, Lucy, *Citizen Indians: Native American Intellectuals, Race, and Reform.* Ithaca, NY: Cornell University, 2005.

Martinez, David. *Dakota Philosopher: Charles Eastman and American Indian Thought.* St. Paul: Minnesota Historical Society Press, 2009.

Mathewson, Christy. *Pitching in a Pinch: or Baseball from the Inside.* Cleveland: L. Van Oeyen, 1912 (http://www.archive.org/stream/pitchinginpincho00mathiala/pitchinginpincho00mathiala_djvu.txt; accessed 1/12/09).

McConaughy, J. W., "M'Graw Picks Meyers for Chief Catcher," August 5, 1909. John Tortes Meyers Players File. National Baseball Hall of Fame Library, Cooperstown, New York.

McDonald, Brian, *Indian Summer: The Forgotten Story of Louis Sockalexis, the First Native American in Major League Baseball*. Emmaus, PA: Rodale, 2003.

McDonald, Jack. "Improved Scouting Biggest Change, Says Chief Meyers." *The Sporting News*, April 18, 1956.

_____. "One for the Chief." *San Francisco Examiner*, August 30, 1966. Reprinted as "Catching Up with Matty's Catcher," *Baseball Digest*, 25, no. 10 (1967).

McGraw, John. "Making a Pennant Winner." *Pearson's Magazine*, November 1912.

McNeil, William. *Backstop: A History of the Catcher and a Sabermetric Ranking of 50 All-time Greats*. Jefferson, NC: McFarland, 2006.

_____. *The California Winter League: America's First Integrated Professional Baseball League*. Jefferson, NC: McFarland, 2002.

Meyers, Chief. "I Am Like An Old Hemlock." *The Third Fireside Book of Baseball*, ed. Charles Einstein. New York: Simon & Schuster, 1968.

Meyers, Colonel John V. Personal Interview, September 22, 2008.

Meyers, John T. "Batters Can Be Developed, Says Meyers." *New York American*, May 11, 1913.

_____. "Chief Meyers Tells of 'The Job' of a Catcher." *New York American*, July 14, 1912.

_____. "Greatest Catcher Believes He 'Booted' Life's Chance by Choosing Diamond Career." *New York American*, June 16, 1912.

_____. "Meyers Lauds Jim Thorpe, Olympic Hero." *New York American*, May 25, 1913.

_____. "When Ball Players Rest." *Sioux City Journal*, September 15, 1912.

Meyers, Shanna. Personal Interview, September 29, 2008.

Mihesuah, Devon A. *American Indians: Stereotypes and Realities*. Atlanta: Clarity Press, 1996.

Morris, Peter. *Catcher: How the Man Behind the Plate Became an American Folk Hero*. Chicago: Ivan R. Dee, 2009.

_____. *A Game of Inches: The Stories Behind the Innovations That Shaped Baseball, Vol. 1: The Game on the Field*. Chicago: Ivan R. Dee, 2006.

Moses, L. G. *Wild West Shows and the Images of American Indians, 1883–1933*. Albuquerque: University of New Mexico Press, 1996.

Murphy, Cait N. *Crazy '08: How a Cast of Cranks, Rogues, Boneheads, and Magnates Created the Greatest Year in Baseball History*. San Francisco: HarperCollins, 2008.

Nelson, Kevin. *Golden Game: The Story of California Baseball*. Berkeley, CA: Heyday Books, 2004.

Neyer, Rob. *Rob Neyer's Big Book of Baseball Lineups: A Complete Guide to the Best, Worst, and Most Memorable Players to Ever Grace the Major Leagues*. New York: Fireside, 2003.

Nies, Judith. *Native American History*. New York: Ballantine Books, 1996.

Norris, Frank. "San Diego Baseball: The Early Years." *The Journal of San Diego History* 10, no. 1 (1984): 1–13.

Oxendine, Joseph B. *American Indian Sports Heritage*. Lincoln: University of Nebraska Press, 1995.

Panero, James, and Stefan Beck, eds. "Indian Wars: The Meaning of a Symbol," *The Dartmouth Review Pleads Innocent: Twenty-five Years of being Threatened, Impugned, Vandalized, Sued, Suspended, and Bitten at the Ivy League's Most Controversial Conservative Newspaper*. Wilmington, DE: ISI Books, 2006.

Paraschak, Victoria. "Native Sport History: Pitfalls and Promise." *Canadian Journal of History of Sport* 20, no. 1 (1989): 57–68.

Patencio, Francisco. *Stories and Legends of the Palm Springs Indians as Told to Margaret Boynton*. Los Angeles: Times-Mirror Press, 1943.

Patterson, Tom. *A Colony for California: Riverside's First Hundred Years*. Riverside, CA: Press-Enterprise, 1971.

Powers, Francis J. "Matty Great at Irking M'Graw, Too." *Chicago Daily News*, January 12, 1945.

Quint, Wilder Dwight. *The Story of Dartmouth*. Boston: Little, Brown, 1914.

Reed, David Lawrence. "Lawrence S. Ritter, the Last New York Giant." *The Baseball Research Journal*, January 1 2004 (http://www.allbusiness.com/heal th-care-social-assistance/social-assis tance-individual/880357–1.html; accessed 1/12/09).

Reyhner, Jon, and Jeanne Eder. *American Indian Education: A History*. Norman: University of Oklahoma Press, 2004.

Rice, Grantland. "A Talk with Chief Meyers." February 14, 1947. John Tortes Meyers Players File. National Baseball Hall of Fame Library, Cooperstown, New York.

_____. "The Greatest Pitcher." January 10, 1939. John Tortes Meyers Players File. National Baseball Hall of Fame Library, Cooperstown, New York.

_____. *The Tumult and the Shouting: My Life in Sport*. New York: A. S. Barnes, 1954.

Riess, Steven A. "Race and Ethnicity in American Baseball: 1900–1919." *Journal of Ethnic Studies* 4, no. 4 (1977), 39–55.

Ringwald, George. "Former Major Leaguer 'Chief' Meyers: Old-timer Analyzes Today's Baseball." *Riverside Press Enterprise* August 23, 1964.

Ritter, Lawrence S. "Chief Meyers." *Baseball's Finest: The Greats, the Flakes, the Weird, and the Wonderful*, ed. Danny Peary. New York: Simon & Schuster, 1990.

_____. *The Glory of Their Times: The Story of the Early Days of Baseball Told by the Men Who Played it, Enlarged Edition*. New York: HarperCollins Perennial, 2002. First published in 1984 by William Morrow; MacMillan published the original edition in 1966; HighBridge published an audio version in 1998.

_____. "Interview Transcript." March 24, 1964, 43 pages. John Tortes Meyers

Players File. National Baseball Hall of Fame Library, Cooperstown, New York.

Roberts, Selena. "Off-Field Hurdles Stymie Indian Athletes." *New York Times*, June 17, 2001.

Robinson, Ray, *Matty: An American Hero — Christy Mathewson of the New York Giants*. New York: Oxford University, 1994.

Rossi, John P., *The National Game: Baseball and American Culture*. Chicago: Ivan Dee, 2000.

Runyon, Damon, and Jim Reisler. *Guys, Dolls, and Curveballs*. New York: Carroll & Graf, 2005 (http://books.google. com/books?id=HCsGghCRBBgC, accessed 2/23/09).

Schechter, Gabriel. *Victory Faust: The Rube Who Saved McGraw's Giants*. Los Gatos, CA: Charles April Publications, 2000.

Seymour, Harold, and Dorothy Seymour. *Baseball: The Golden Age*, Vol. II. New York: Oxford University Press, 1971.

_____. *Baseball: The People's Game*. New York: Oxford University Press, 1990.

Sieb, Philip. *The Player: Christy Mathewson, Baseball, and the American Century*. New York: Four Walls Eight Windows, 2003.

Simon, Tom, ed. *Deadball Stars of the National League*. Washington, DC: Brassey's, 2004.

Skipper, James. *Baseball Nicknames: A Dictionary of Origins and Meanings*. Jefferson, NC: McFarland, 1992.

Spalding Baseball Guides, 1910–13, 1915–17 (http://memory.loc.gov/ammem/co llections/spalding/index.html; accessed 2/25/09).

Spillman, Benjamin. "Fall Classic Stirs Family Memories of Player." *The Desert Sun*, November 4, 2001.

Spink, J. G. Taylor. "Albert Bender's Four Decades on the Mound." *The Sporting News*, December 31, 1942.

Staurowsky, Ellen J. "Sockalexis and the Making of the Myth at the Core of Cleveland's 'Indian' Image." *Team Spir-*

*its: The Native American Mascots Controversy*, ed. C. Richard King and Charles Fruehling Springwood. Lincoln: University of Nebraska Press, 2001.

Stout, Glenn, and Richard A. Johnson. *The Dodgers: 120 Years of Dodgers Baseball*. Boston: Houghton Mifflin, 2004.

Strong, William Duncan. "Cahuilla." In "Aboriginal Society in Southern California," *University of California Publications in American Archaeology and Ethnology, Vol. 26*, 36–182. Berkeley: University of California Press, 1929.

Swank, Bill. *Baseball in San Diego: From the Plaza to the Padres*. Mount Pleasant, SC: Arcadia, 2005.

Swift, Tom. *Chief Bender's Burden: The Silent Struggle of a Baseball Star*. Lincoln: University of Nebraska Press, 2008.

Thompson, Stephen I. "The American Indian in the Major Leagues." *Baseball Research Journal* 12 (1983).

Thorne, Tavis. *The World's Richest Indian: The Scandal over Jackson Barnett's Oil Fortune*. New York: Oxford University Press, 2003.

Tucker, Nichola W. "Dartmouth Reviewed: Community Protests Anti-Native American Imagery." *The Nation*, December 5, 2006 (http://www.then ation.com/doc/20061218/dartmouth; accessed 2/8/09).

Vacarro, Mike. *The First Fall Classic: The Red Sox, the Giants, and the Cast of Players, Pugs, and Politicos Who Reinvented the World Series in 1912*. New York: Doubleday, 2009.

Ward, Geoffrey, and Ken Burns. *Baseball: An Illustrated History*. New York: Alfred A. Knopf, 1996.

Watson, Don. "Famed Indian Ball Player Dies at 91." *The Daily Enterprise: A Newspaper for Riverside County*, July 27, 1971.

Wheeler, Robert. *Jim Thorpe: World's Greatest Athlete*. Norman: University of Oklahoma Press, 1981.

Wiggins, Robert Peyton. *Chief Bender: A Baseball Biography*. Jefferson, NC: McFarland, 2010.

_____. *The Federal League of Base Ball Clubs: The History of an Outlaw Major League, 1914–1915*. Jefferson, NC: McFarland, 2008.

Wilson, James. *The Earth Shall Weep: A History of Native America*. New York: Atlantic Monthly Press, 1999.

Zoss, Joel, and John Bowman. "Native Americans at Bat." *Diamonds in the Rough: The Untold History of Baseball*. New York: Macmillan, 1989.

# Index

Numbers in **bold italics** indicate pages with photographs.